STUMPTOWN™

PORTLAND, OREGON

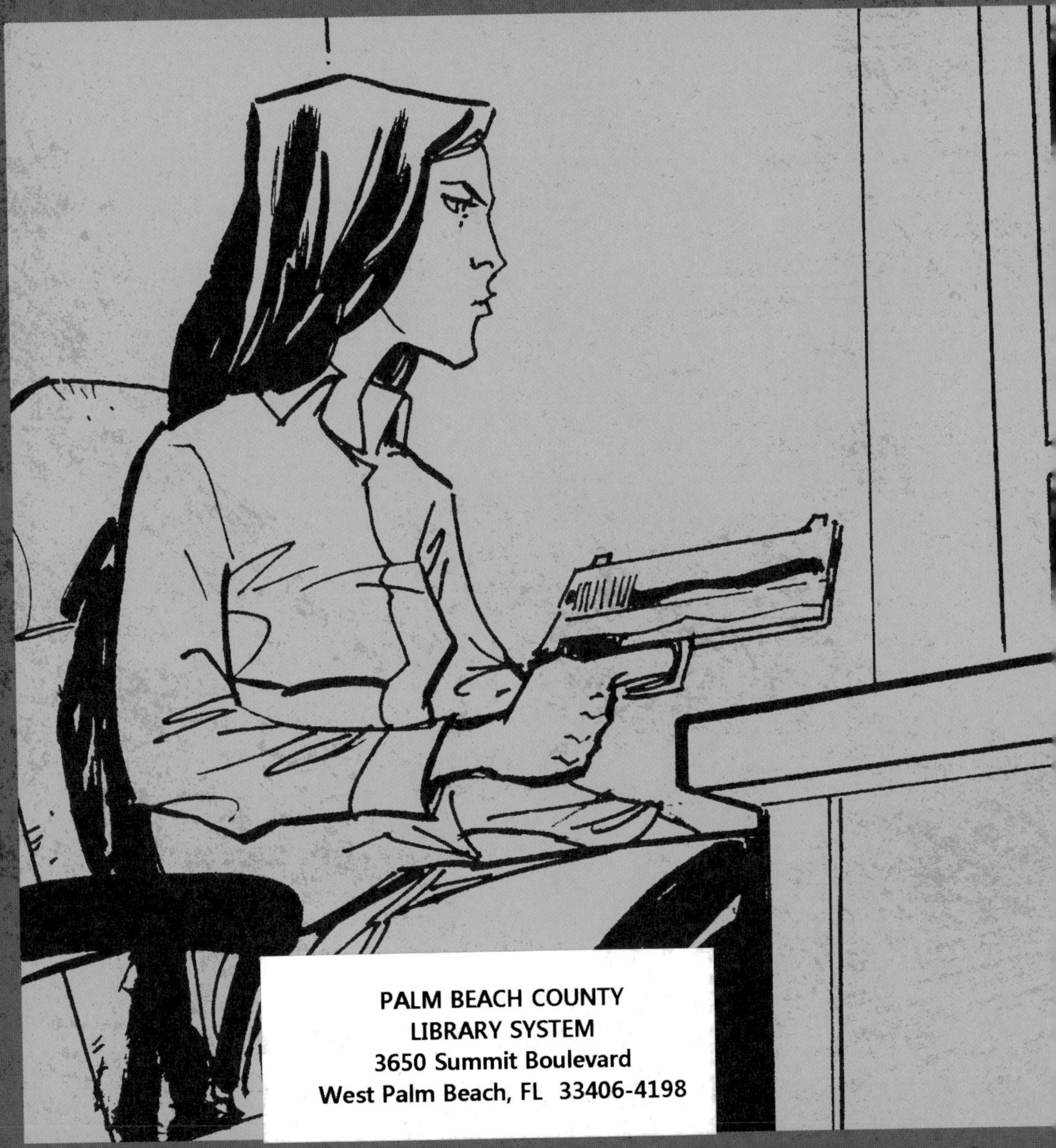

STUMPTOWN™

INVESTIGATIONS • PORTLAND, OREGON

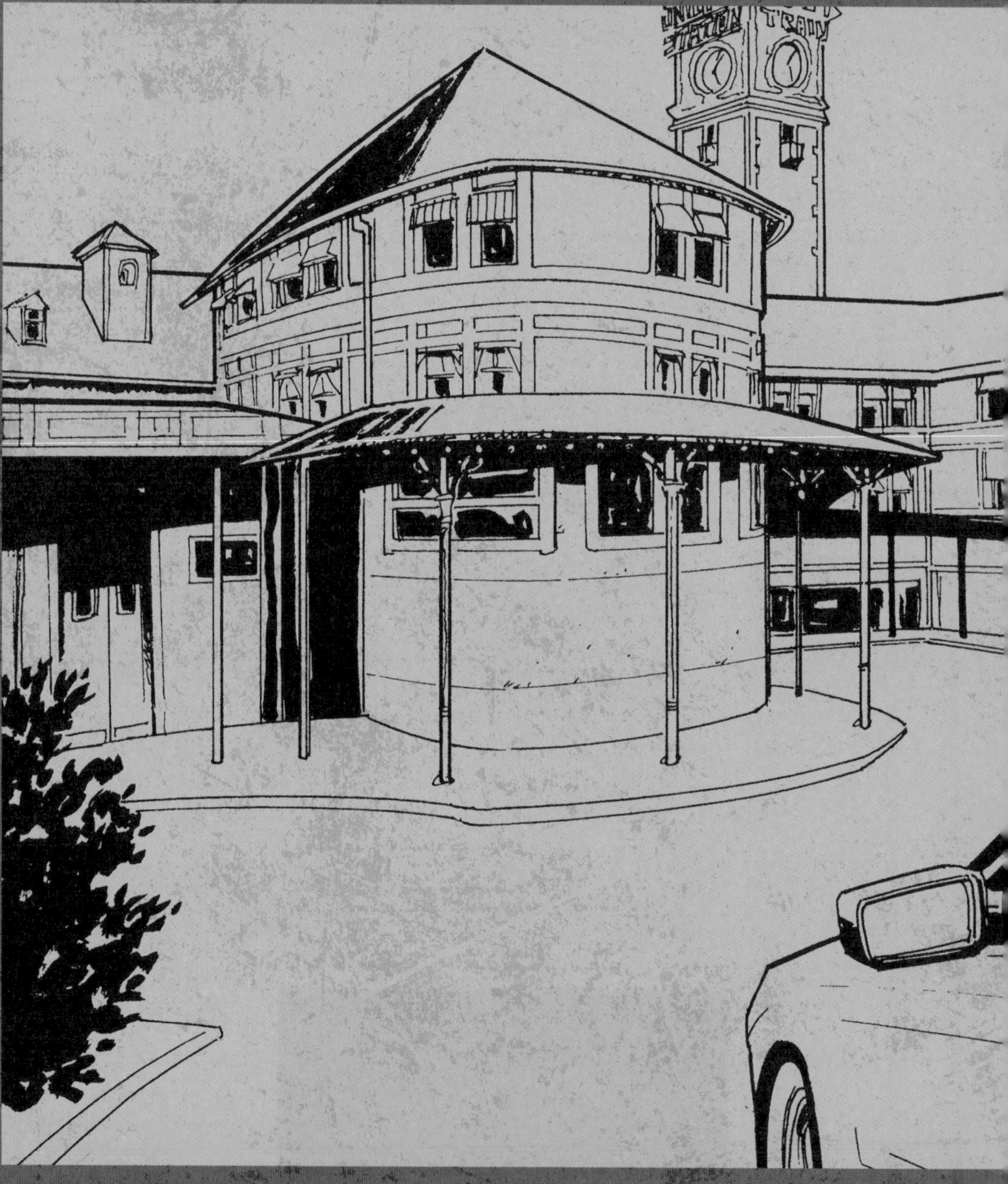

The Case of the Cup of Joe

written by
GREG RUCKA

illustrated by
JUSTIN GREENWOOD

colored by
RYAN HILL

lettered by
CRANK!

Edited by
JAMES LUCAS JONES and
ARI YARWOOD

Designed by
KEITH WOOD with
HILARY THOMPSON

AN ONI PRESS PRODUCTION

PUBLISHED BY ONI PRESS, INC.

Joe Nozemack, founder & chief financial officer
James Lucas Jones, publisher
Charlie Chu, v.p. of creative & business development
Brad Rooks, director of operations
Melissa Meszaros, director of publicity
Margot Wood, director of sales
Sandy Tanaka, marketing design manager
Amber O'Neill, special projects manager
Troy Look, director of design & production
Kate Z. Stone, senior graphic designer
Sonja Synak, graphic designer
Angie Knowles, digital prepress lead
Ari Yarwood, executive editor
Sarah Gaydos, editorial director of licensed publishing
Robin Herrera, senior editor
Desiree Wilson, associate editor
Michelle Nguyen, executive assistant
Jung Lee, logistics coordinator
Scott Sharkey, warehouse assistant

ONI PRESS, INC.
1319 SE Martin Luther King, Jr. Blvd.
Suite 240
Portland, OR 97214

onipress.com
facebook.com/onipress
twitter.com/onipress
onipress.tumblr.com
instagram.com/onipress

@ruckawriter / gregrucka.com
@jkgreenwood_art / justingreenwoodart.com
@josephryanhill

First edition: March 2019
ISBN 978-1-62010-579-5
eISBN 978-1-62010-302-9

Library of Congress Control Number: 2018950886

1 3 5 7 9 10 8 6 4 2

STUMPTOWN, VOLUME FOUR: THE CASE OF THE CUP OF JOE, March 2019. Published by Oni
Press, Inc. 1319 SE Martin Luther King Jr. Blvd., Suite 240, Portland, OR 97214. STUMPTOWN
is ™ & © 2019 Greg Rucka. Oni Press logo and icon are ™ & © 2019 Oni Press, Inc. All rights
reserved. Oni Press logo and icon artwork created by Keith A. Wood. The events, institutions,
and characters presented in this book are fictional. Any resemblance to actual persons, living or
dead, is purely coincidental. No portion of this publication may be reproduced, by any means,
without the express written permission of the copyright holders.

PRINTED IN CHINA.

Chapter One

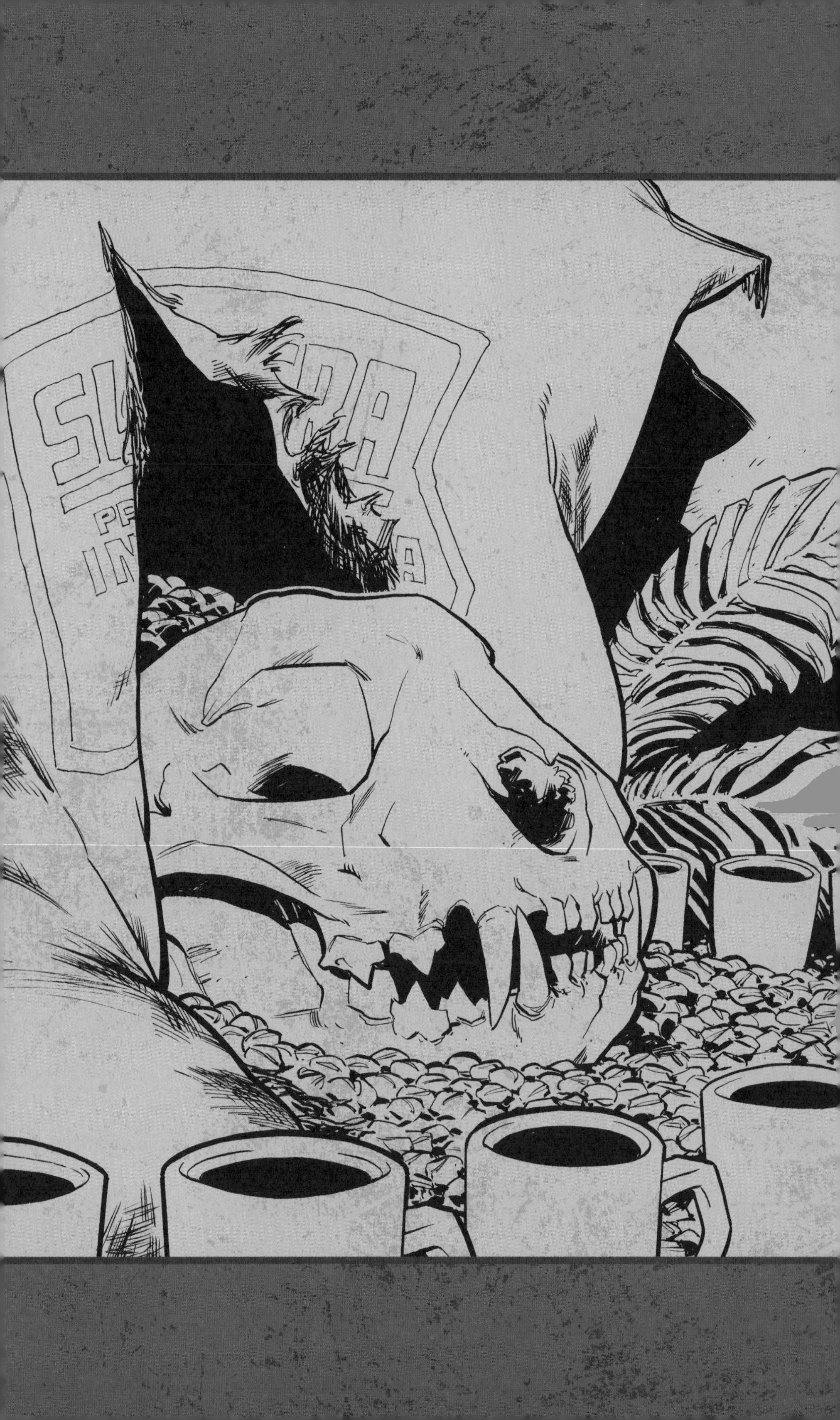

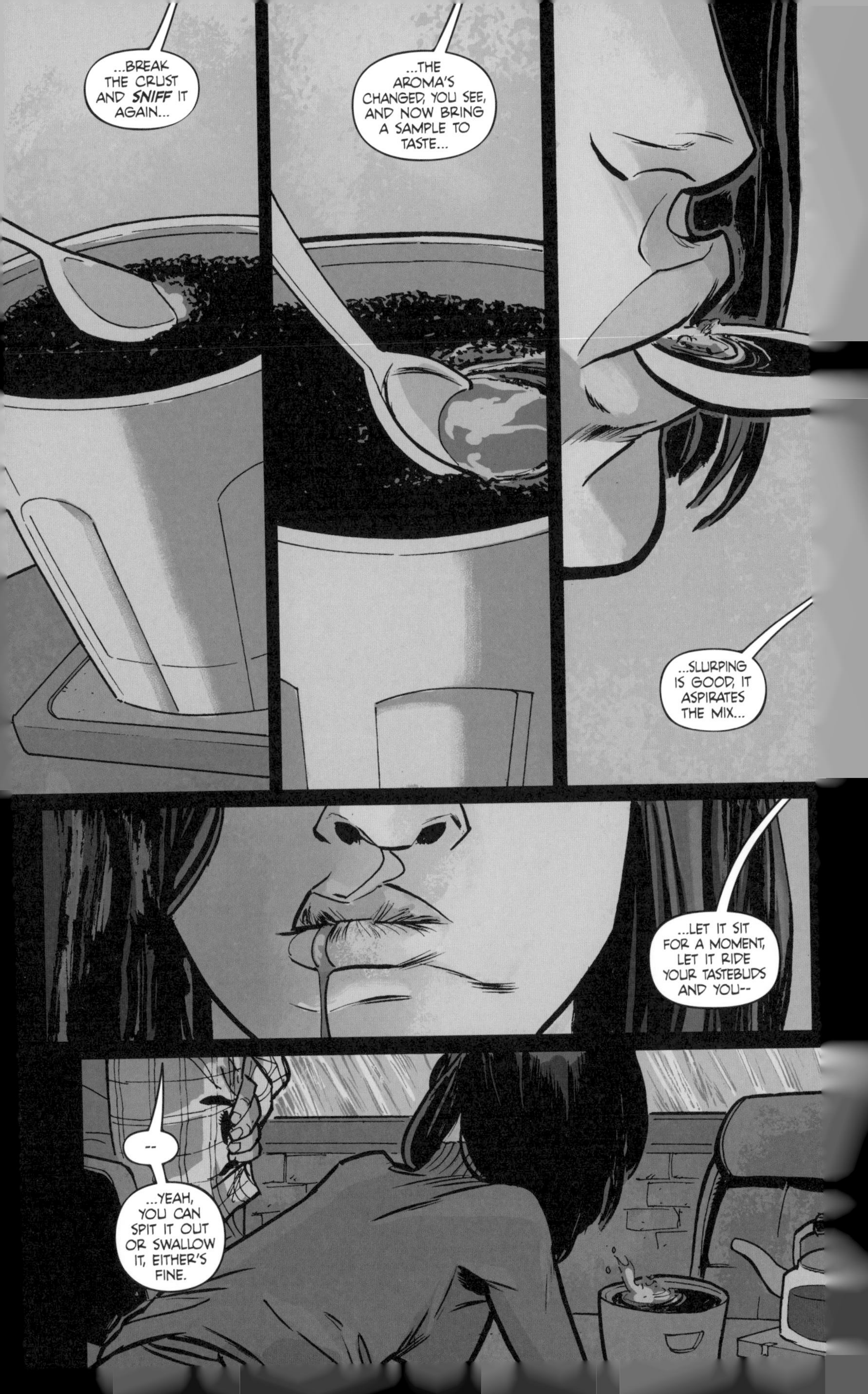
...BREAK THE CRUST AND SNIFF IT AGAIN...
...THE AROMA'S CHANGED, YOU SEE, AND NOW BRING A SAMPLE TO TASTE...
...SLURPING IS GOOD, IT ASPIRATES THE MIX...
...LET IT SIT FOR A MOMENT, LET IT RIDE YOUR TASTEBUDS AND YOU--
--
...YEAH, YOU CAN SPIT IT OUT OR SWALLOW IT, EITHER'S FINE.

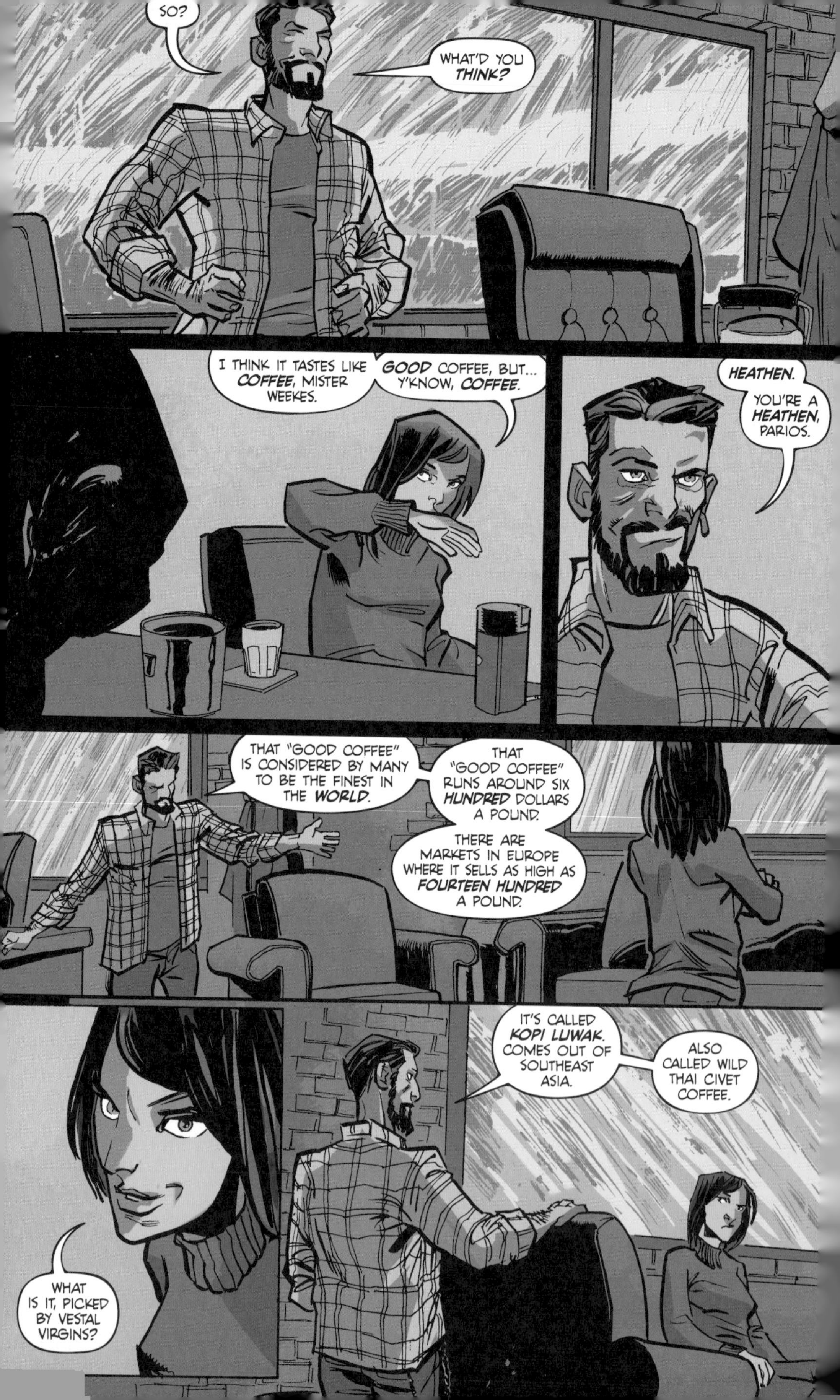
SO?
WHAT'D YOU THINK?
I THINK IT TASTES LIKE COFFEE, MISTER WEEKES.
GOOD COFFEE, BUT... Y'KNOW, COFFEE.
HEATHEN.
YOU'RE A HEATHEN, PARIOS.
THAT "GOOD COFFEE" IS CONSIDERED BY MANY TO BE THE FINEST IN THE WORLD.
THAT "GOOD COFFEE" RUNS AROUND SIX HUNDRED DOLLARS A POUND.
THERE ARE MARKETS IN EUROPE WHERE IT SELLS AS HIGH AS FOURTEEN HUNDRED A POUND.
IT'S CALLED KOPI LUWAK. COMES OUT OF SOUTHEAST ASIA.
ALSO CALLED WILD THAI CIVET COFFEE.
WHAT IS IT, PICKED BY VESTAL VIRGINS?

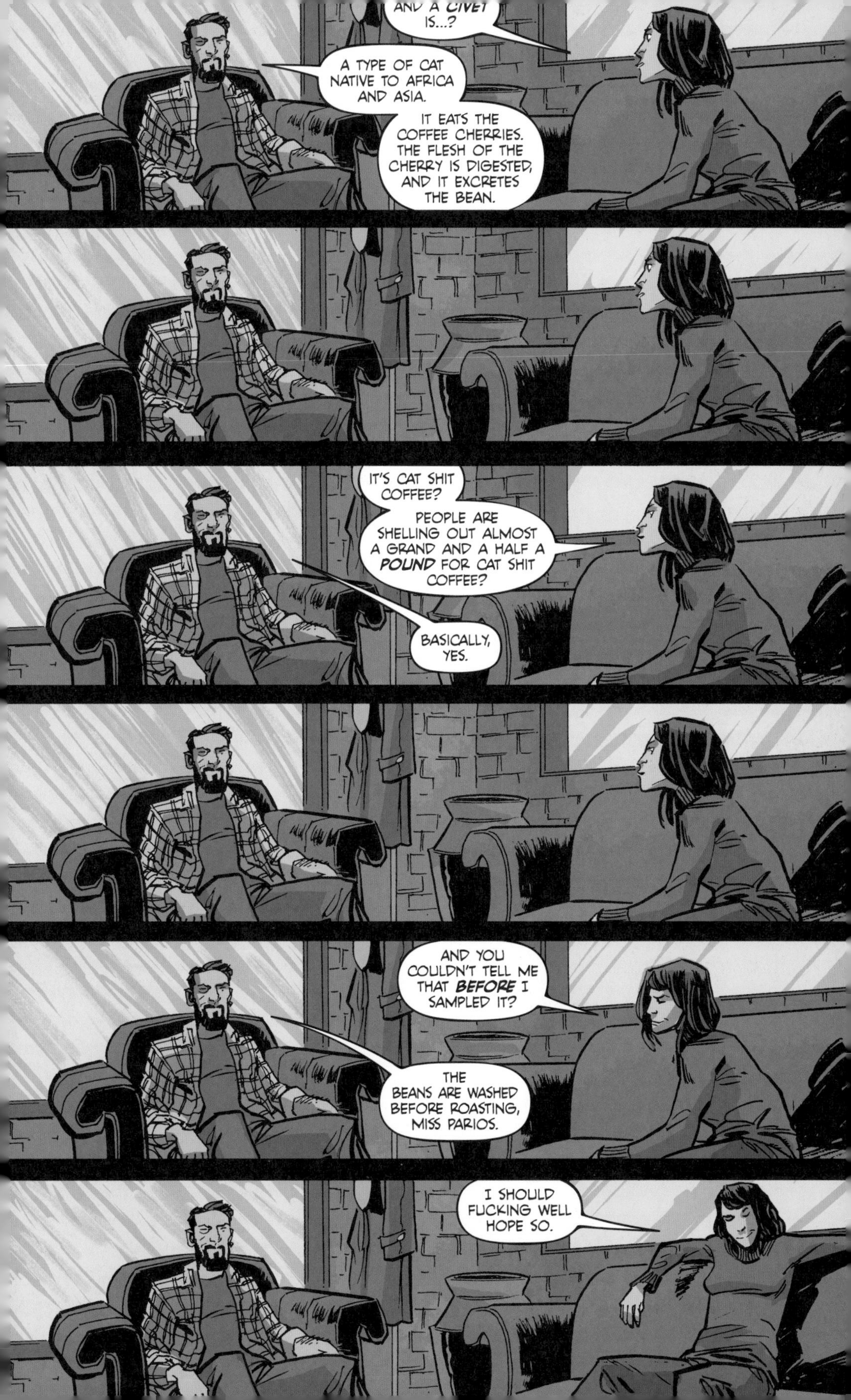
AND A *CIVET* IS...?
A TYPE OF CAT NATIVE TO AFRICA AND ASIA.
IT EATS THE COFFEE CHERRIES. THE FLESH OF THE CHERRY IS DIGESTED, AND IT EXCRETES THE BEAN.
IT'S CAT SHIT COFFEE?
PEOPLE ARE SHELLING OUT ALMOST A GRAND AND A HALF A *POUND* FOR CAT SHIT COFFEE?
BASICALLY, YES.
AND YOU COULDN'T TELL ME THAT *BEFORE* I SAMPLED IT?
THE BEANS ARE WASHED BEFORE ROASTING, MISS PARIOS.
I SHOULD FUCKING WELL HOPE SO.

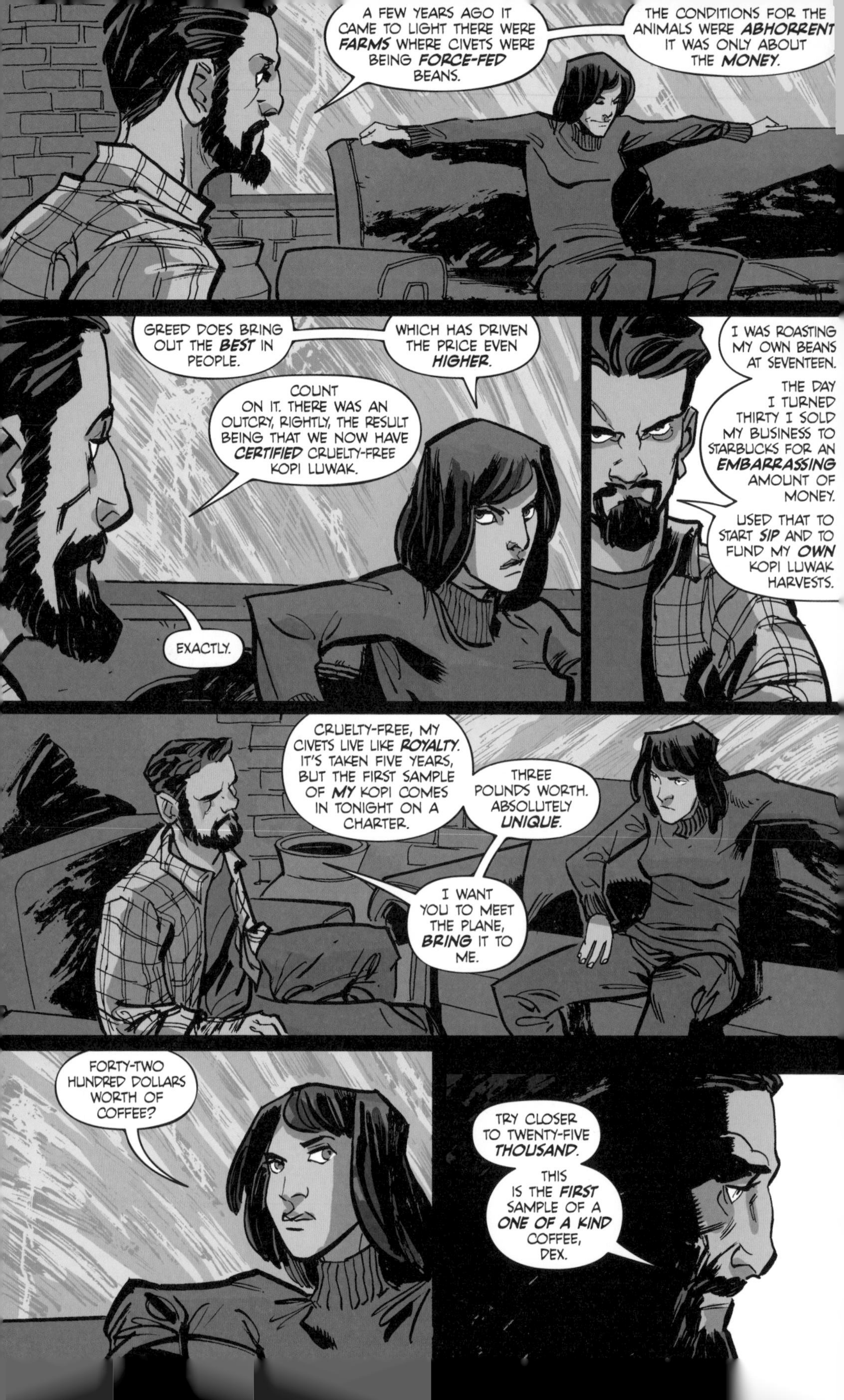
A FEW YEARS AGO IT CAME TO LIGHT THERE WERE FARMS WHERE CIVETS WERE BEING FORCE-FED BEANS.
THE CONDITIONS FOR THE ANIMALS WERE ABHORRENT IT WAS ONLY ABOUT THE MONEY.
GREED DOES BRING OUT THE BEST IN PEOPLE.
WHICH HAS DRIVEN THE PRICE EVEN HIGHER.
COUNT ON IT. THERE WAS AN OUTCRY, RIGHTLY, THE RESULT BEING THAT WE NOW HAVE CERTIFIED CRUELTY-FREE KOPI LUWAK.
EXACTLY.
I WAS ROASTING MY OWN BEANS AT SEVENTEEN.
THE DAY I TURNED THIRTY I SOLD MY BUSINESS TO STARBUCKS FOR AN EMBARRASSING AMOUNT OF MONEY.
USED THAT TO START SIP AND TO FUND MY OWN KOPI LUWAK HARVESTS.
CRUELTY-FREE, MY CIVETS LIVE LIKE ROYALTY. IT'S TAKEN FIVE YEARS, BUT THE FIRST SAMPLE OF MY KOPI COMES IN TONIGHT ON A CHARTER.
THREE POUNDS WORTH. ABSOLUTELY UNIQUE.
I WANT YOU TO MEET THE PLANE, BRING IT TO ME.
FORTY-TWO HUNDRED DOLLARS WORTH OF COFFEE?
TRY CLOSER TO TWENTY-FIVE THOUSAND.
THIS IS THE FIRST SAMPLE OF A ONE OF A KIND COFFEE, DEX.

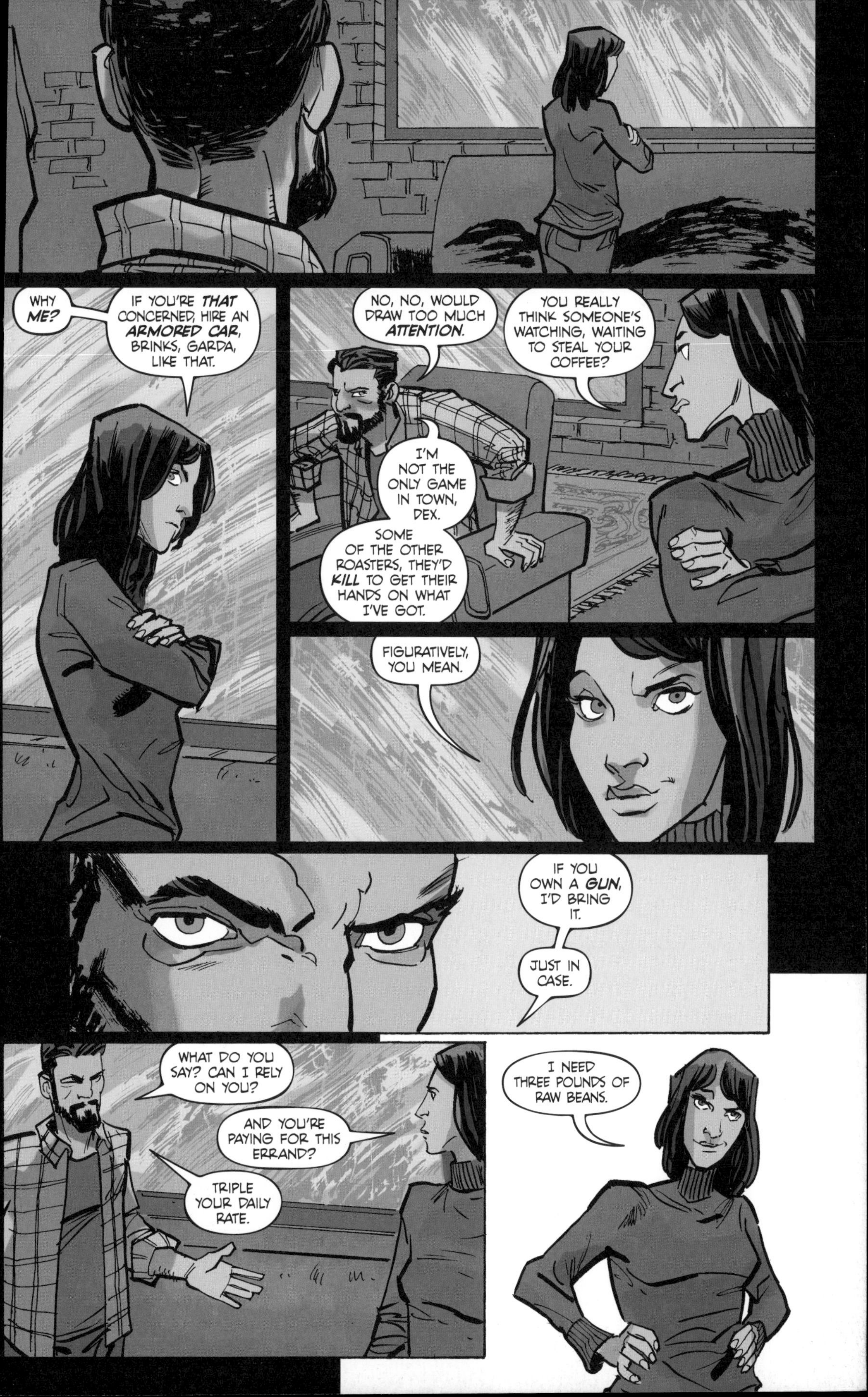
WHY ME?
IF YOU'RE THAT CONCERNED, HIRE AN ARMORED CAR, BRINKS, GARDA, LIKE THAT.
NO, NO, WOULD DRAW TOO MUCH ATTENTION.
YOU REALLY THINK SOMEONE'S WATCHING, WAITING TO STEAL YOUR COFFEE?
I'M NOT THE ONLY GAME IN TOWN, DEX.
SOME OF THE OTHER ROASTERS, THEY'D KILL TO GET THEIR HANDS ON WHAT I'VE GOT.
FIGURATIVELY, YOU MEAN.
IF YOU OWN A GUN, I'D BRING IT.
JUST IN CASE.
WHAT DO YOU SAY? CAN I RELY ON YOU?
AND YOU'RE PAYING FOR THIS ERRAND?
TRIPLE YOUR DAILY RATE.
I NEED THREE POUNDS OF RAW BEANS.

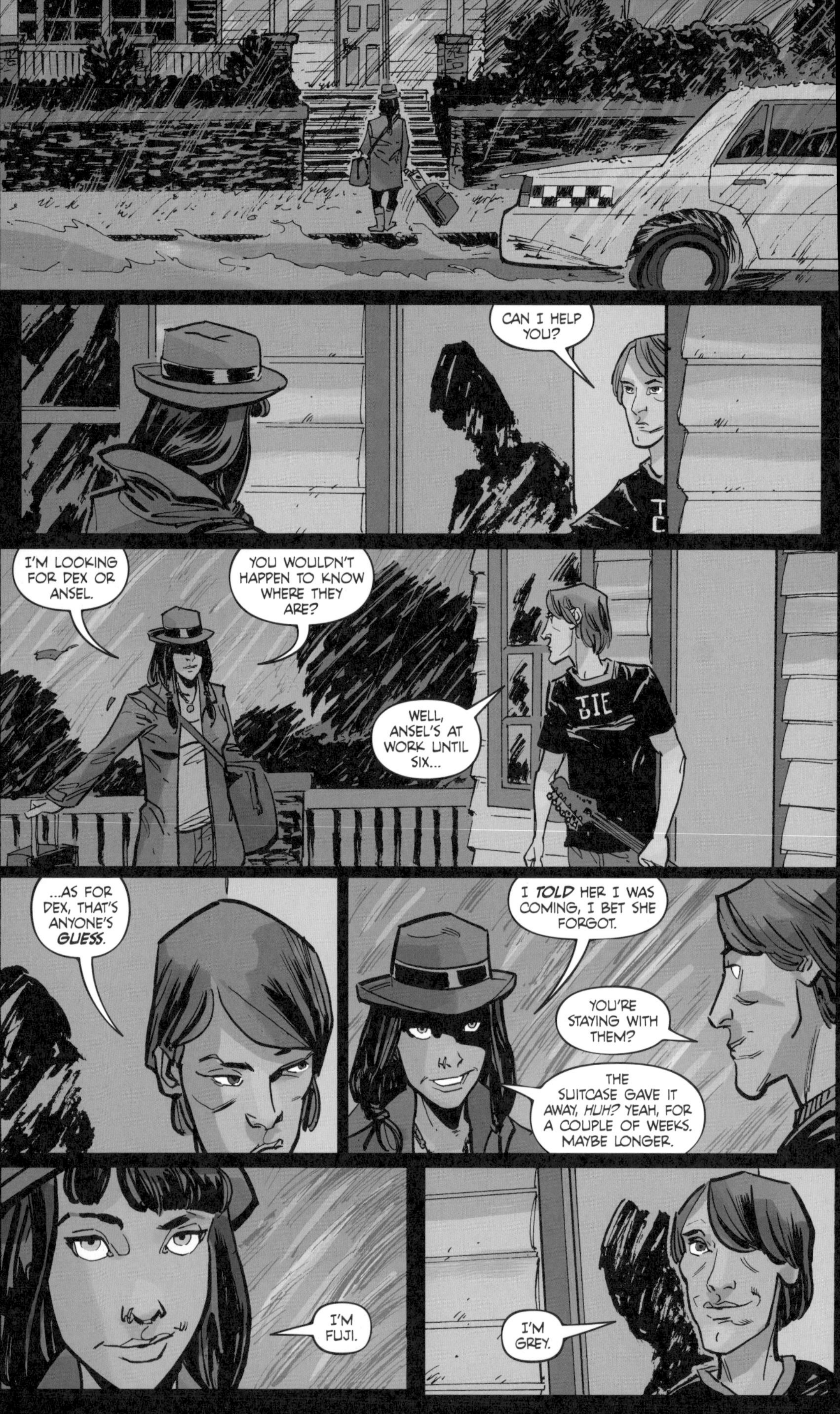

CAN I HELP YOU?
I'M LOOKING FOR DEX OR ANSEL.
YOU WOULDN'T HAPPEN TO KNOW WHERE THEY ARE?
WELL, ANSEL'S AT WORK UNTIL SIX...
...AS FOR DEX, THAT'S ANYONE'S GUESS.
I TOLD HER I WAS COMING, I BET SHE FORGOT.
YOU'RE STAYING WITH THEM?
THE SUITCASE GAVE IT AWAY, HUH? YEAH, FOR A COUPLE OF WEEKS. MAYBE LONGER.
I'M FUJI.
I'M GREY.

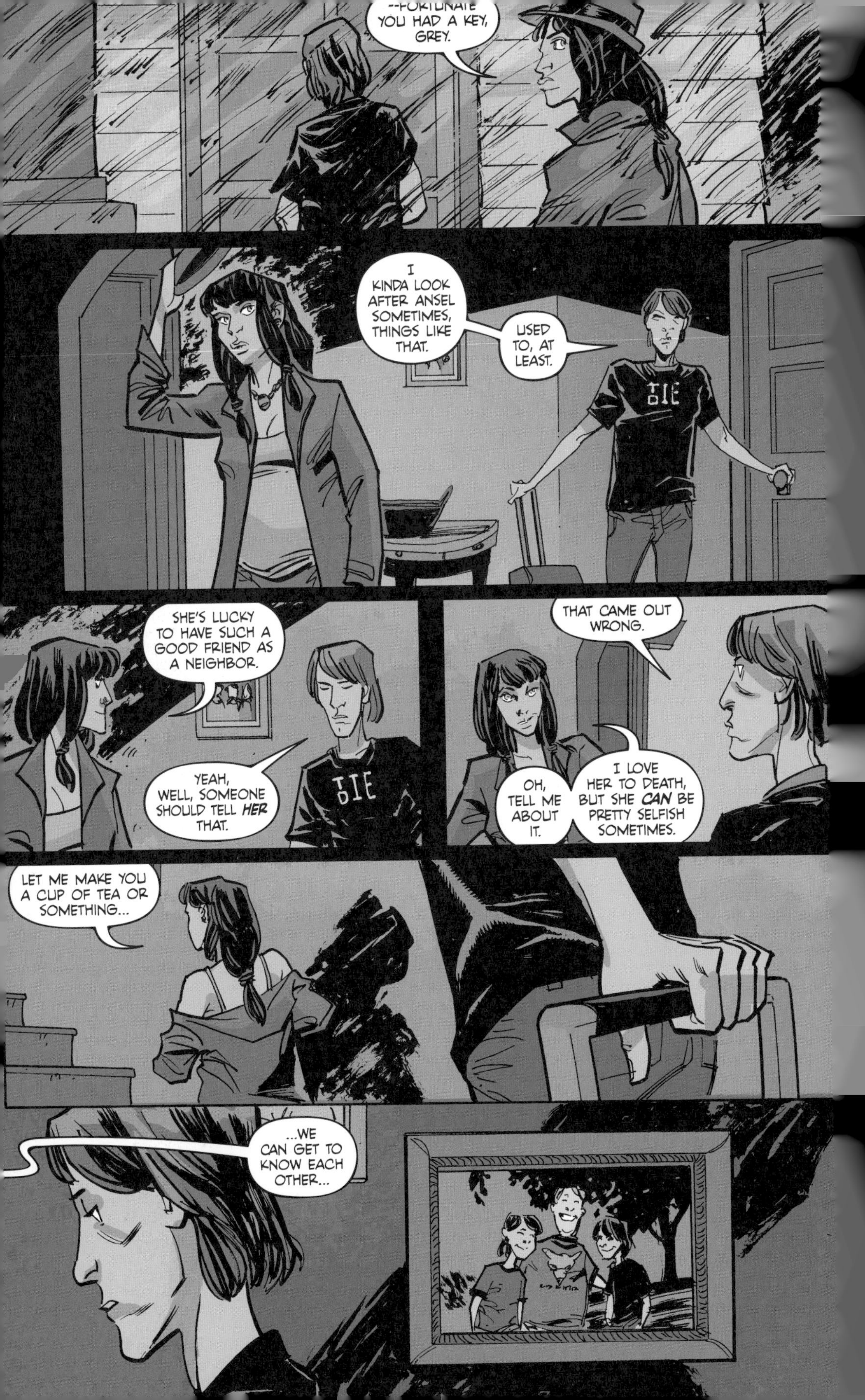
--FORTUNATE YOU HAD A KEY, GREY.
I KINDA LOOK AFTER ANSEL SOMETIMES, THINGS LIKE THAT.
USED TO, AT LEAST.
TIE DIE
SHE'S LUCKY TO HAVE SUCH A GOOD FRIEND AS A NEIGHBOR.
YEAH, WELL, SOMEONE SHOULD TELL HER THAT.
TIE DIE
THAT CAME OUT WRONG.
I LOVE HER TO DEATH, BUT SHE CAN BE PRETTY SELFISH SOMETIMES.
OH, TELL ME ABOUT IT.
LET ME MAKE YOU A CUP OF TEA OR SOMETHING...
...WE CAN GET TO KNOW EACH OTHER...

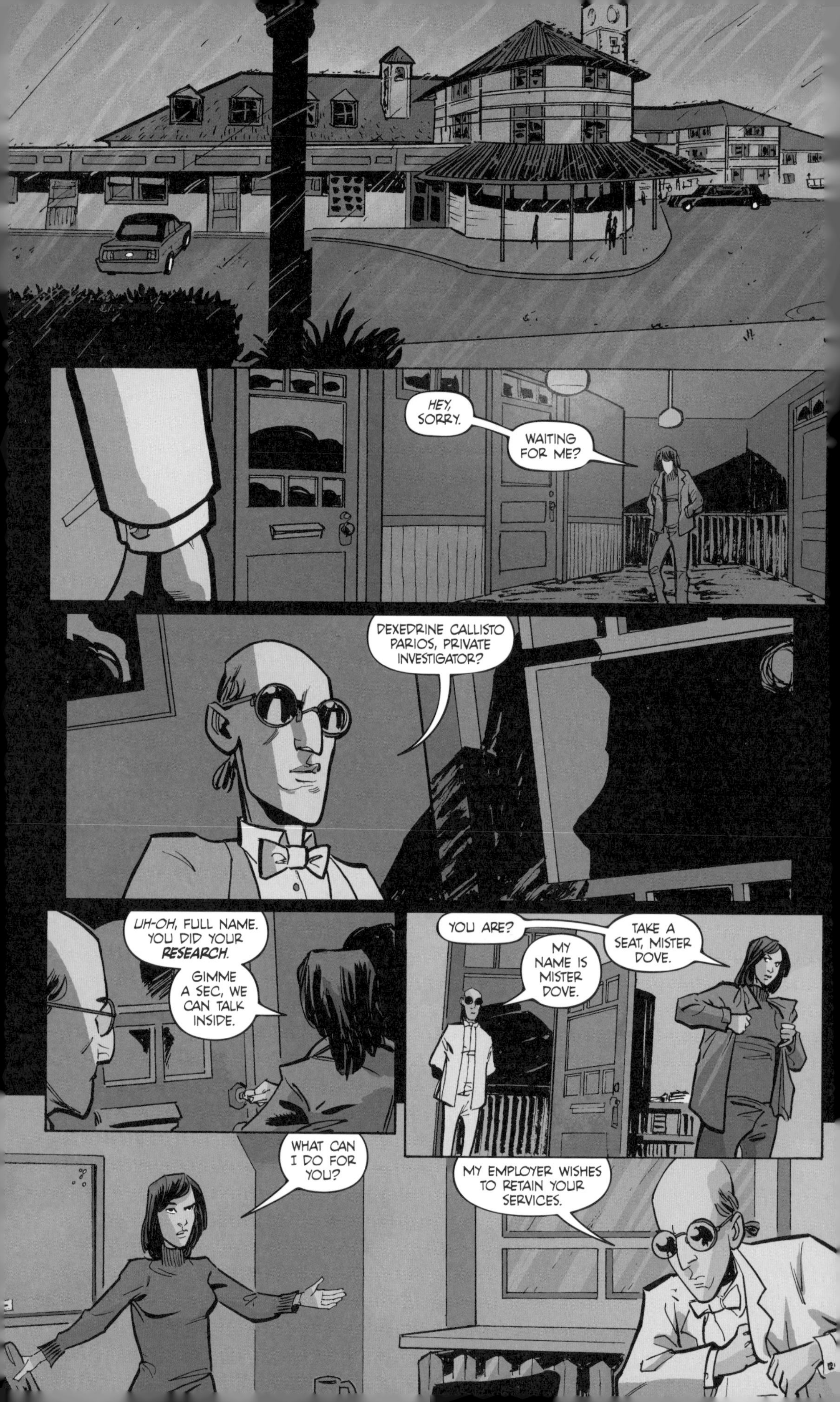

HEY, SORRY.
WAITING FOR ME?
DEXEDRINE CALLISTO PARIOS, PRIVATE INVESTIGATOR?
UH-OH, FULL NAME. YOU DID YOUR RESEARCH.
GIMME A SEC, WE CAN TALK INSIDE.
YOU ARE?
MY NAME IS MISTER DOVE.
TAKE A SEAT, MISTER DOVE.
WHAT CAN I DO FOR YOU?
MY EMPLOYER WISHES TO RETAIN YOUR SERVICES.

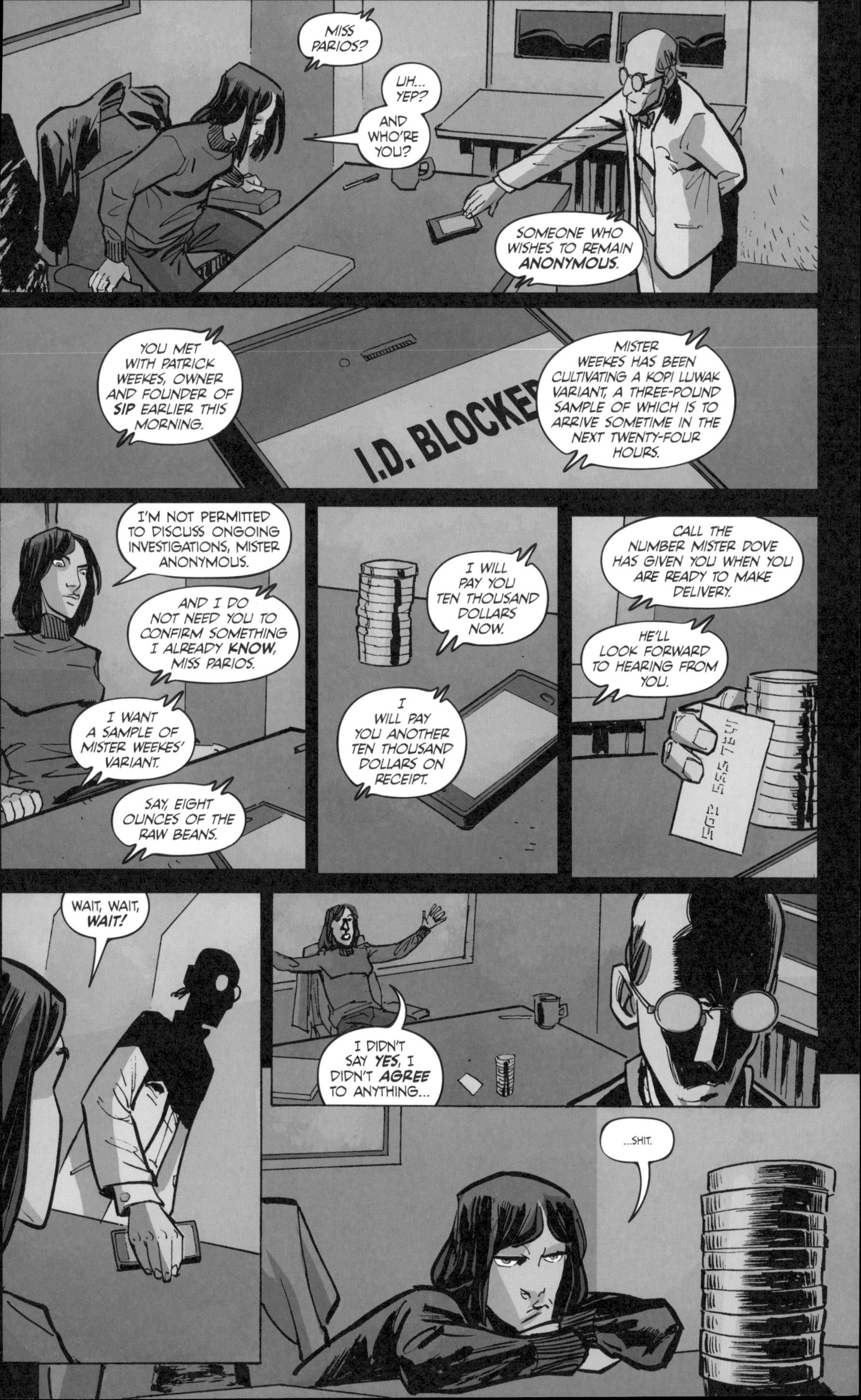
MISS PARIOS?
UH... YEP?
AND WHO'RE YOU?
SOMEONE WHO WISHES TO REMAIN ANONYMOUS.
YOU MET WITH PATRICK WEEKES, OWNER AND FOUNDER OF SIP EARLIER THIS MORNING.
I.D. BLOCKED
MISTER WEEKES HAS BEEN CULTIVATING A KOPI LUWAK VARIANT, A THREE-POUND SAMPLE OF WHICH IS TO ARRIVE SOMETIME IN THE NEXT TWENTY-FOUR HOURS.
I'M NOT PERMITTED TO DISCUSS ONGOING INVESTIGATIONS, MISTER ANONYMOUS.
AND I DO NOT NEED YOU TO CONFIRM SOMETHING I ALREADY KNOW, MISS PARIOS.
I WANT A SAMPLE OF MISTER WEEKES' VARIANT.
SAY, EIGHT OUNCES OF THE RAW BEANS.
I WILL PAY YOU TEN THOUSAND DOLLARS NOW.
I WILL PAY YOU ANOTHER TEN THOUSAND DOLLARS ON RECEIPT.
CALL THE NUMBER MISTER DOVE HAS GIVEN YOU WHEN YOU ARE READY TO MAKE DELIVERY.
HE'LL LOOK FORWARD TO HEARING FROM YOU.
WAIT, WAIT, WAIT!
I DIDN'T SAY YES, I DIDN'T AGREE TO ANYTHING...
...SHIT.

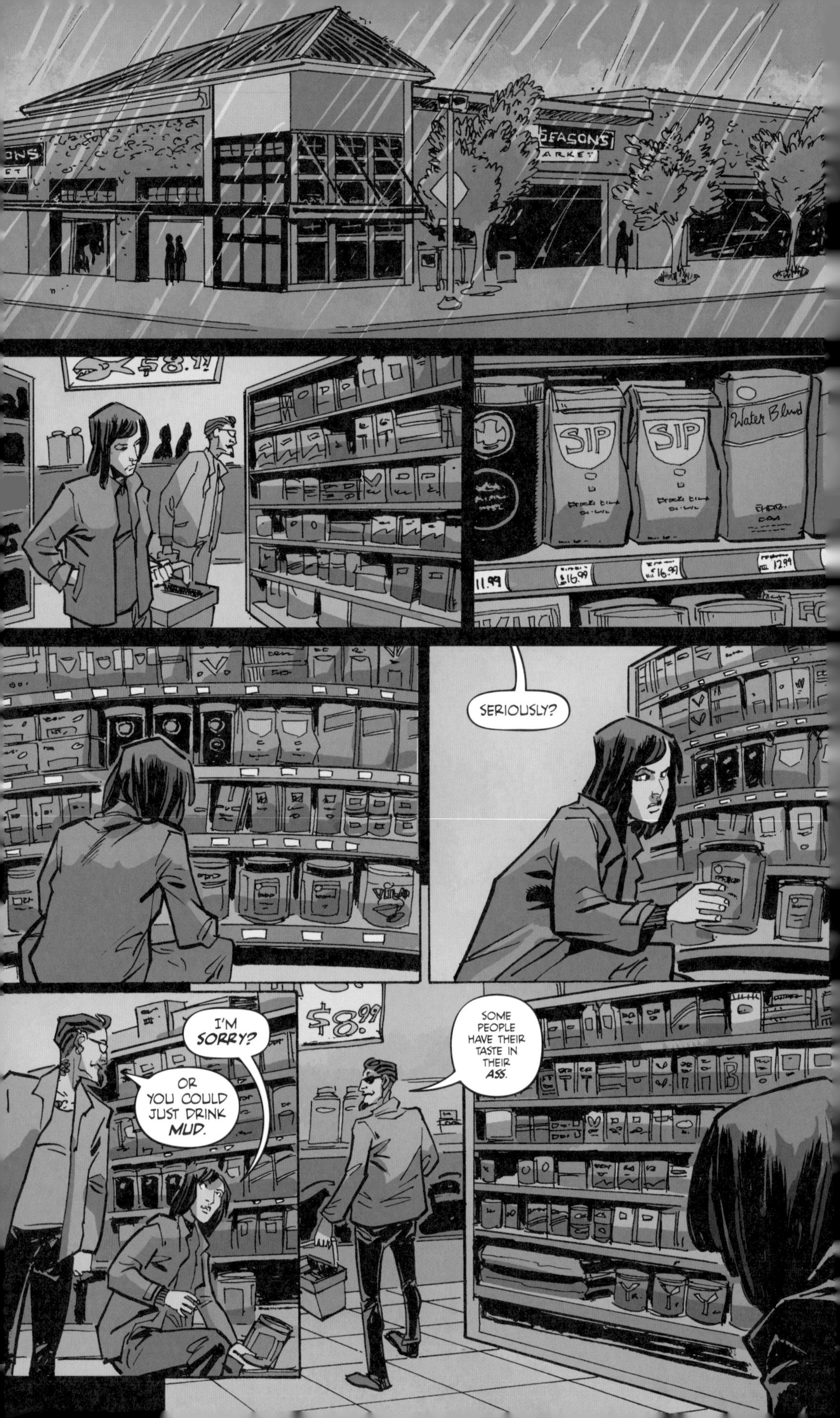
SEASONS
MARKET
$8.99
SIP
SIP
Water Blend
11.99
$16.99
$16.99
12.99
SERIOUSLY?
I'M SORRY?
OR YOU COULD JUST DRINK MUD.
SOME PEOPLE HAVE THEIR TASTE IN THEIR ASS.

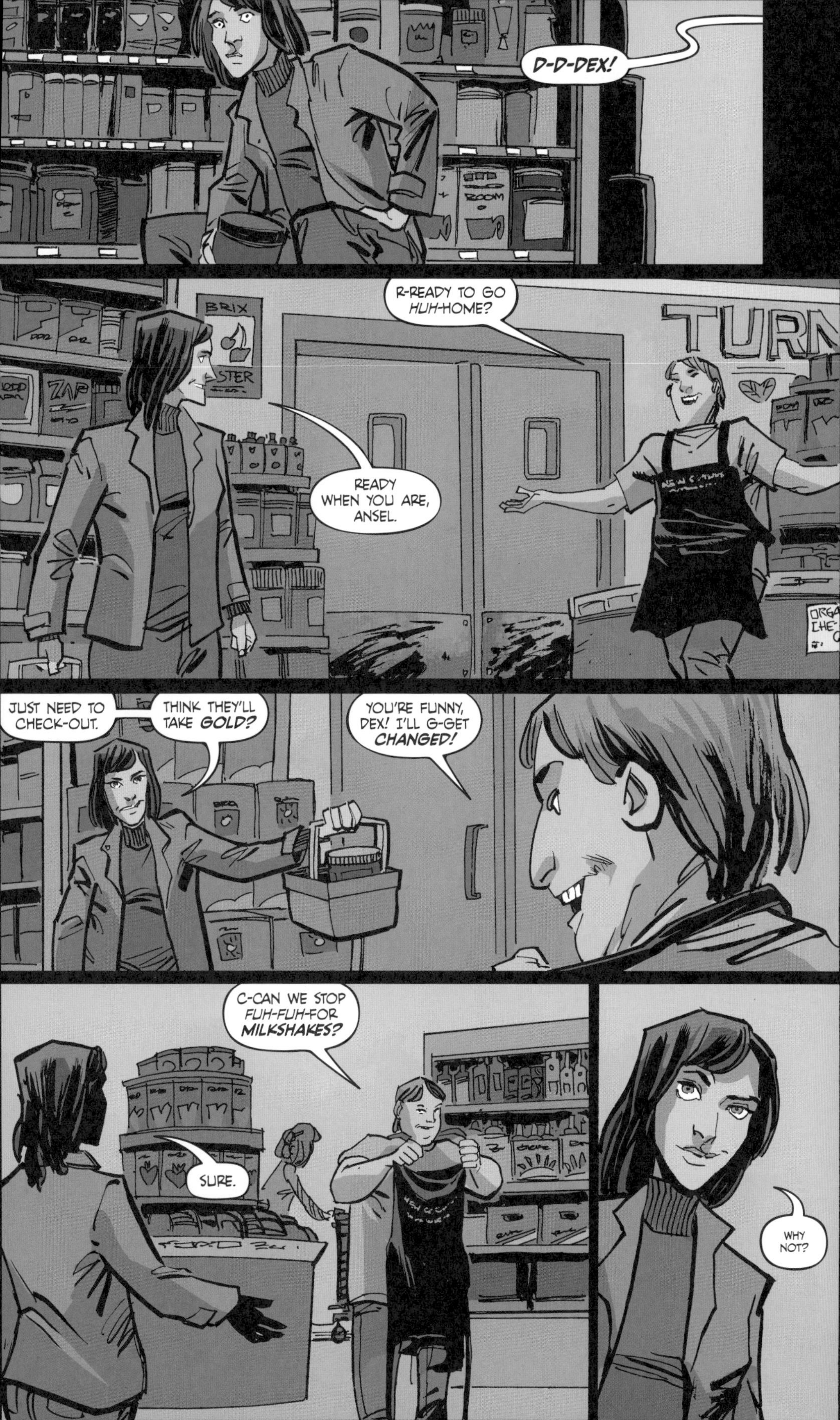
D-D-DEX!
R-READY TO GO HUH-HOME?
READY WHEN YOU ARE, ANSEL.
TURN
BRIX
JUST NEED TO CHECK-OUT.
THINK THEY'LL TAKE GOLD?
YOU'RE FUNNY, DEX! I'LL G-GET CHANGED!
C-CAN WE STOP FUH-FUH-FOR MILKSHAKES?
SURE.
WHY NOT?

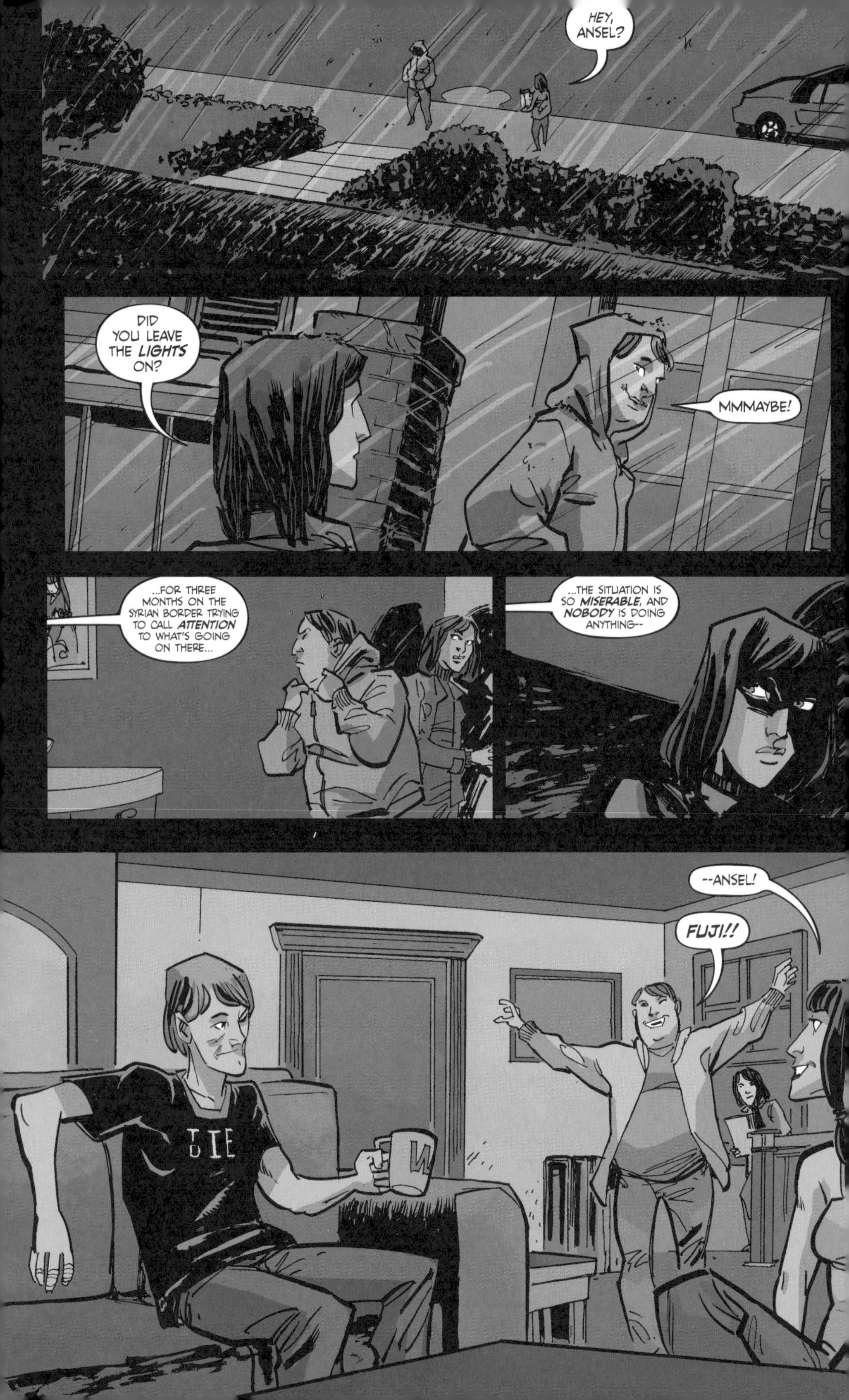
HEY, ANSEL?
DID YOU LEAVE THE LIGHTS ON?
MMMAYBE!
...FOR THREE MONTHS ON THE SYRIAN BORDER TRYING TO CALL ATTENTION TO WHAT'S GOING ON THERE...
...THE SITUATION IS SO MISERABLE, AND NOBODY IS DOING ANYTHING--
--ANSEL!
FUJI!!

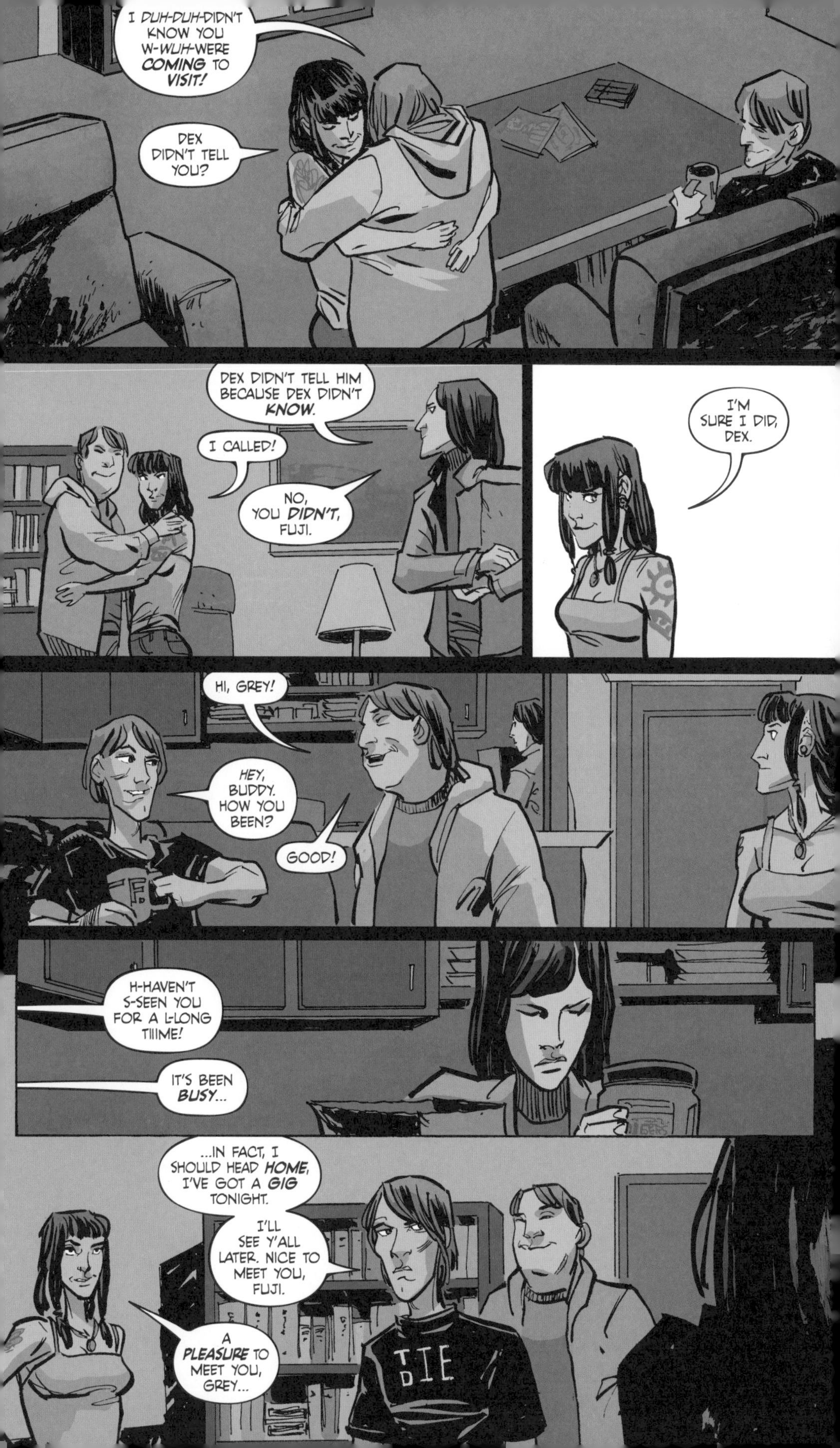

I DUH-DUH-DIDN'T KNOW YOU W-WUH-WERE *COMING* TO *VISIT!*
DEX DIDN'T TELL YOU?
DEX DIDN'T TELL HIM BECAUSE DEX DIDN'T *KNOW*.
I CALLED!
NO, YOU *DIDN'T*, FUJI.
I'M SURE I DID, DEX.
HI, GREY!
HEY, BUDDY. HOW YOU BEEN?
GOOD!
H-HAVEN'T S-SEEN YOU FOR A L-LONG TIIIME!
IT'S BEEN *BUSY*...
...IN FACT, I SHOULD HEAD *HOME*, I'VE GOT A *GIG* TONIGHT.
I'LL SEE Y'ALL LATER. NICE TO MEET YOU, FUJI.
A *PLEASURE* TO MEET YOU, GREY...

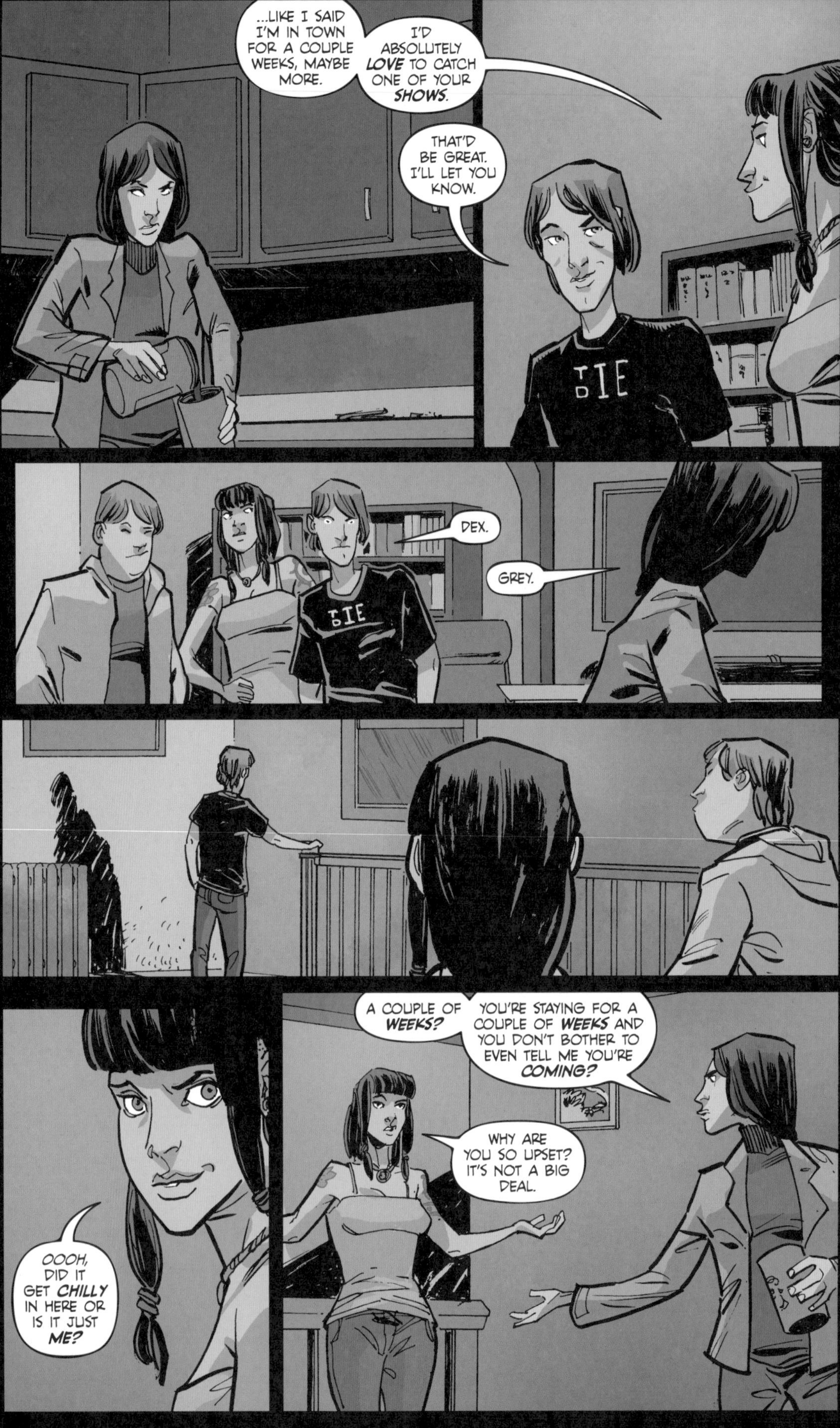
...LIKE I SAID I'M IN TOWN FOR A COUPLE WEEKS, MAYBE MORE.
I'D ABSOLUTELY LOVE TO CATCH ONE OF YOUR SHOWS.
THAT'D BE GREAT. I'LL LET YOU KNOW.
DEX.
GREY.
A COUPLE OF WEEKS?
YOU'RE STAYING FOR A COUPLE OF WEEKS AND YOU DON'T BOTHER TO EVEN TELL ME YOU'RE COMING?
WHY ARE YOU SO UPSET? IT'S NOT A BIG DEAL.
OOOH, DID IT GET CHILLY IN HERE OR IS IT JUST ME?

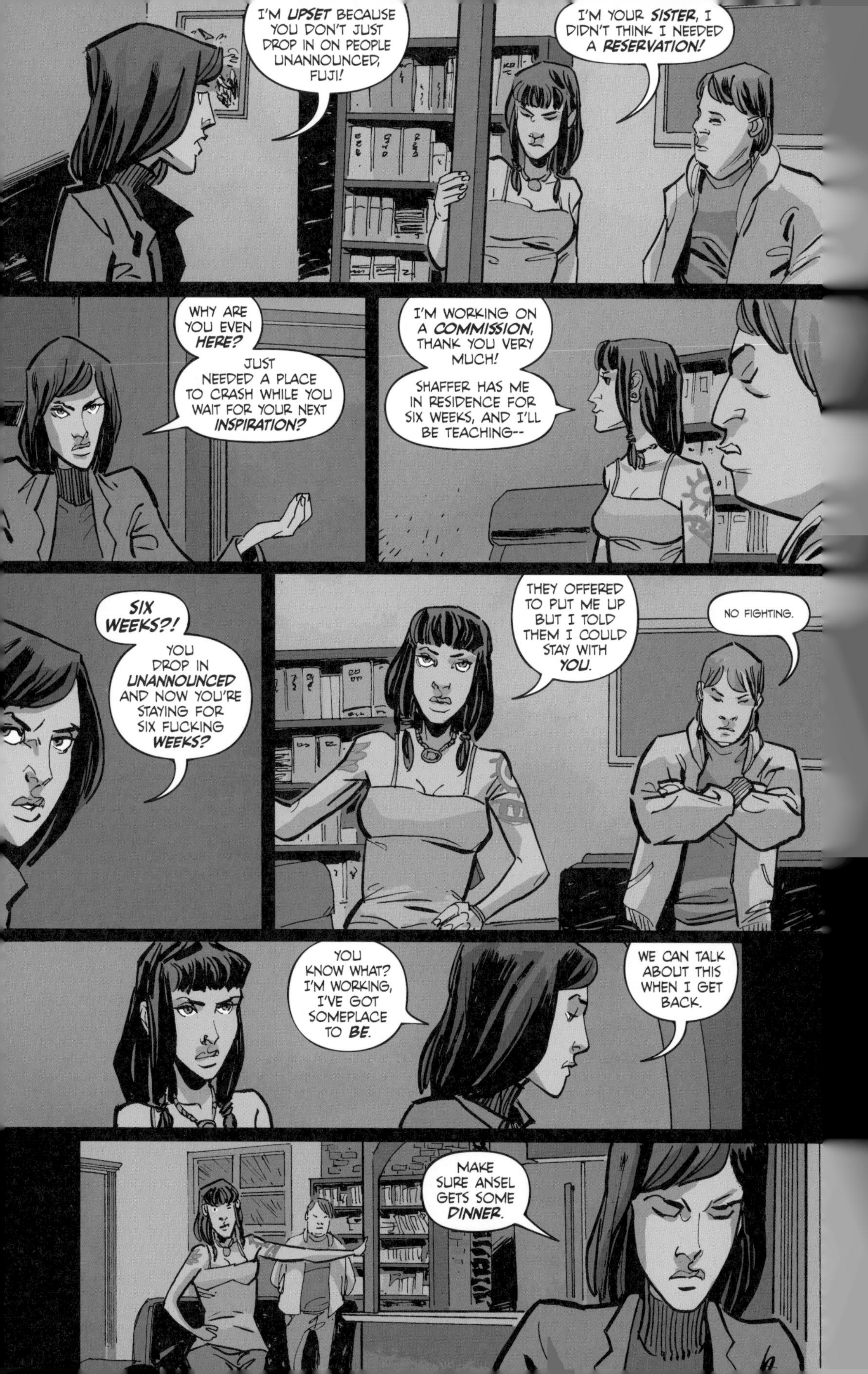
I'M UPSET BECAUSE YOU DON'T JUST DROP IN ON PEOPLE UNANNOUNCED, FUJI!
I'M YOUR SISTER, I DIDN'T THINK I NEEDED A RESERVATION!
WHY ARE YOU EVEN HERE?
JUST NEEDED A PLACE TO CRASH WHILE YOU WAIT FOR YOUR NEXT INSPIRATION?
I'M WORKING ON A COMMISSION, THANK YOU VERY MUCH!
SHAFFER HAS ME IN RESIDENCE FOR SIX WEEKS, AND I'LL BE TEACHING--
SIX WEEKS?!
YOU DROP IN UNANNOUNCED AND NOW YOU'RE STAYING FOR SIX FUCKING WEEKS?
THEY OFFERED TO PUT ME UP BUT I TOLD THEM I COULD STAY WITH YOU.
NO FIGHTING.
YOU KNOW WHAT? I'M WORKING, I'VE GOT SOMEPLACE TO BE.
WE CAN TALK ABOUT THIS WHEN I GET BACK.
MAKE SURE ANSEL GETS SOME DINNER.

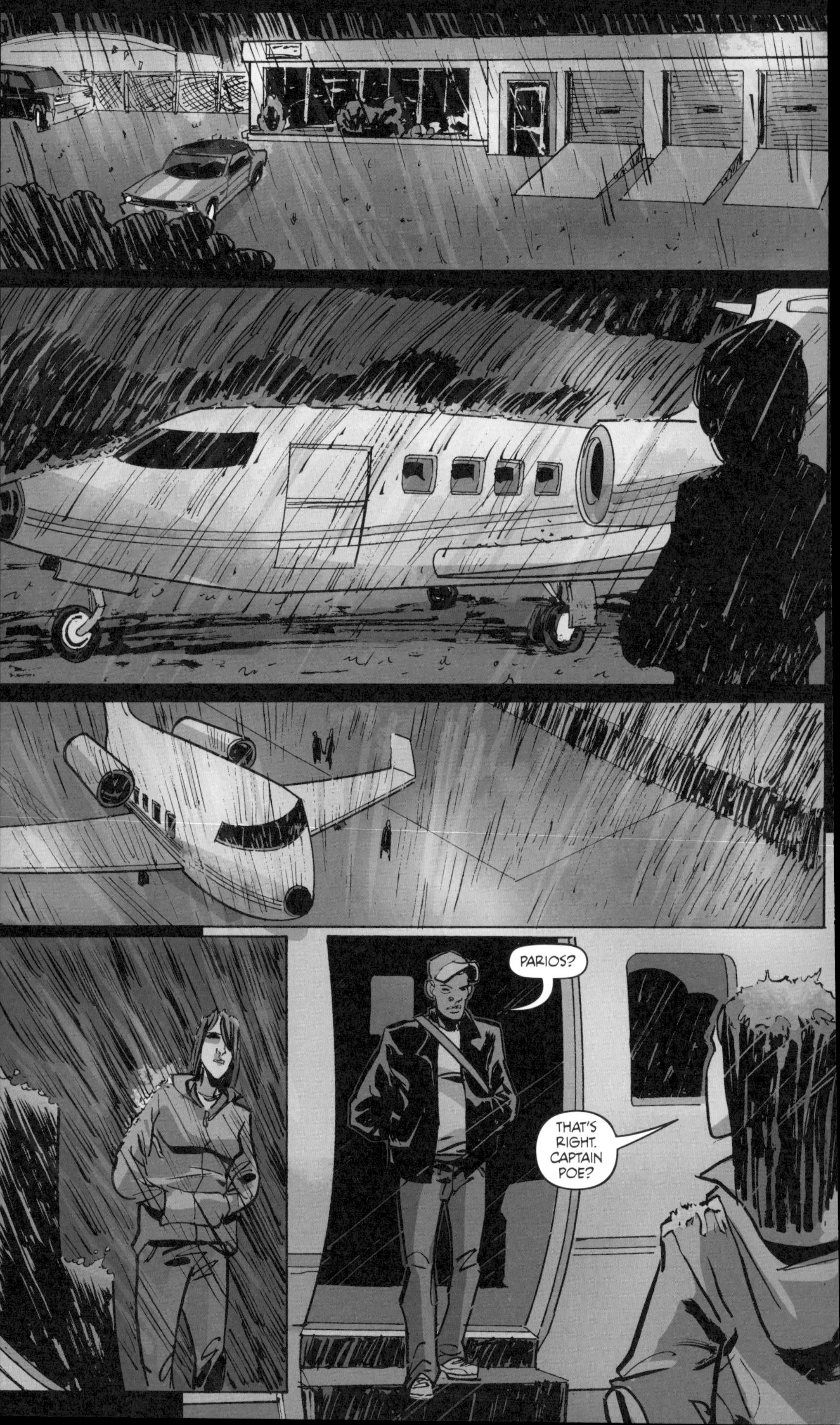
PARIOS?
THAT'S RIGHT. CAPTAIN POE?

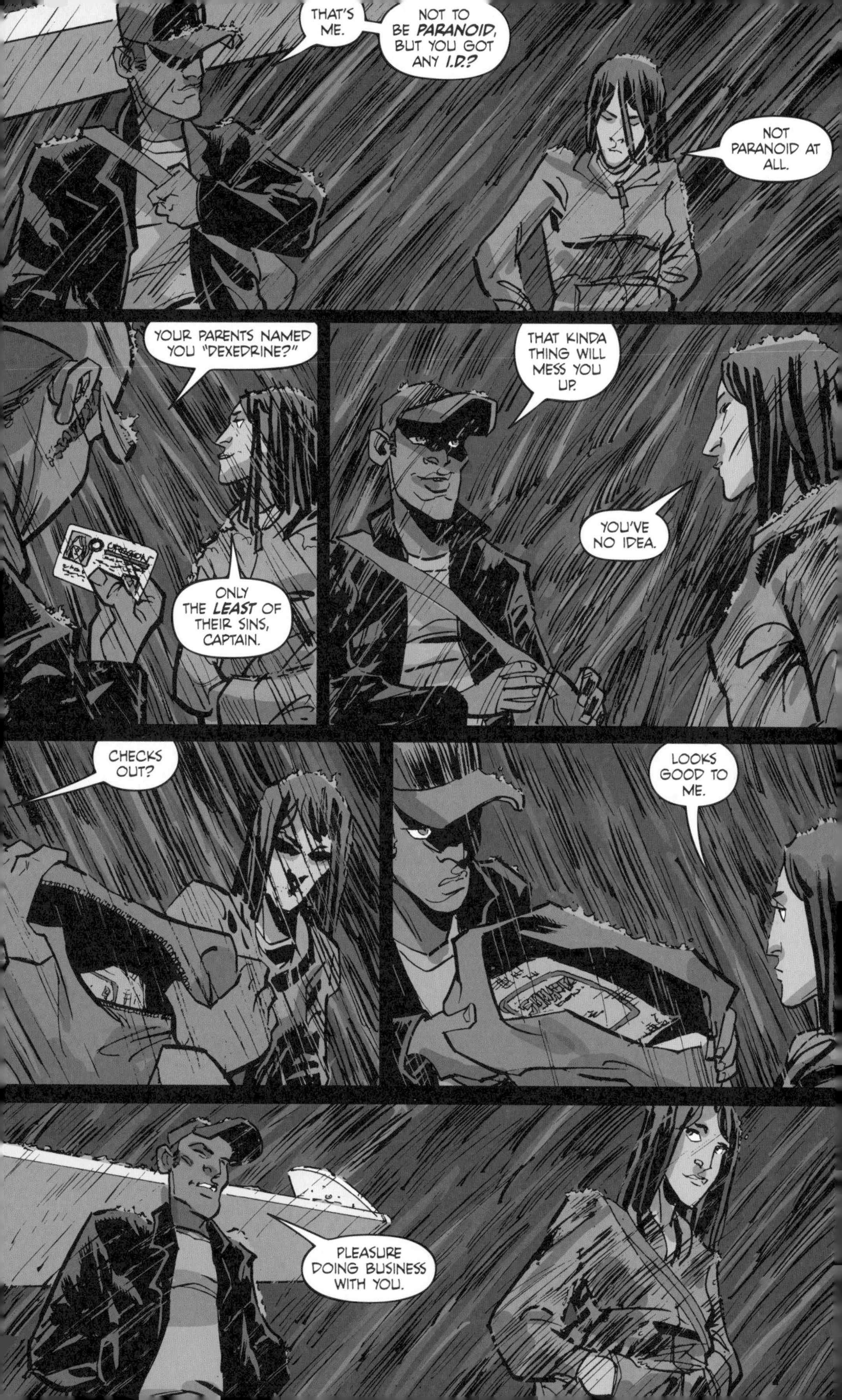
THAT'S ME.
NOT TO BE *PARANOID*, BUT YOU GOT ANY *I.D.?*
NOT PARANOID AT ALL.
YOUR PARENTS NAMED YOU "DEXEDRINE?"
ONLY THE *LEAST* OF THEIR SINS, CAPTAIN.
THAT KINDA THING WILL MESS YOU UP.
YOU'VE NO IDEA.
CHECKS OUT?
LOOKS GOOD TO ME.
PLEASURE DOING BUSINESS WITH YOU.

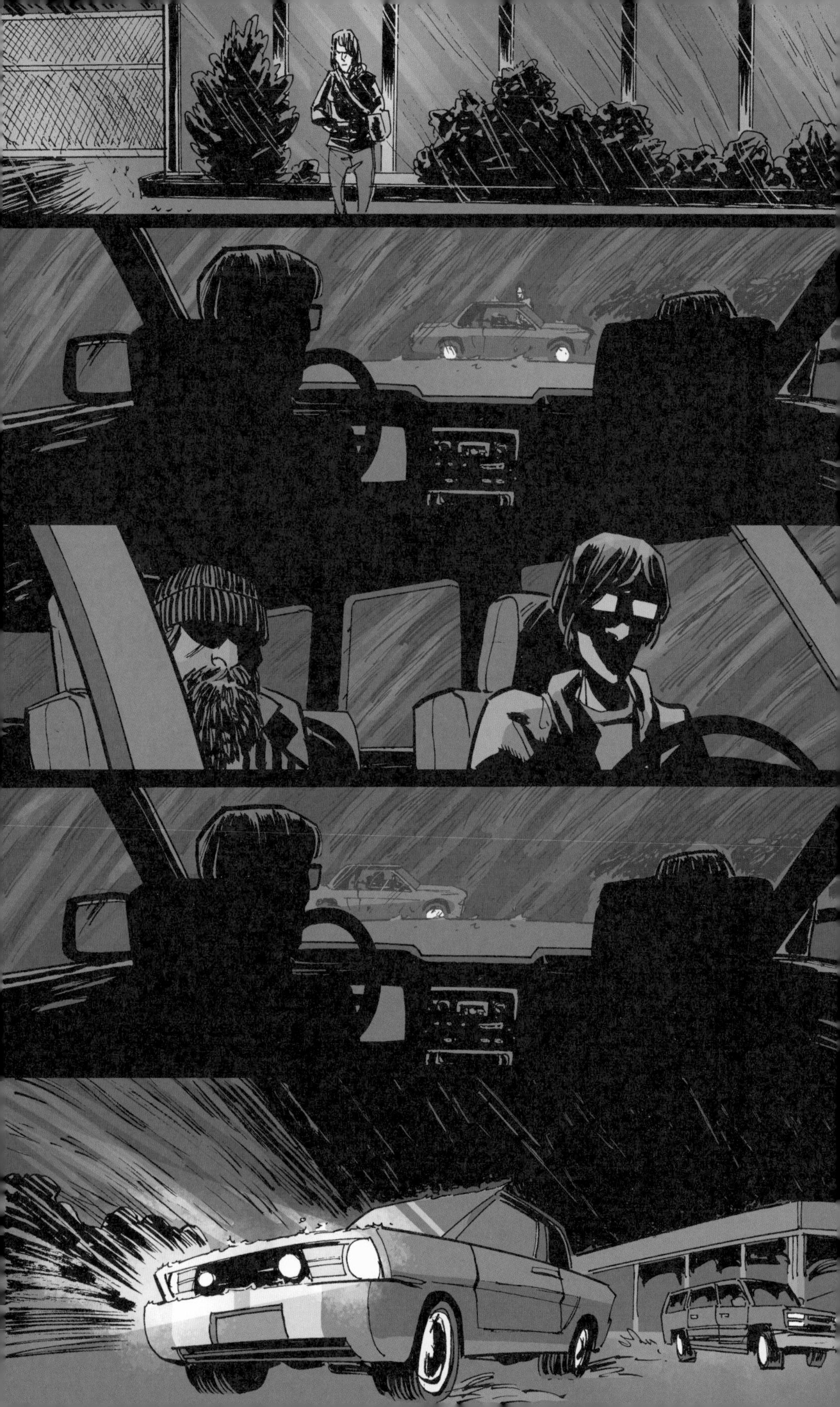

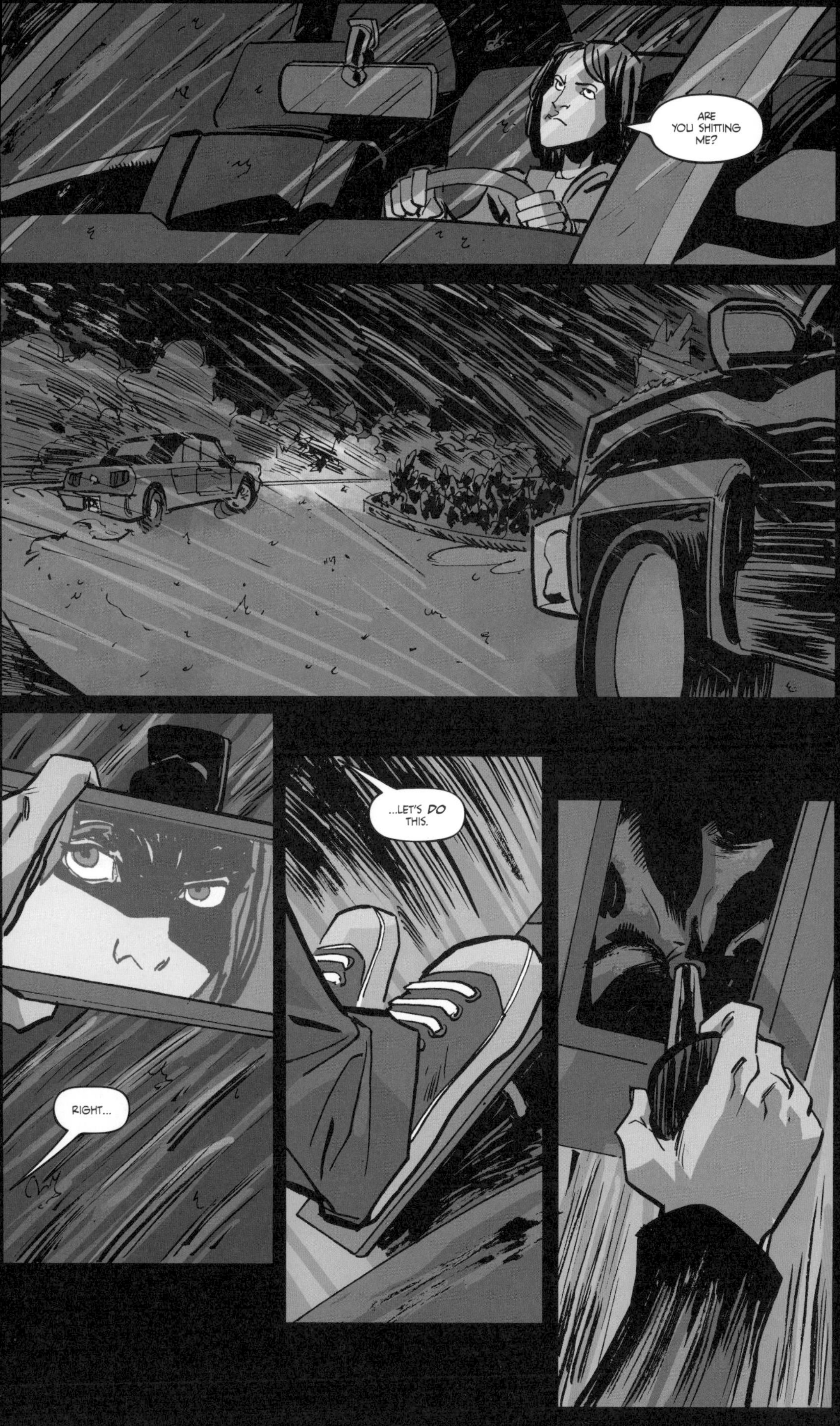
ARE YOU SHITTING ME?
RIGHT...
...LET'S DO THIS.

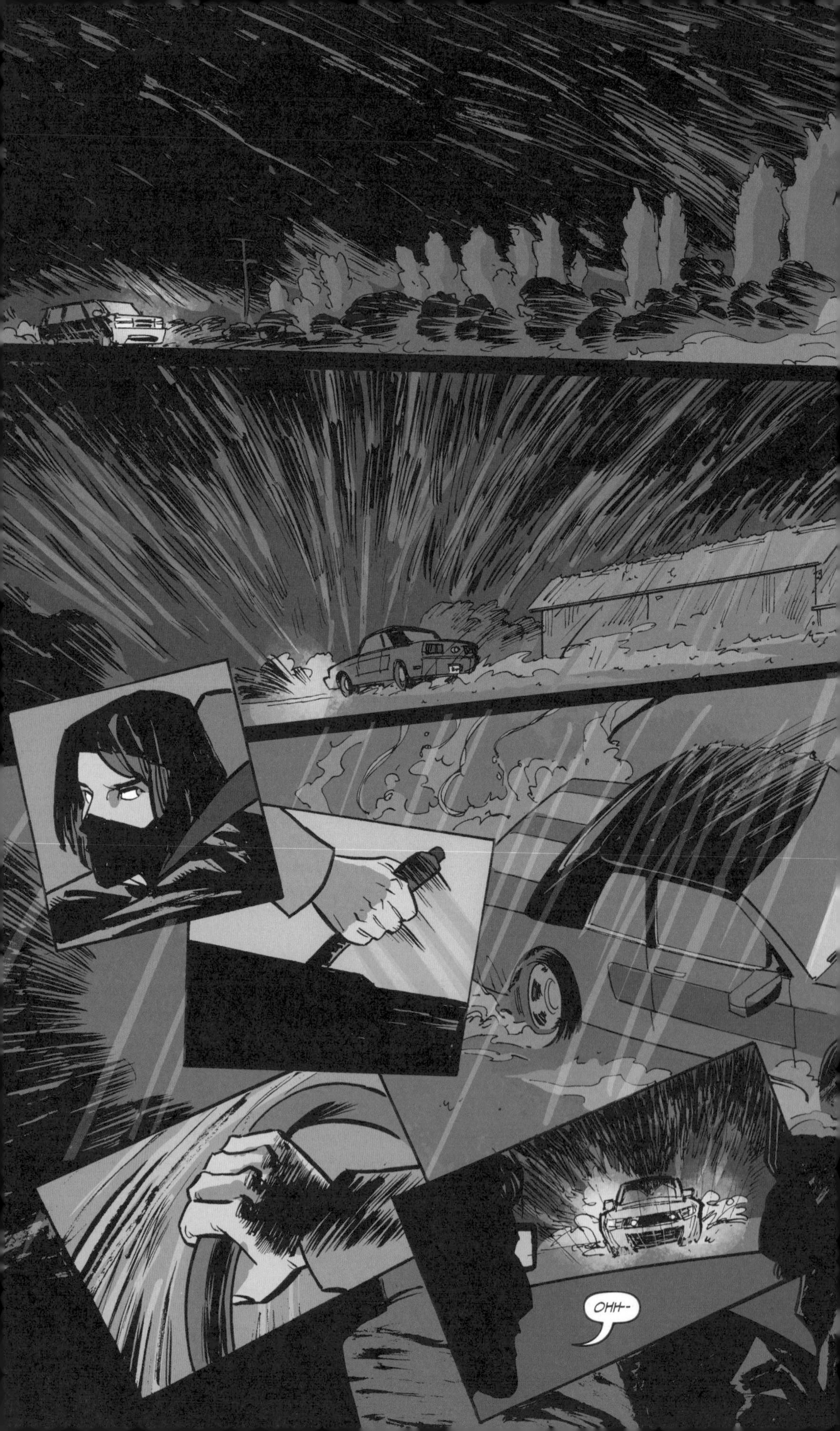
OHH--

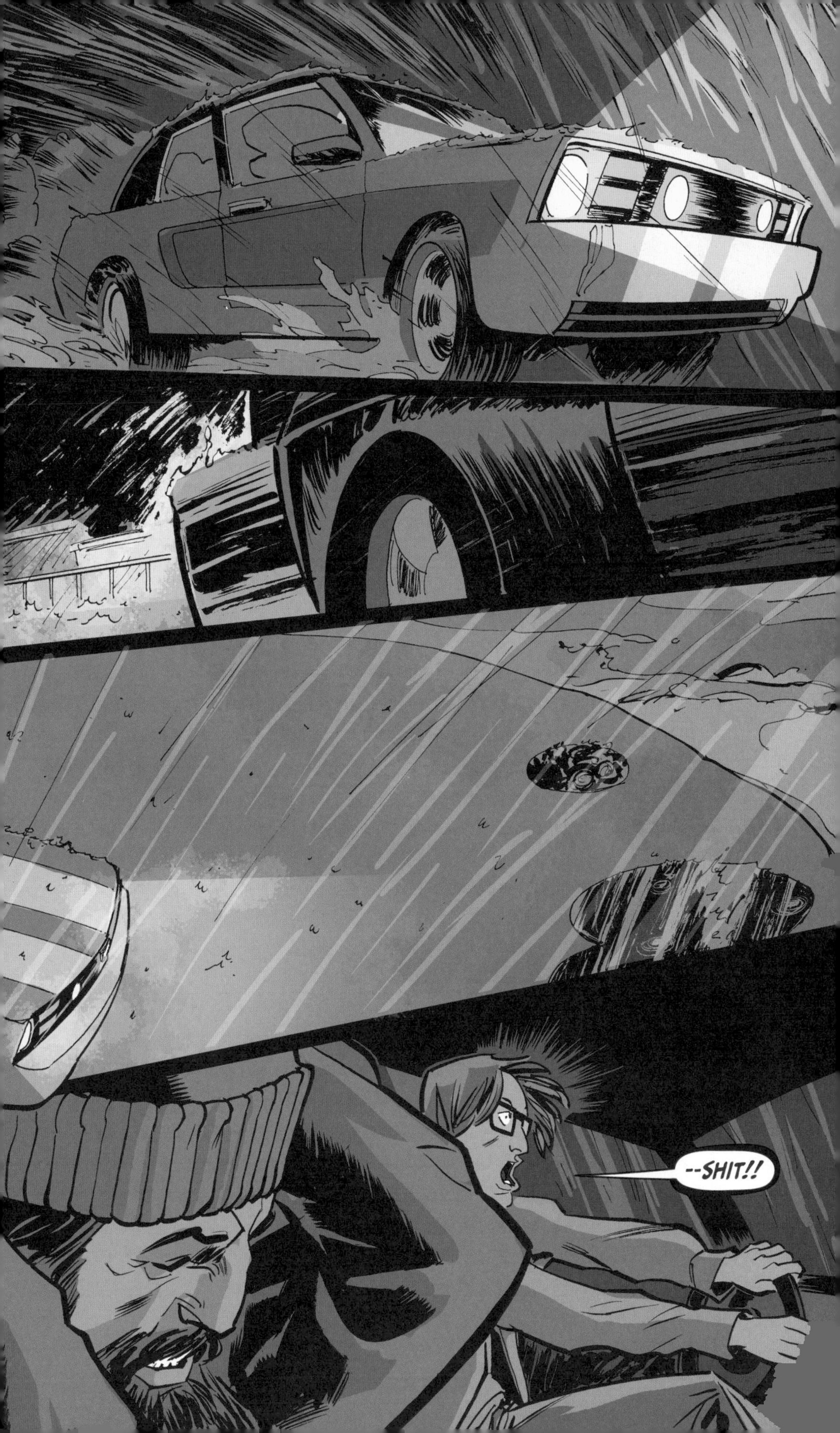
--SHIT!!

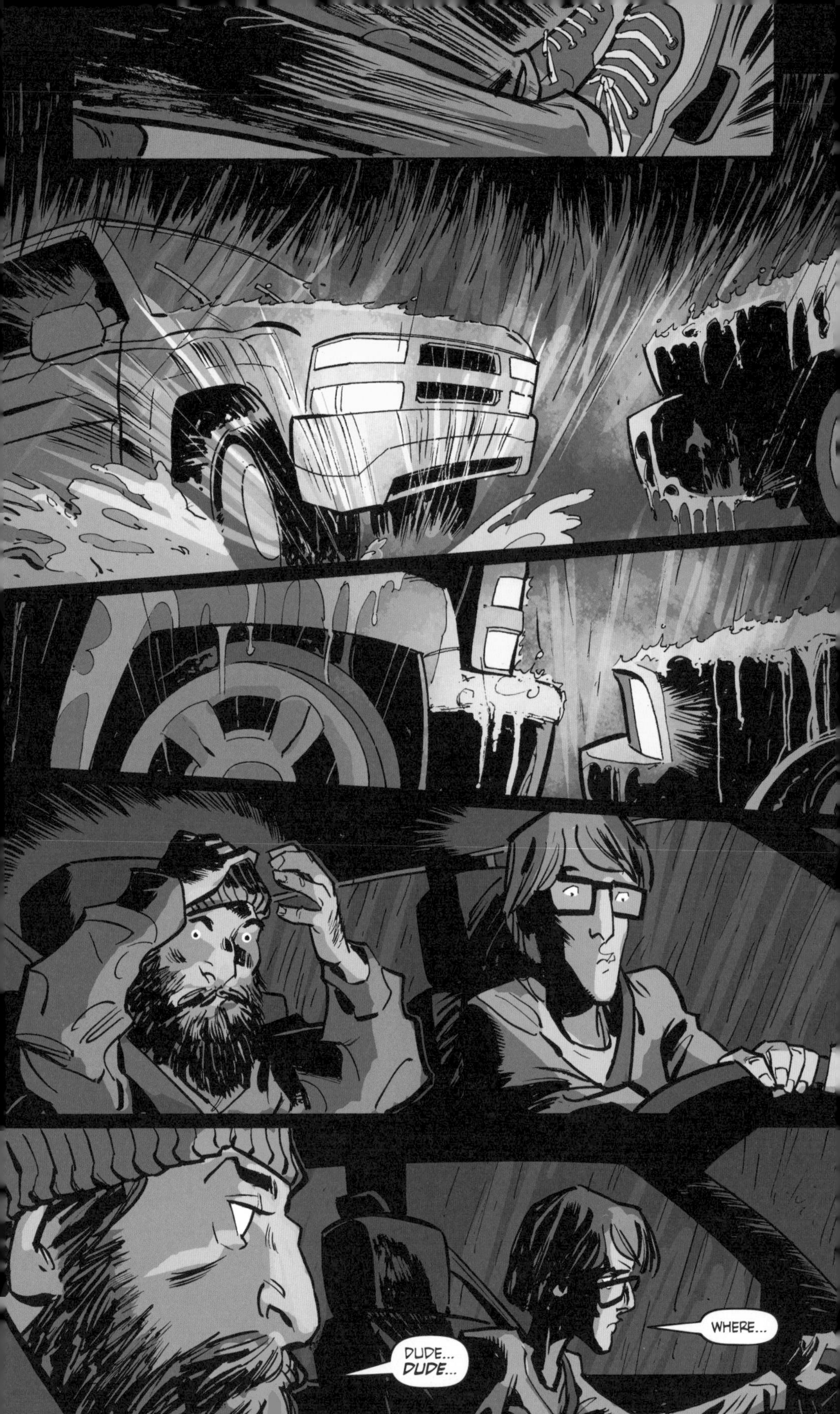
WHERE...
DUDE...
DUDE...

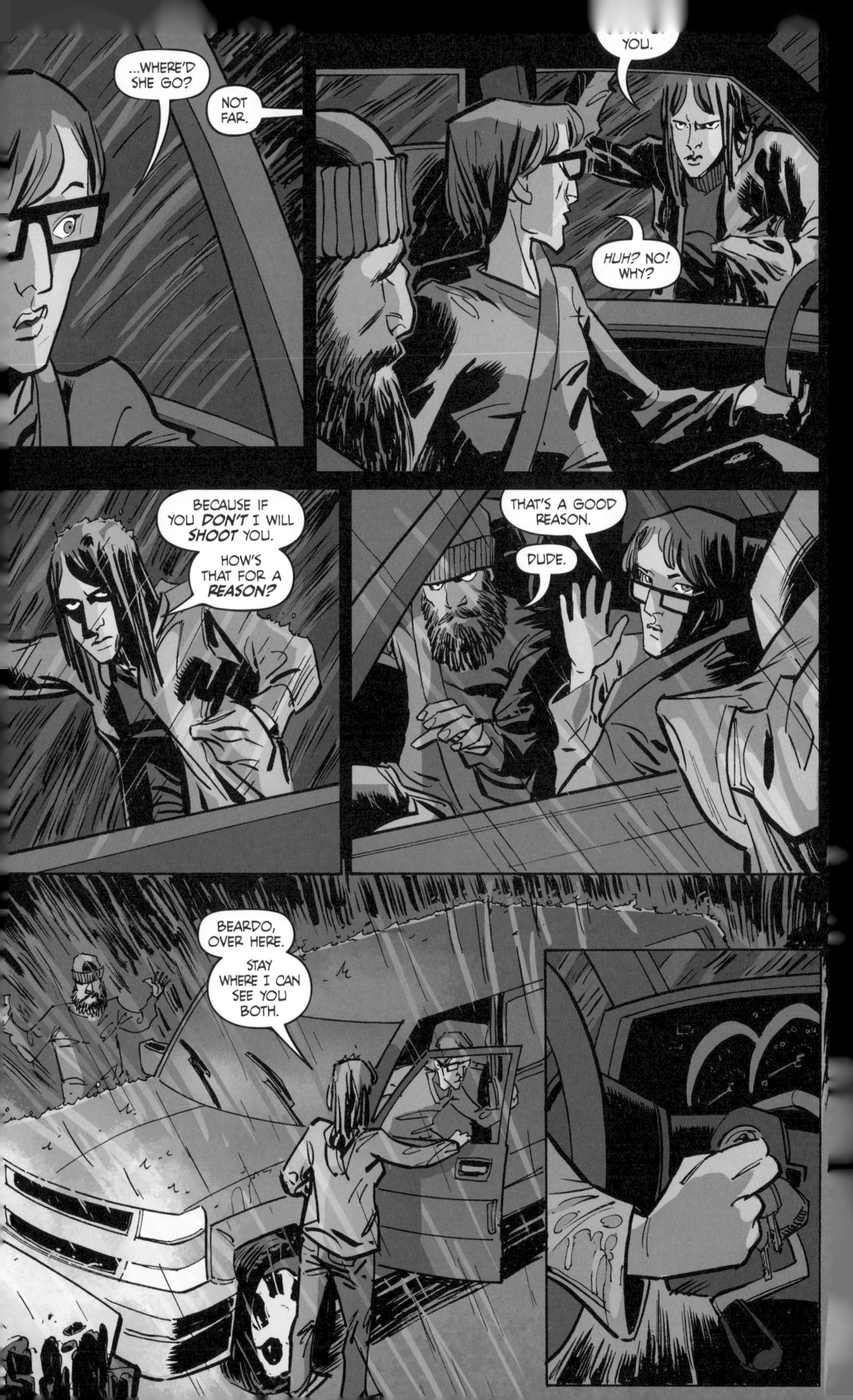
...WHERE'D SHE GO?
NOT FAR.
YOU.
HUH? NO! WHY?
BECAUSE IF YOU DON'T I WILL SHOOT YOU.
HOW'S THAT FOR A REASON?
THAT'S A GOOD REASON.
DUDE.
BEARDO, OVER HERE.
STAY WHERE I CAN SEE YOU BOTH.

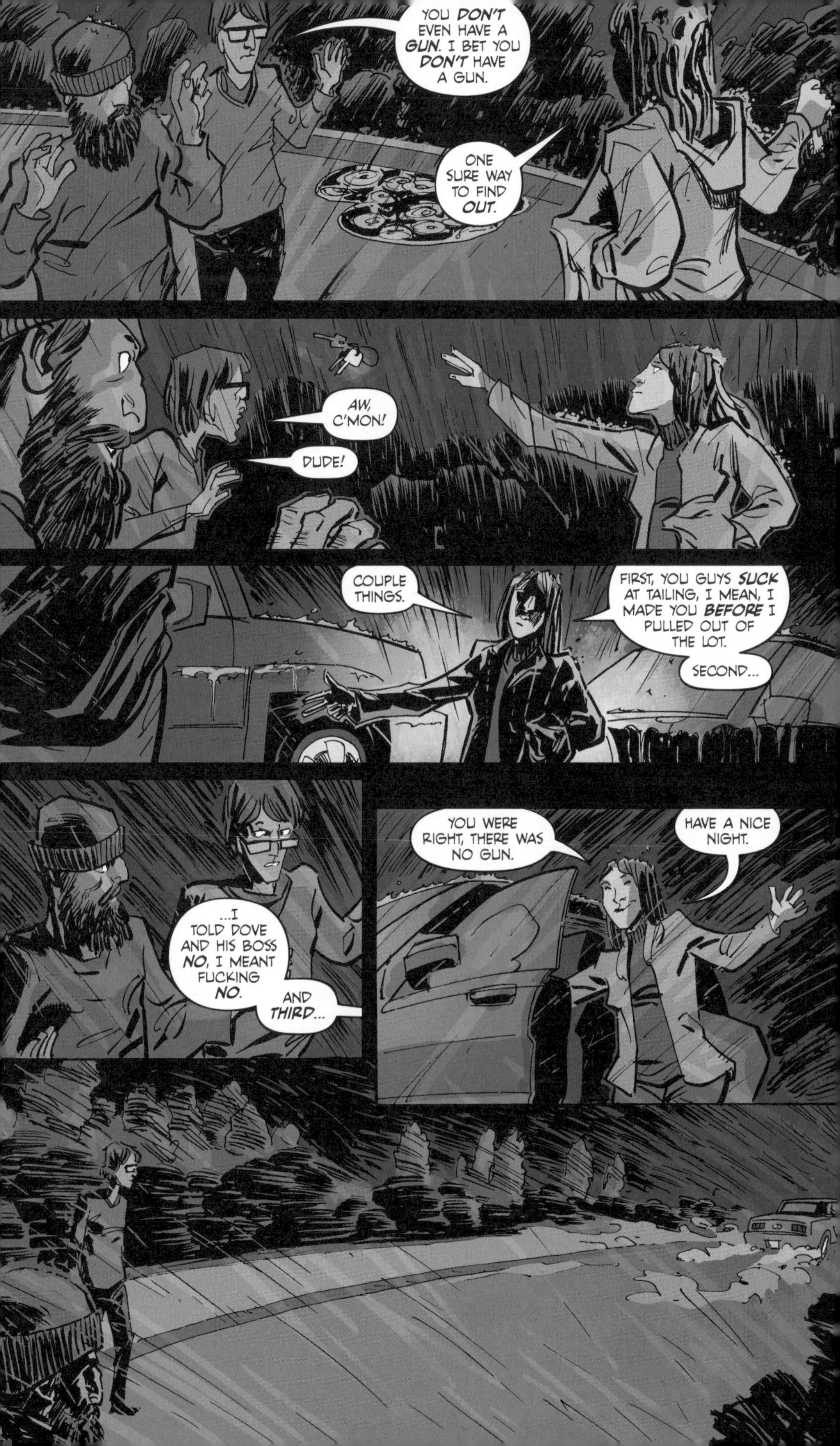

YOU **DON'T** EVEN HAVE A **GUN**. I BET YOU **DON'T** HAVE A GUN.
ONE SURE WAY TO FIND **OUT**.
AW, C'MON!
DUDE!
COUPLE THINGS.
FIRST, YOU GUYS ***SUCK*** AT TAILING, I MEAN, I MADE YOU ***BEFORE*** I PULLED OUT OF THE LOT.
SECOND...
...I TOLD DOVE AND HIS BOSS **NO**, I MEANT FUCKING **NO**.
AND ***THIRD***...
YOU WERE RIGHT, THERE WAS NO GUN.
HAVE A NICE NIGHT.

Chapter Two

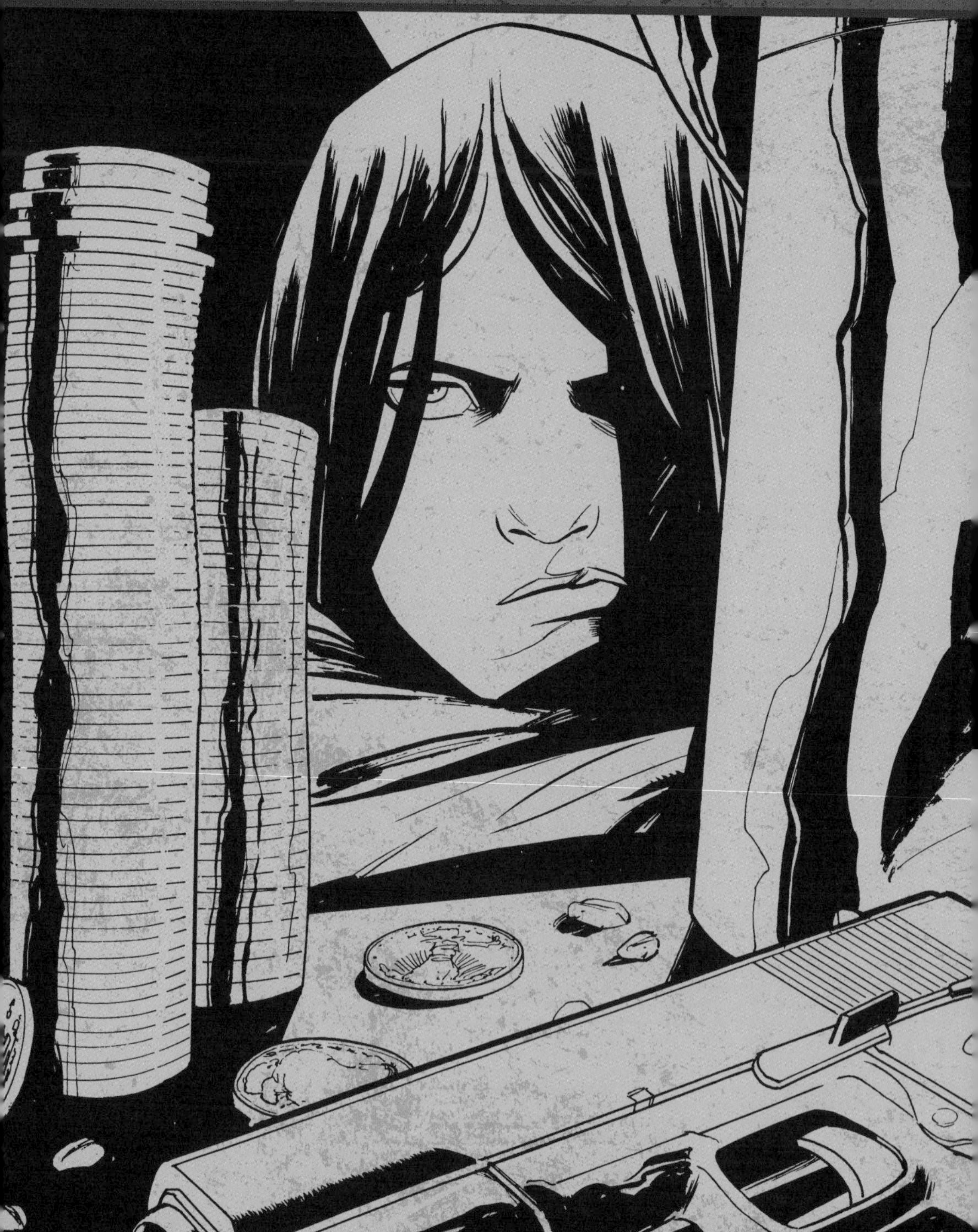

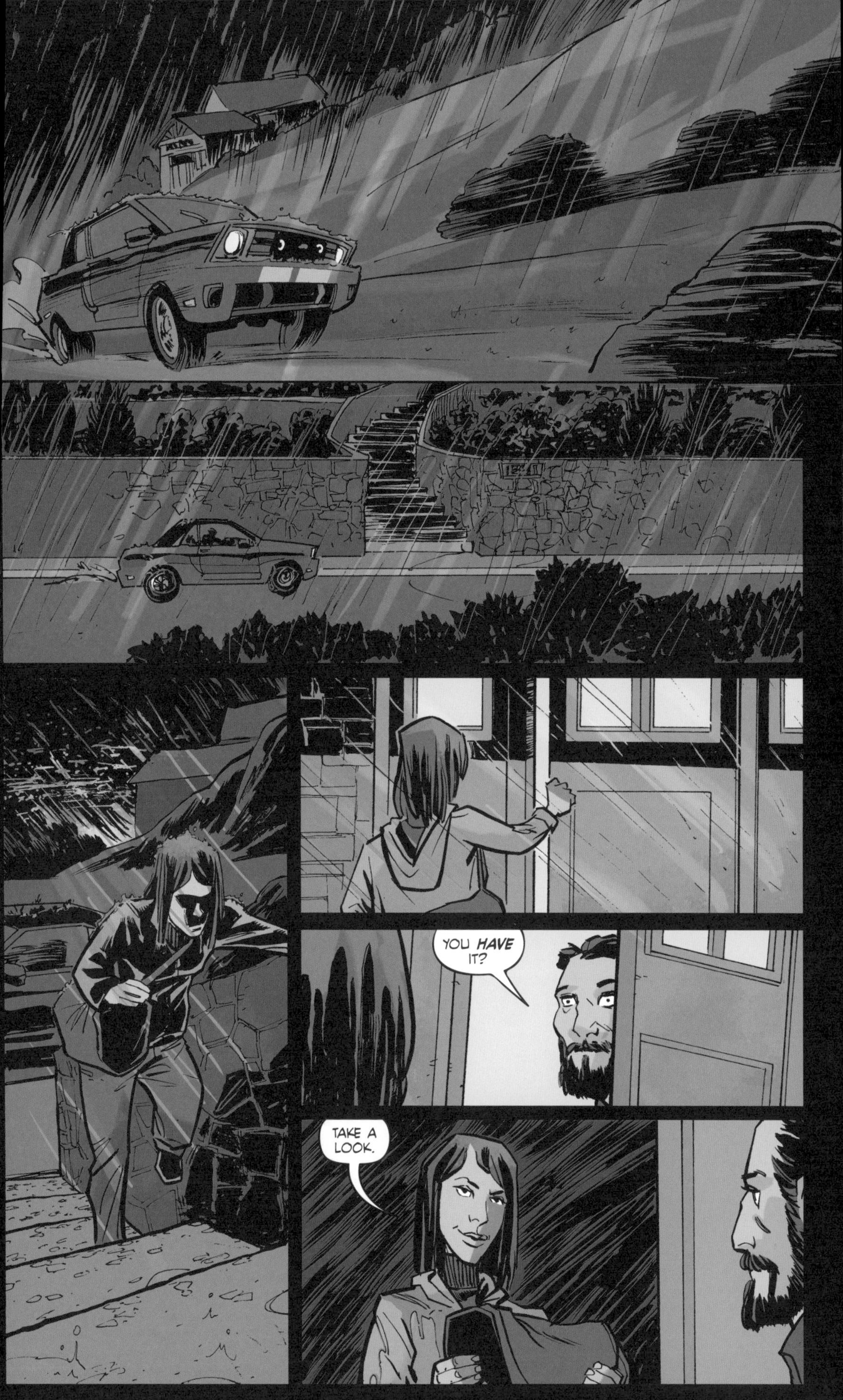
YOU *HAVE* IT?
TAKE A LOOK.

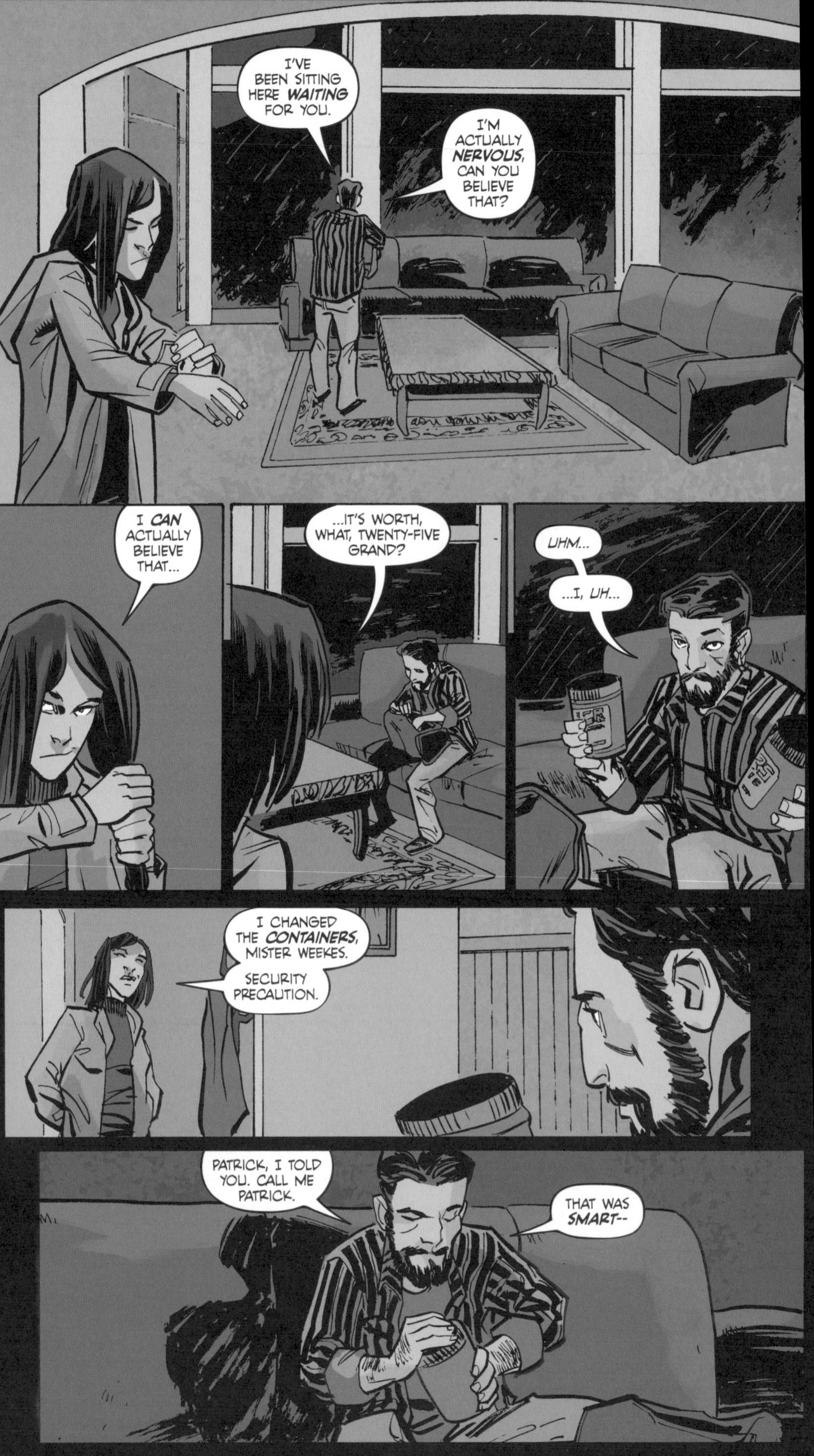
I'VE BEEN SITTING HERE WAITING FOR YOU.
I'M ACTUALLY NERVOUS, CAN YOU BELIEVE THAT?
I CAN ACTUALLY BELIEVE THAT...
...IT'S WORTH, WHAT, TWENTY-FIVE GRAND?
UHM...
...I, UH...
I CHANGED THE CONTAINERS, MISTER WEEKES.
SECURITY PRECAUTION.
PATRICK, I TOLD YOU. CALL ME PATRICK.
THAT WAS SMART--

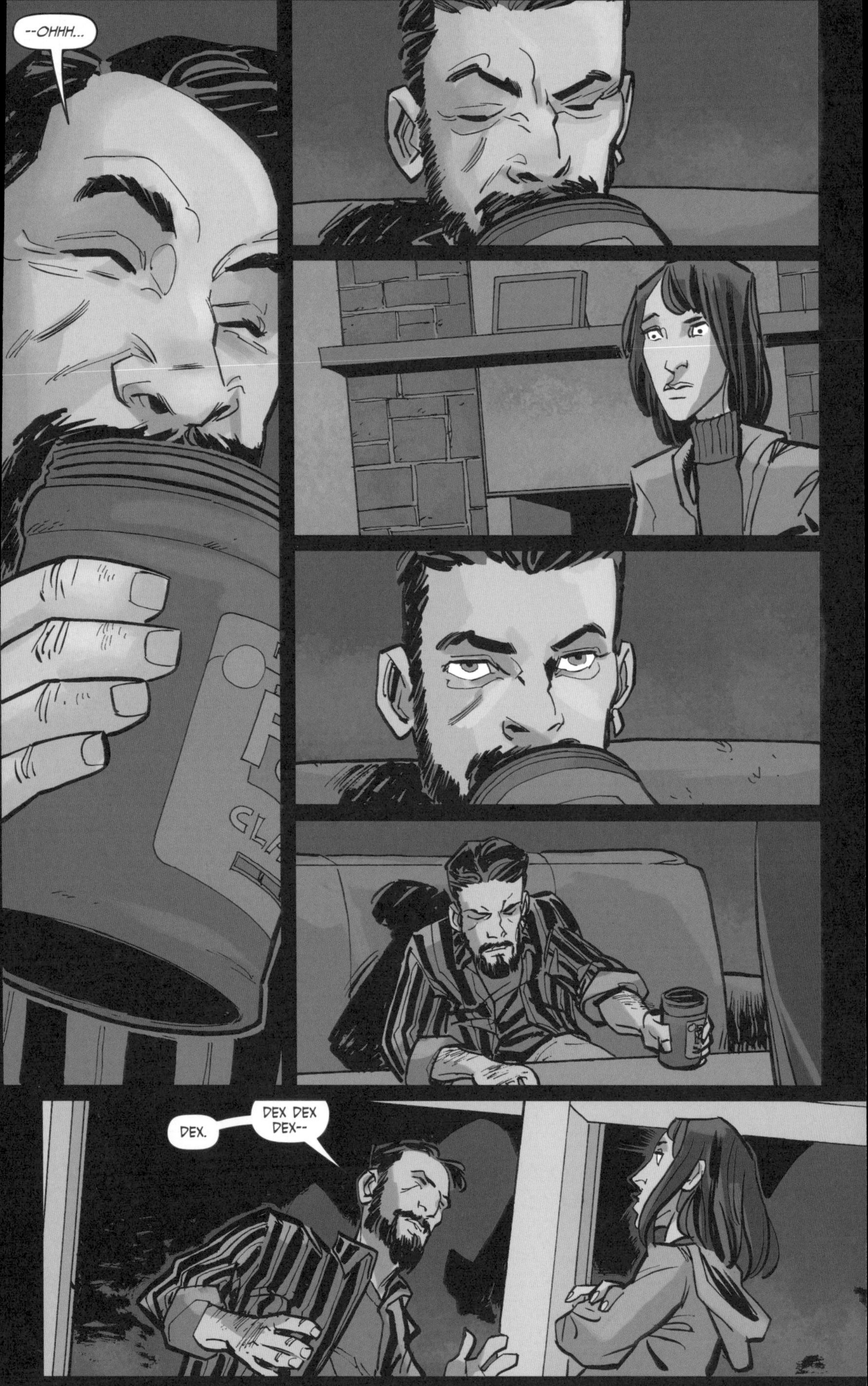
--OHHH...
DEX.
DEX DEX DEX--

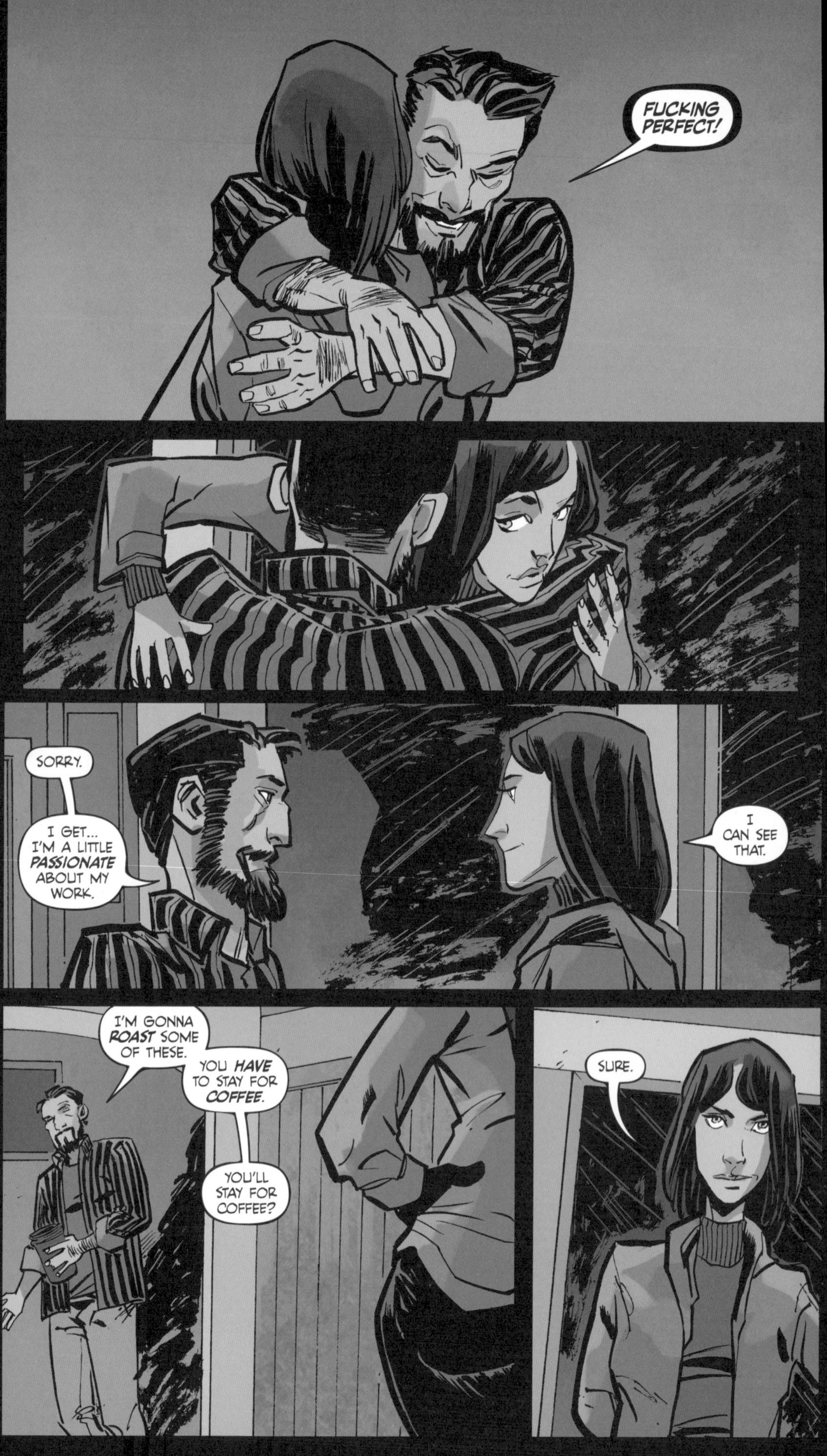
FUCKING PERFECT!
SORRY.
I GET... I'M A LITTLE PASSIONATE ABOUT MY WORK.
I CAN SEE THAT.
I'M GONNA ROAST SOME OF THESE.
YOU HAVE TO STAY FOR COFFEE.
YOU'LL STAY FOR COFFEE?
SURE.

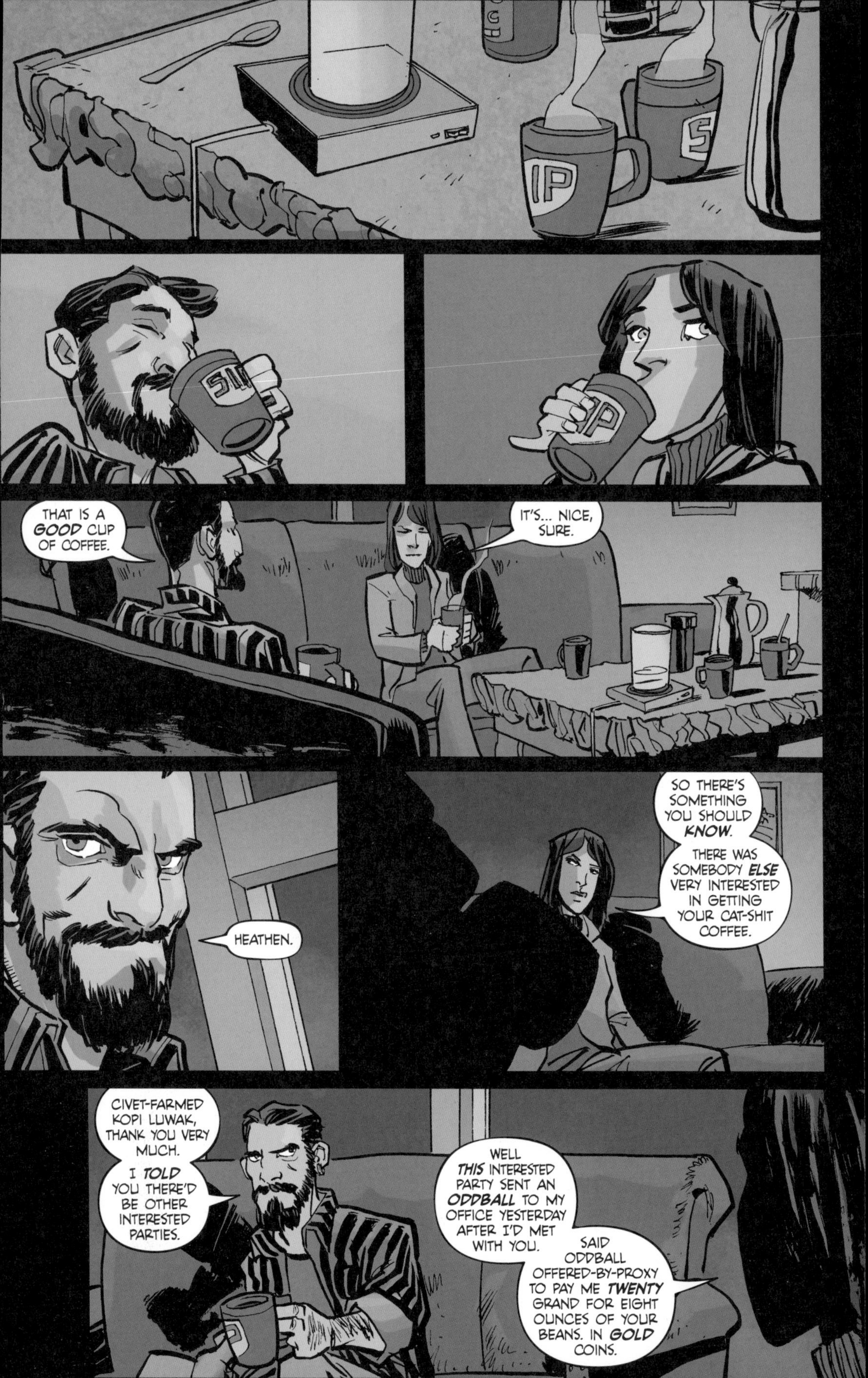
THAT IS A GOOD CUP OF COFFEE.
IT'S... NICE, SURE.
HEATHEN.
SO THERE'S SOMETHING YOU SHOULD KNOW.
THERE WAS SOMEBODY ELSE VERY INTERESTED IN GETTING YOUR CAT-SHIT COFFEE.
CIVET-FARMED KOPI LUWAK, THANK YOU VERY MUCH.
I TOLD YOU THERE'D BE OTHER INTERESTED PARTIES.
WELL THIS INTERESTED PARTY SENT AN ODDBALL TO MY OFFICE YESTERDAY AFTER I'D MET WITH YOU.
SAID ODDBALL OFFERED-BY-PROXY TO PAY ME TWENTY GRAND FOR EIGHT OUNCES OF YOUR BEANS. IN GOLD COINS.

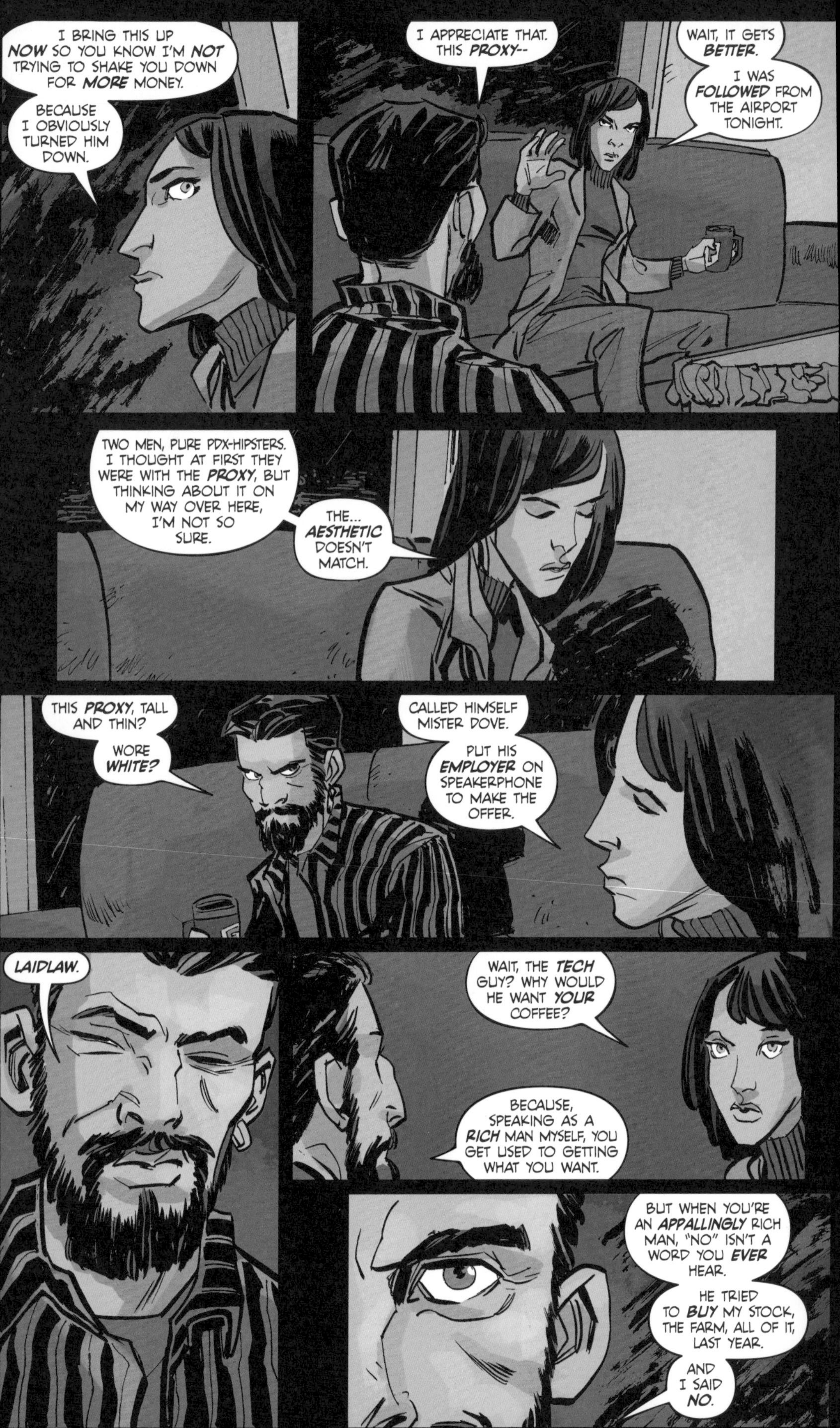
I BRING THIS UP NOW SO YOU KNOW I'M NOT TRYING TO SHAKE YOU DOWN FOR MORE MONEY.
BECAUSE I OBVIOUSLY TURNED HIM DOWN.
I APPRECIATE THAT. THIS PROXY--
WAIT, IT GETS BETTER.
I WAS FOLLOWED FROM THE AIRPORT TONIGHT.
TWO MEN, PURE PDX-HIPSTERS. I THOUGHT AT FIRST THEY WERE WITH THE PROXY, BUT THINKING ABOUT IT ON MY WAY OVER HERE, I'M NOT SO SURE.
THE... AESTHETIC DOESN'T MATCH.
THIS PROXY, TALL AND THIN?
WORE WHITE?
CALLED HIMSELF MISTER DOVE.
PUT HIS EMPLOYER ON SPEAKERPHONE TO MAKE THE OFFER.
LAIDLAW.
WAIT, THE TECH GUY? WHY WOULD HE WANT YOUR COFFEE?
BECAUSE, SPEAKING AS A RICH MAN MYSELF, YOU GET USED TO GETTING WHAT YOU WANT.
BUT WHEN YOU'RE AN APPALLINGLY RICH MAN, "NO" ISN'T A WORD YOU EVER HEAR.
HE TRIED TO BUY MY STOCK, THE FARM, ALL OF IT, LAST YEAR.
AND I SAID NO.

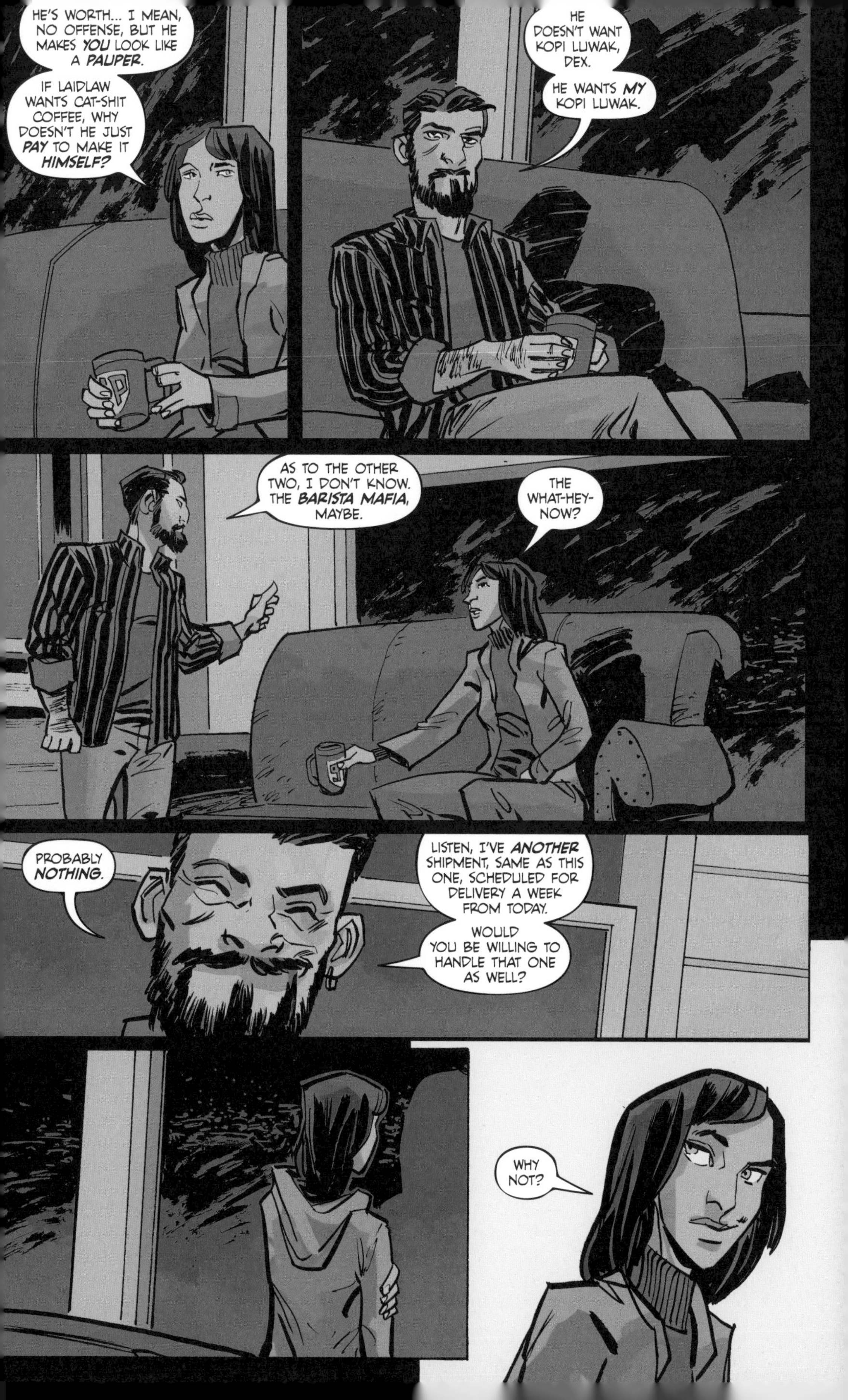
HE'S WORTH... I MEAN, NO OFFENSE, BUT HE MAKES YOU LOOK LIKE A PAUPER.
IF LAIDLAW WANTS CAT-SHIT COFFEE, WHY DOESN'T HE JUST PAY TO MAKE IT HIMSELF?
HE DOESN'T WANT KOPI LUWAK, DEX.
HE WANTS MY KOPI LUWAK.
AS TO THE OTHER TWO, I DON'T KNOW. THE BARISTA MAFIA, MAYBE.
THE WHAT-HEY-NOW?
PROBABLY NOTHING.
LISTEN, I'VE ANOTHER SHIPMENT, SAME AS THIS ONE, SCHEDULED FOR DELIVERY A WEEK FROM TODAY.
WOULD YOU BE WILLING TO HANDLE THAT ONE AS WELL?
WHY NOT?

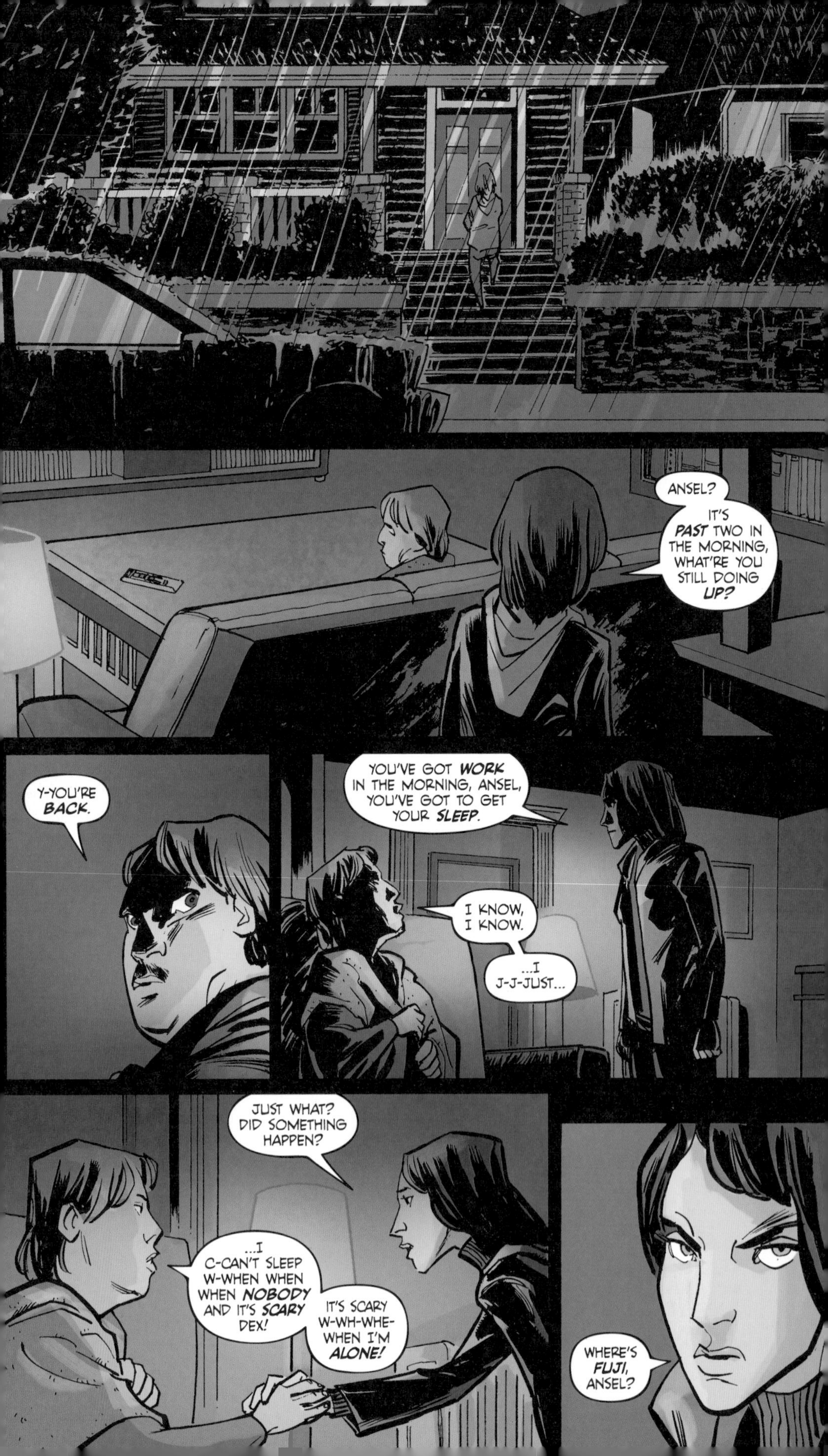
ANSEL?
IT'S PAST TWO IN THE MORNING, WHAT'RE YOU STILL DOING UP?
Y-YOU'RE BACK.
YOU'VE GOT WORK IN THE MORNING, ANSEL, YOU'VE GOT TO GET YOUR SLEEP.
I KNOW, I KNOW.
...I J-J-JUST...
JUST WHAT? DID SOMETHING HAPPEN?
...I C-CAN'T SLEEP W-WHEN WHEN WHEN NOBODY AND IT'S SCARY DEX!
IT'S SCARY W-WH-WHE-WHEN I'M ALONE!
WHERE'S FUJI, ANSEL?

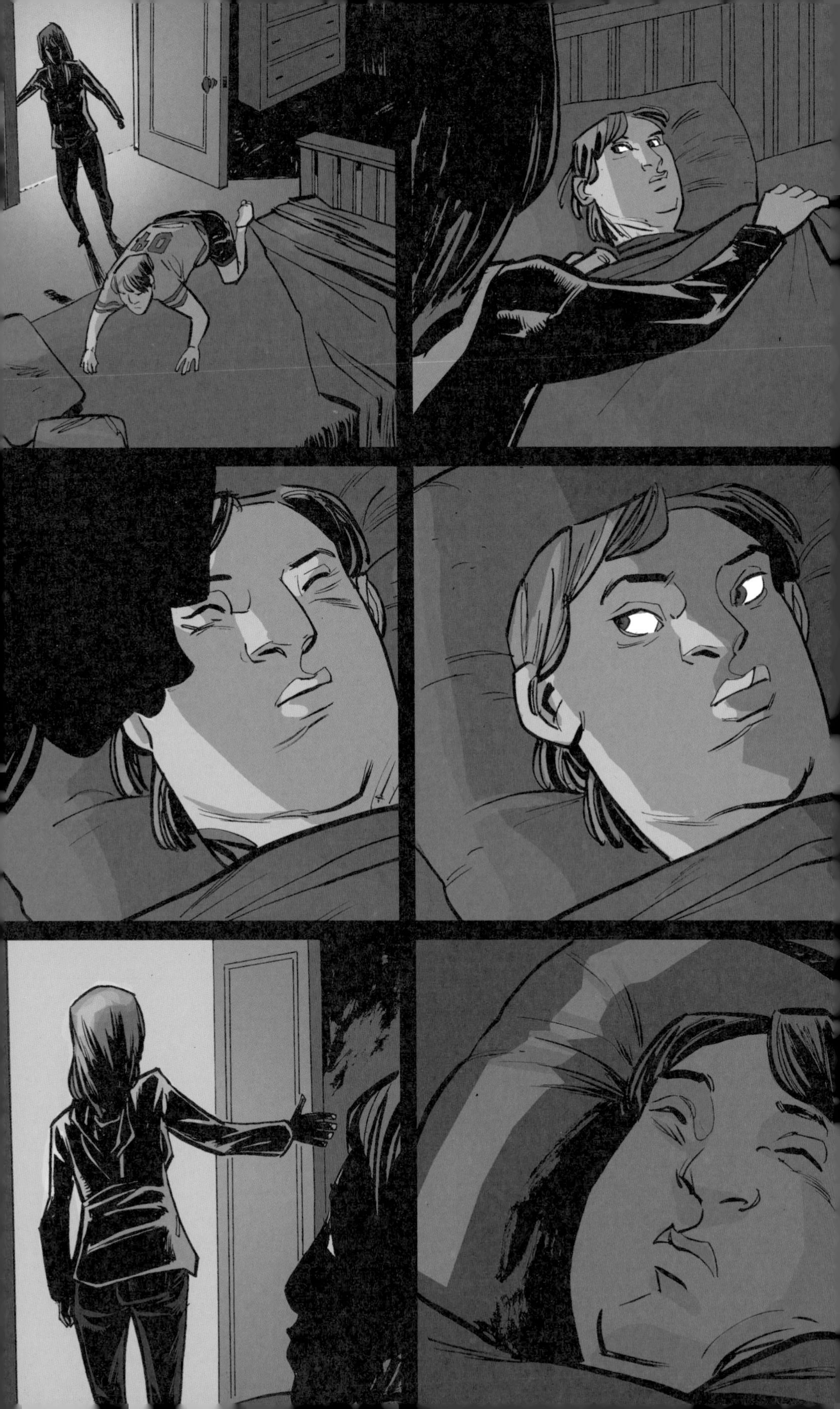

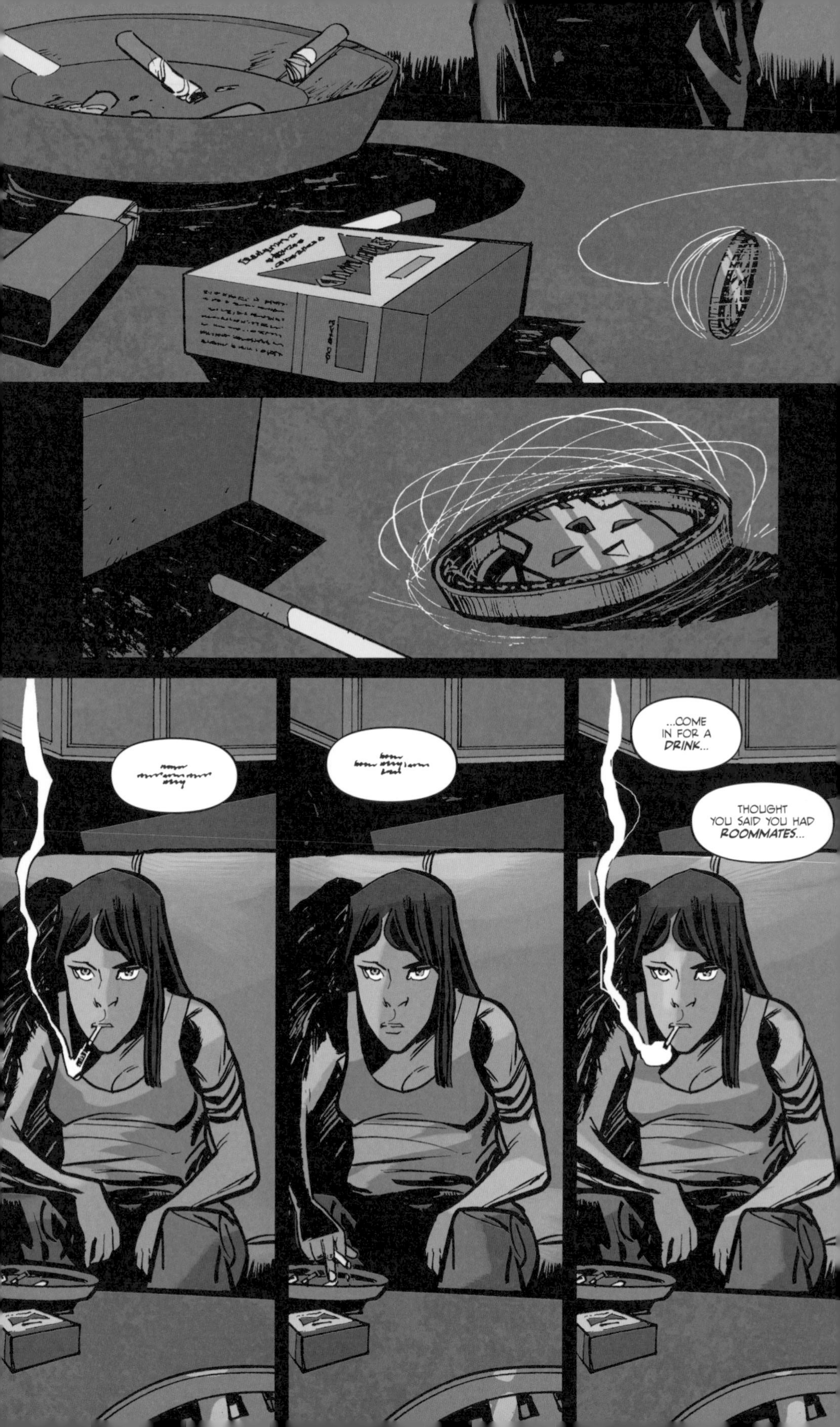
...COME IN FOR A DRINK...
THOUGHT YOU SAID YOU HAD ROOMMATES...

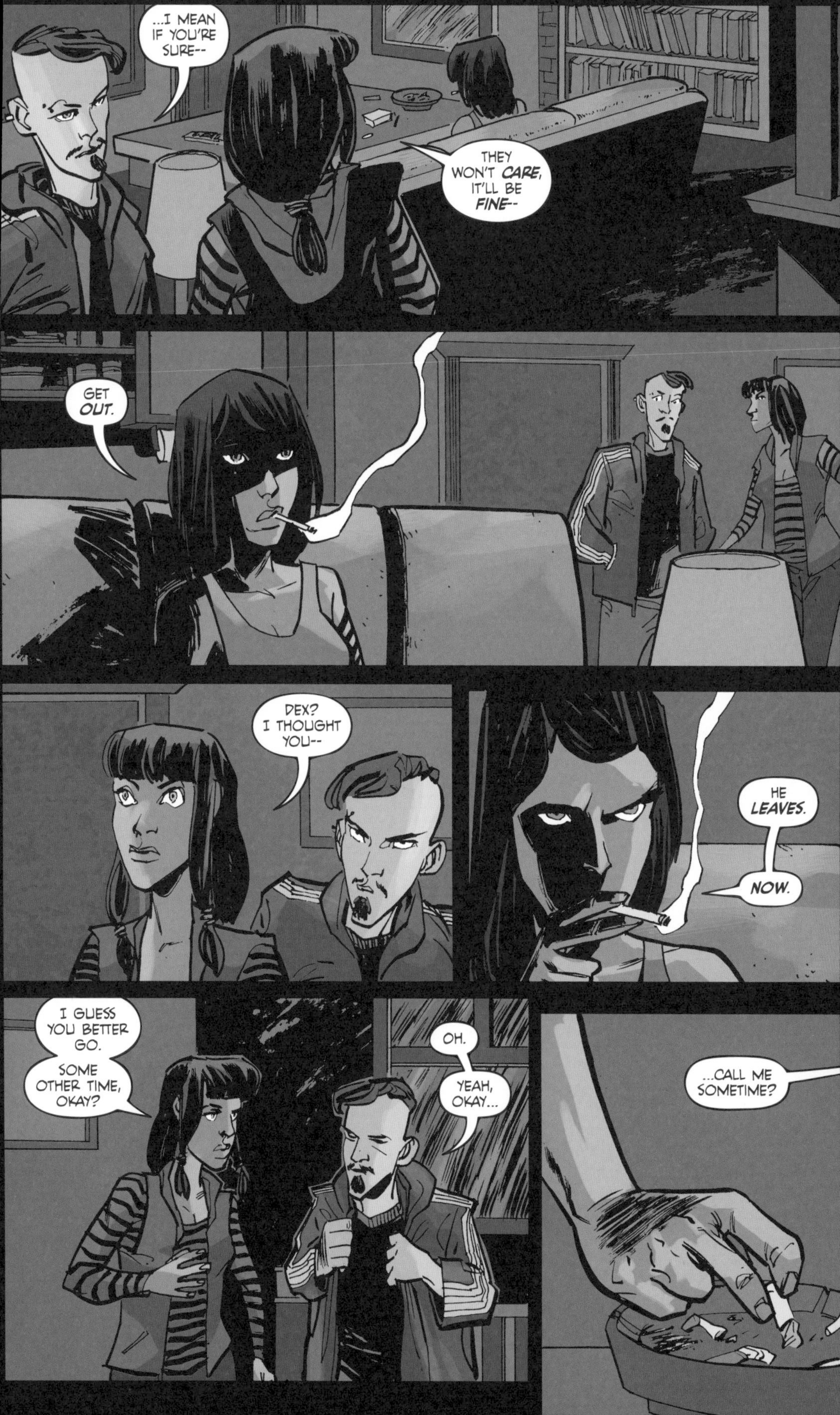
...I MEAN IF YOU'RE SURE--
THEY WON'T CARE, IT'LL BE FINE--
GET OUT.
DEX? I THOUGHT YOU--
HE LEAVES.
NOW.
I GUESS YOU BETTER GO.
SOME OTHER TIME, OKAY?
OH.
YEAH, OKAY...
...CALL ME SOMETIME?

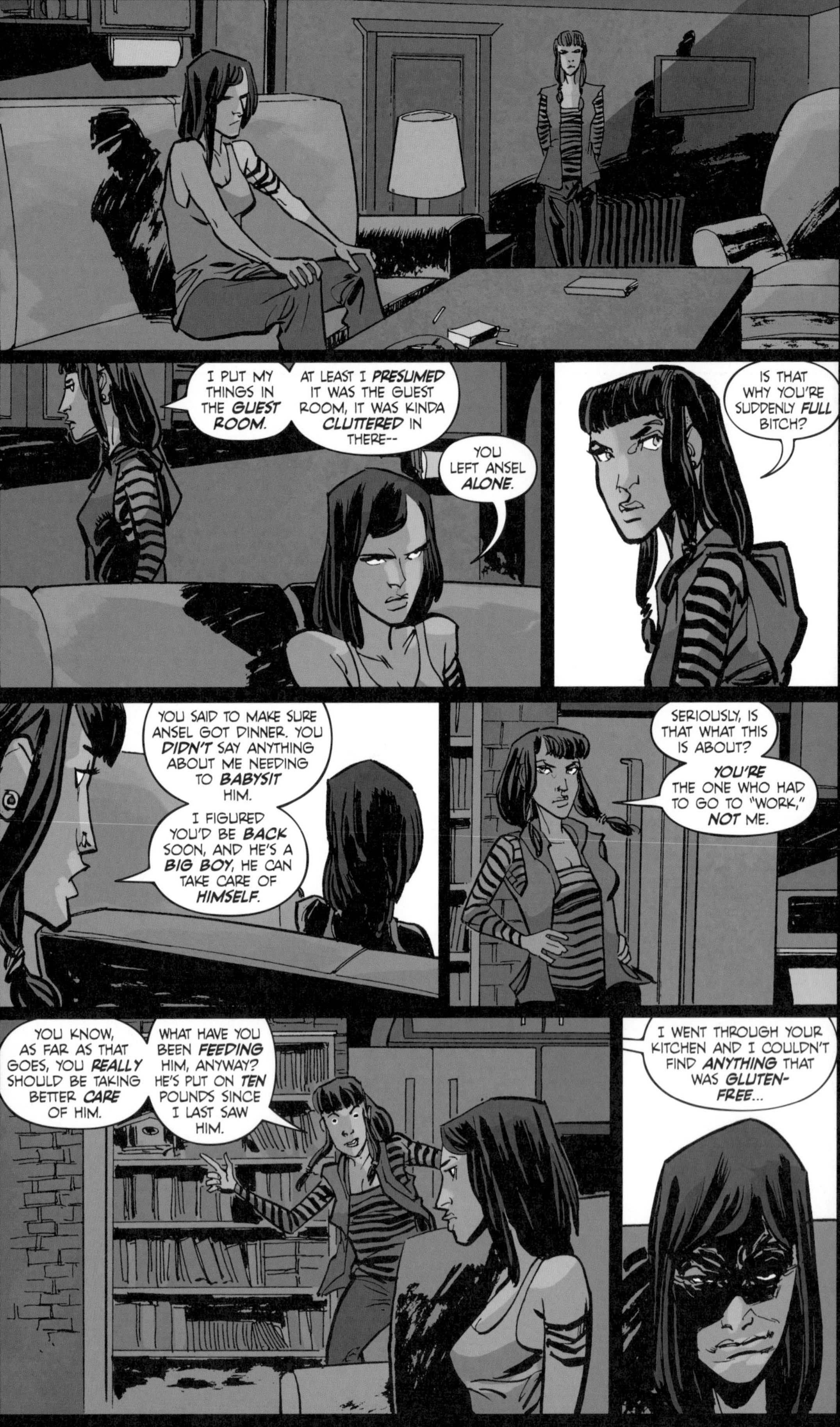
I PUT MY THINGS IN THE GUEST ROOM.
AT LEAST I PRESUMED IT WAS THE GUEST ROOM, IT WAS KINDA CLUTTERED IN THERE--
YOU LEFT ANSEL ALONE.
IS THAT WHY YOU'RE SUDDENLY FULL BITCH?
YOU SAID TO MAKE SURE ANSEL GOT DINNER. YOU DIDN'T SAY ANYTHING ABOUT ME NEEDING TO BABYSIT HIM.
I FIGURED YOU'D BE BACK SOON, AND HE'S A BIG BOY, HE CAN TAKE CARE OF HIMSELF.
SERIOUSLY, IS THAT WHAT THIS IS ABOUT?
YOU'RE THE ONE WHO HAD TO GO TO "WORK," NOT ME.
YOU KNOW, AS FAR AS THAT GOES, YOU REALLY SHOULD BE TAKING BETTER CARE OF HIM.
WHAT HAVE YOU BEEN FEEDING HIM, ANYWAY? HE'S PUT ON TEN POUNDS SINCE I LAST SAW HIM.
I WENT THROUGH YOUR KITCHEN AND I COULDN'T FIND ANYTHING THAT WAS GLUTEN-FREE...

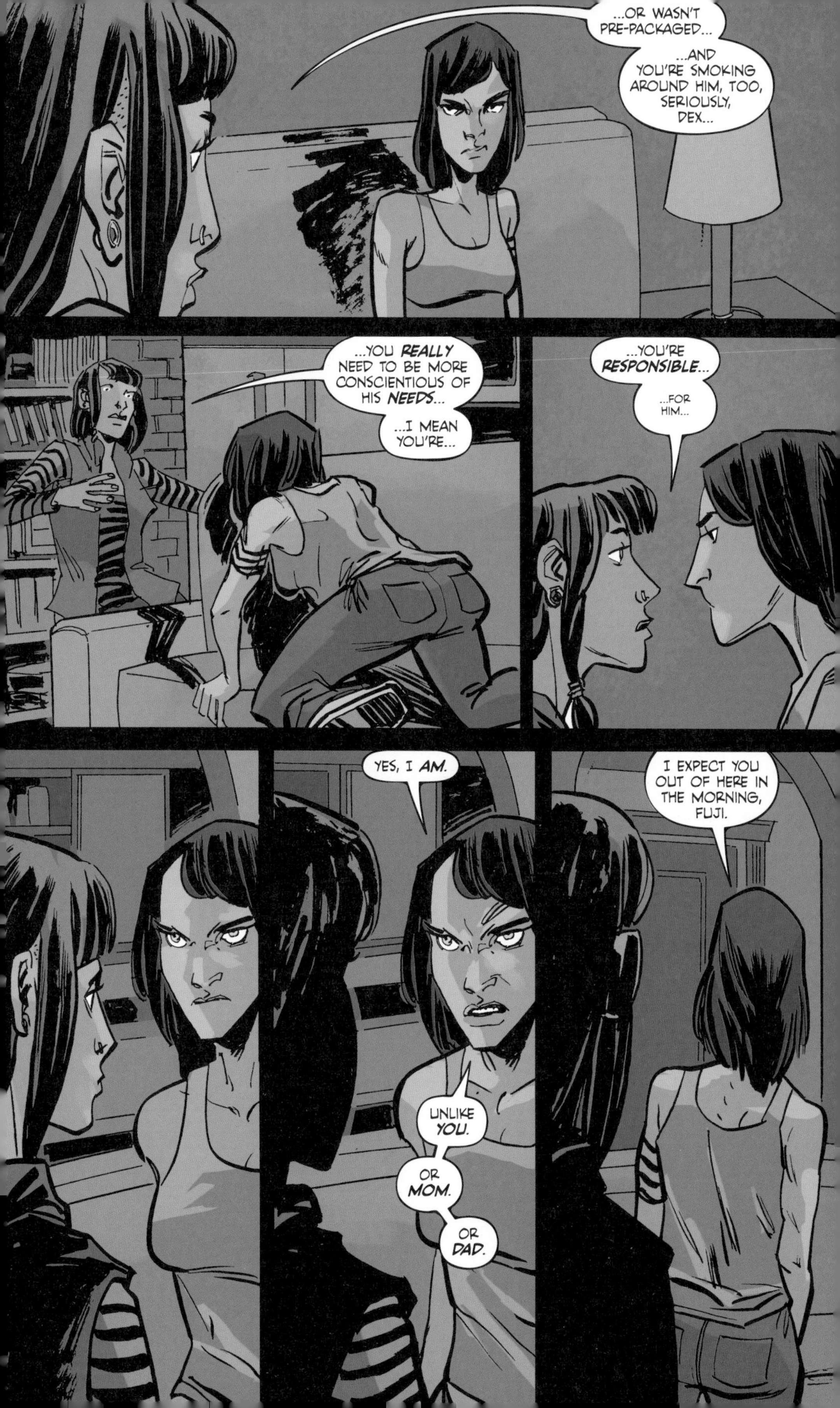

...OR WASN'T PRE-PACKAGED...
...AND YOU'RE SMOKING AROUND HIM, TOO, SERIOUSLY, DEX...
...YOU REALLY NEED TO BE MORE CONSCIENTIOUS OF HIS NEEDS...
...I MEAN YOU'RE...
...YOU'RE RESPONSIBLE...
...FOR HIM...
YES, I AM.
UNLIKE YOU.
OR MOM.
OR DAD.
I EXPECT YOU OUT OF HERE IN THE MORNING, FUJI.

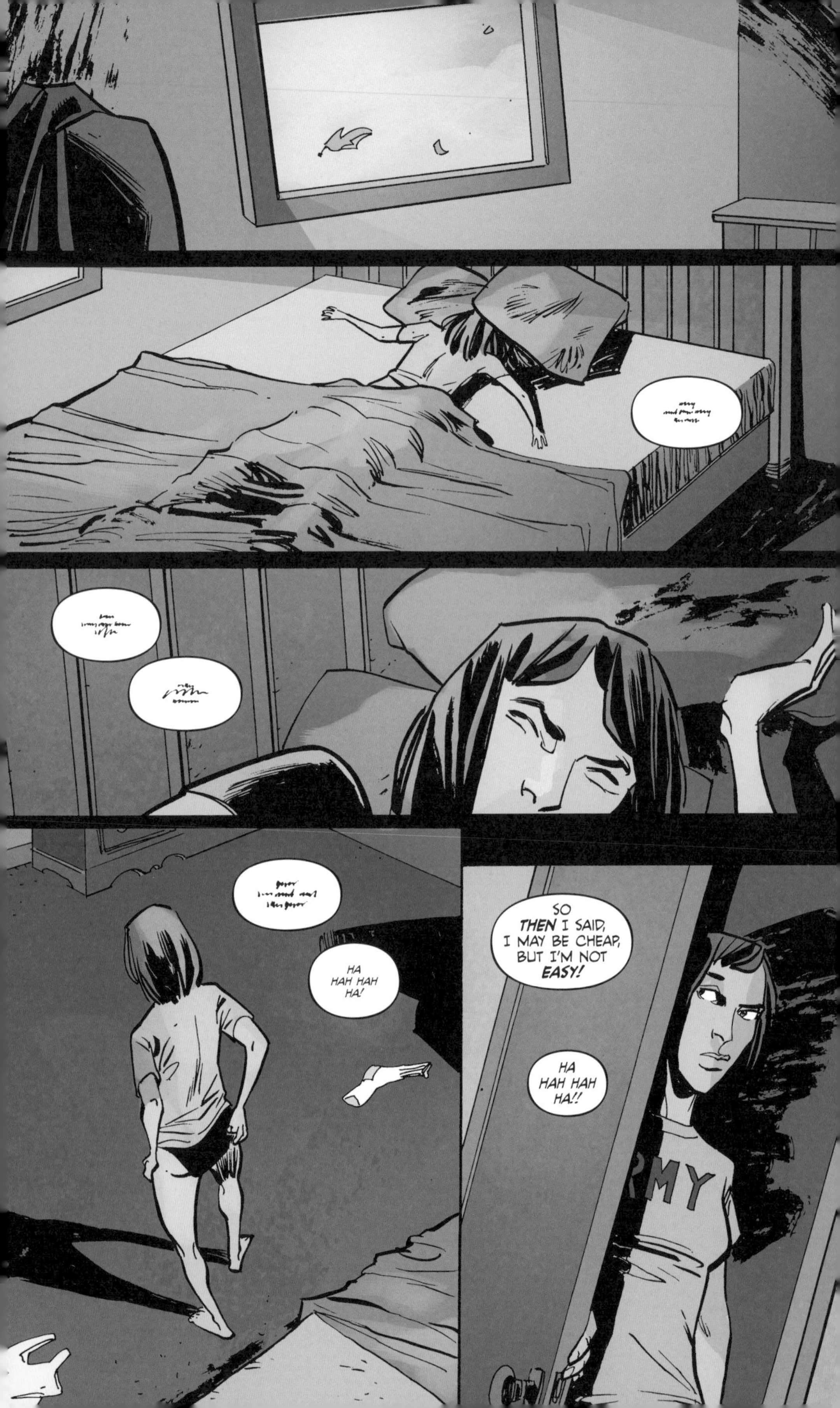
HA
HAH HAH
HA!
SO
THEN I SAID,
I MAY BE CHEAP,
BUT I'M NOT
EASY!
HA
HAH HAH
HA!!
RMY

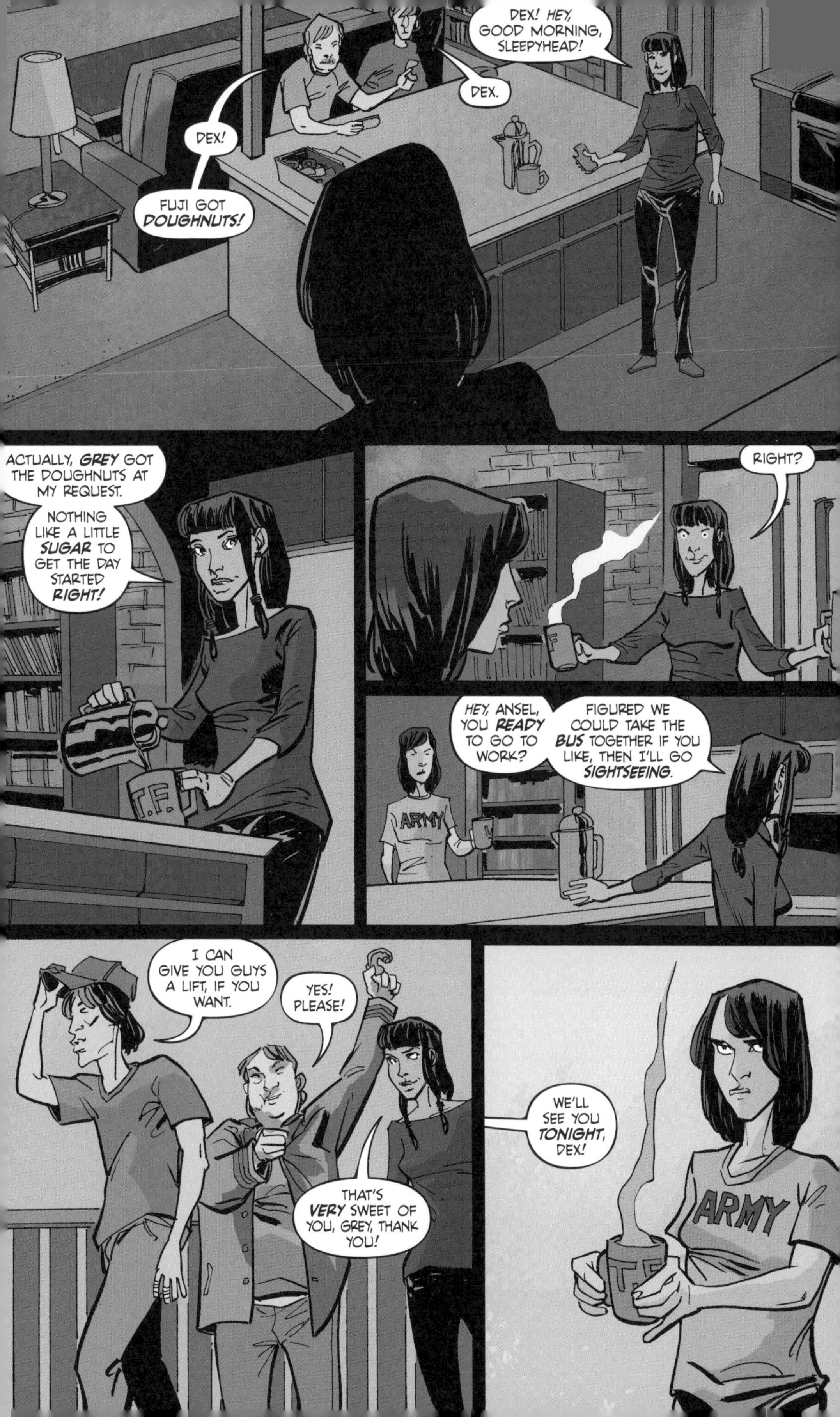
DEX! HEY, GOOD MORNING, SLEEPYHEAD!
DEX.
DEX!
FUJI GOT DOUGHNUTS!
ACTUALLY, GREY GOT THE DOUGHNUTS AT MY REQUEST.
NOTHING LIKE A LITTLE SUGAR TO GET THE DAY STARTED RIGHT!
RIGHT?
HEY, ANSEL, YOU READY TO GO TO WORK?
FIGURED WE COULD TAKE THE BUS TOGETHER IF YOU LIKE, THEN I'LL GO SIGHTSEEING.
ARMY
I CAN GIVE YOU GUYS A LIFT, IF YOU WANT.
YES! PLEASE!
THAT'S VERY SWEET OF YOU, GREY, THANK YOU!
WE'LL SEE YOU TONIGHT, DEX!
ARMY

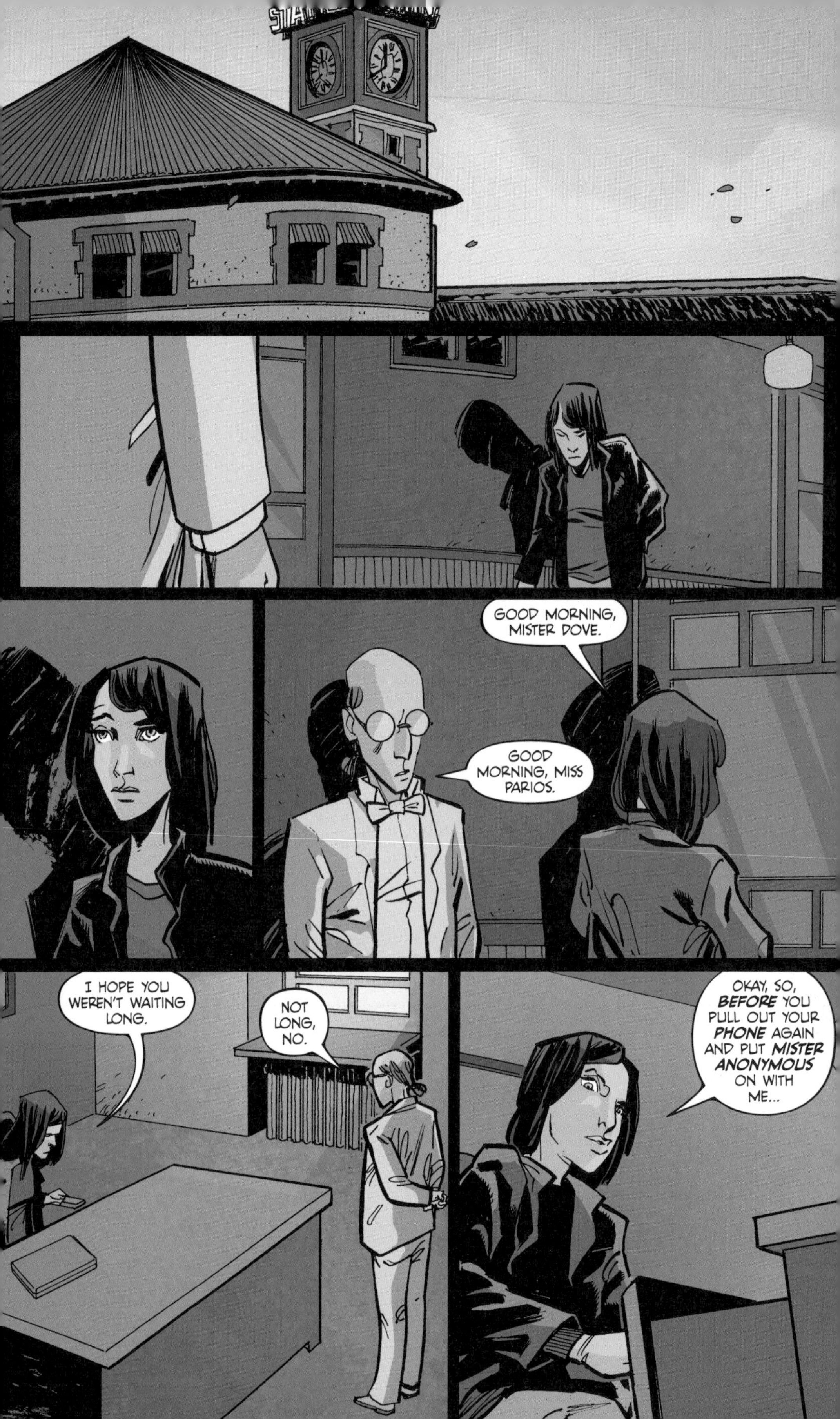
GOOD MORNING, MISTER DOVE.
GOOD MORNING, MISS PARIOS.
I HOPE YOU WEREN'T WAITING LONG.
NOT LONG, NO.
OKAY, SO, BEFORE YOU PULL OUT YOUR PHONE AGAIN AND PUT MISTER ANONYMOUS ON WITH ME...

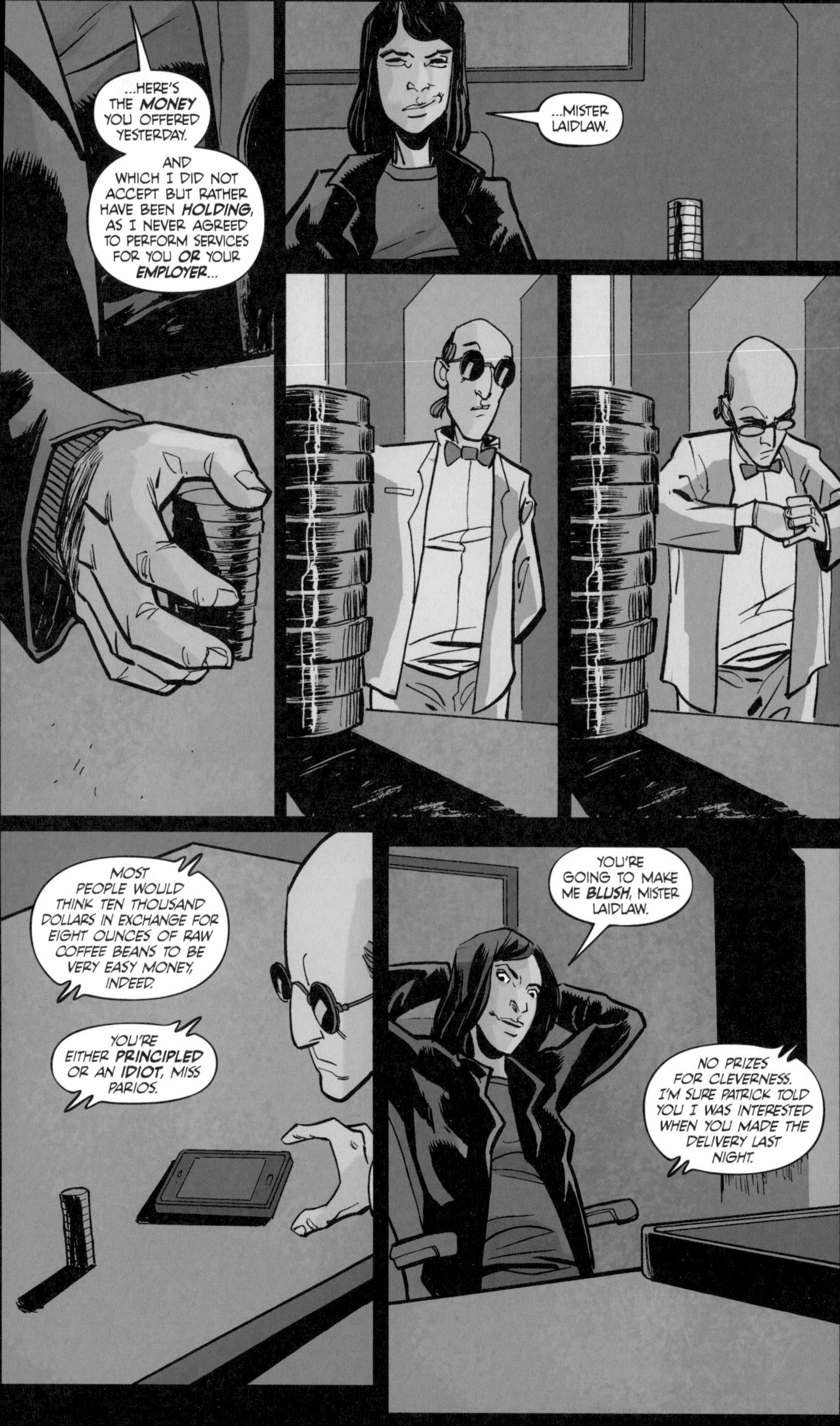
...HERE'S THE MONEY YOU OFFERED YESTERDAY.
AND WHICH I DID NOT ACCEPT BUT RATHER HAVE BEEN HOLDING, AS I NEVER AGREED TO PERFORM SERVICES FOR YOU OR YOUR EMPLOYER...
...MISTER LAIDLAW.
MOST PEOPLE WOULD THINK TEN THOUSAND DOLLARS IN EXCHANGE FOR EIGHT OUNCES OF RAW COFFEE BEANS TO BE VERY EASY MONEY, INDEED.
YOU'RE EITHER PRINCIPLED OR AN IDIOT, MISS PARIOS.
YOU'RE GOING TO MAKE ME BLUSH, MISTER LAIDLAW.
NO PRIZES FOR CLEVERNESS. I'M SURE PATRICK TOLD YOU I WAS INTERESTED WHEN YOU MADE THE DELIVERY LAST NIGHT.

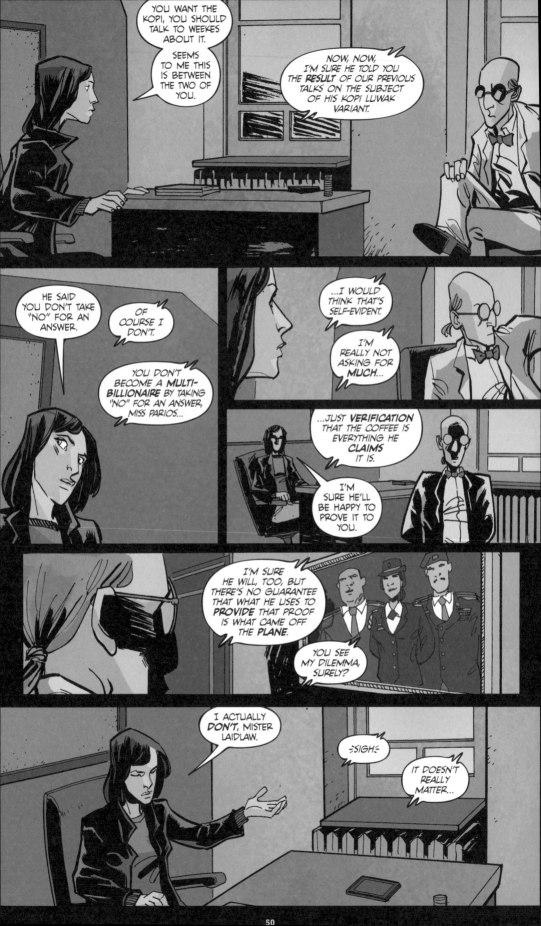

YOU WANT THE KOPI, YOU SHOULD TALK TO WEEKES ABOUT IT.

SEEMS TO ME THIS IS BETWEEN THE TWO OF YOU.

NOW, NOW, I'M SURE HE TOLD YOU THE **RESULT** OF OUR PREVIOUS TALKS ON THE SUBJECT OF HIS KOPI LUWAK VARIANT.

HE SAID YOU DON'T TAKE "NO" FOR AN ANSWER.

OF COURSE I DON'T.

YOU DON'T BECOME A **MULTI-BILLIONAIRE** BY TAKING "NO" FOR AN ANSWER, MISS PARIOS...

...I WOULD THINK THAT'S SELF-EVIDENT.

I'M REALLY NOT ASKING FOR **MUCH**...

...JUST **VERIFICATION** THAT THE COFFEE IS EVERYTHING HE **CLAIMS** IT IS.

I'M SURE HE'LL BE HAPPY TO PROVE IT TO YOU.

I'M SURE HE WILL, TOO, BUT THERE'S NO GUARANTEE THAT WHAT HE USES TO **PROVIDE** THAT PROOF IS WHAT CAME OFF THE **PLANE.**

YOU SEE MY DILEMMA, SURELY?

I ACTUALLY **DON'T**, MISTER LAIDLAW.

=SIGH=

IT DOESN'T REALLY MATTER...

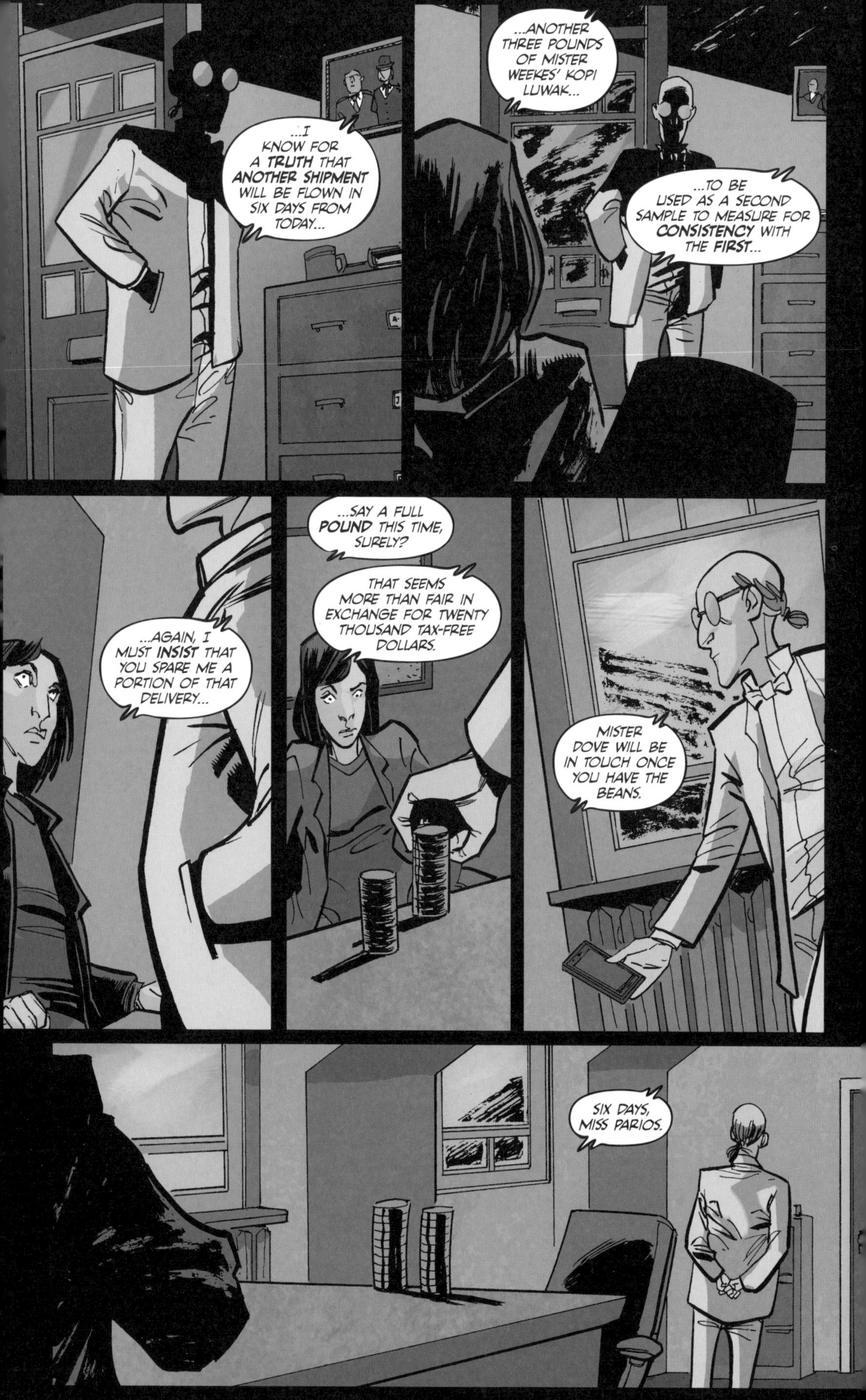
...I KNOW FOR A TRUTH THAT ANOTHER SHIPMENT WILL BE FLOWN IN SIX DAYS FROM TODAY...
...ANOTHER THREE POUNDS OF MISTER WEEKES' KOPI LUWAK...
...TO BE USED AS A SECOND SAMPLE TO MEASURE FOR CONSISTENCY WITH THE FIRST...
...AGAIN, I MUST INSIST THAT YOU SPARE ME A PORTION OF THAT DELIVERY...
...SAY A FULL POUND THIS TIME, SURELY?
THAT SEEMS MORE THAN FAIR IN EXCHANGE FOR TWENTY THOUSAND TAX-FREE DOLLARS.
MISTER DOVE WILL BE IN TOUCH ONCE YOU HAVE THE BEANS.
SIX DAYS, MISS PARIOS.

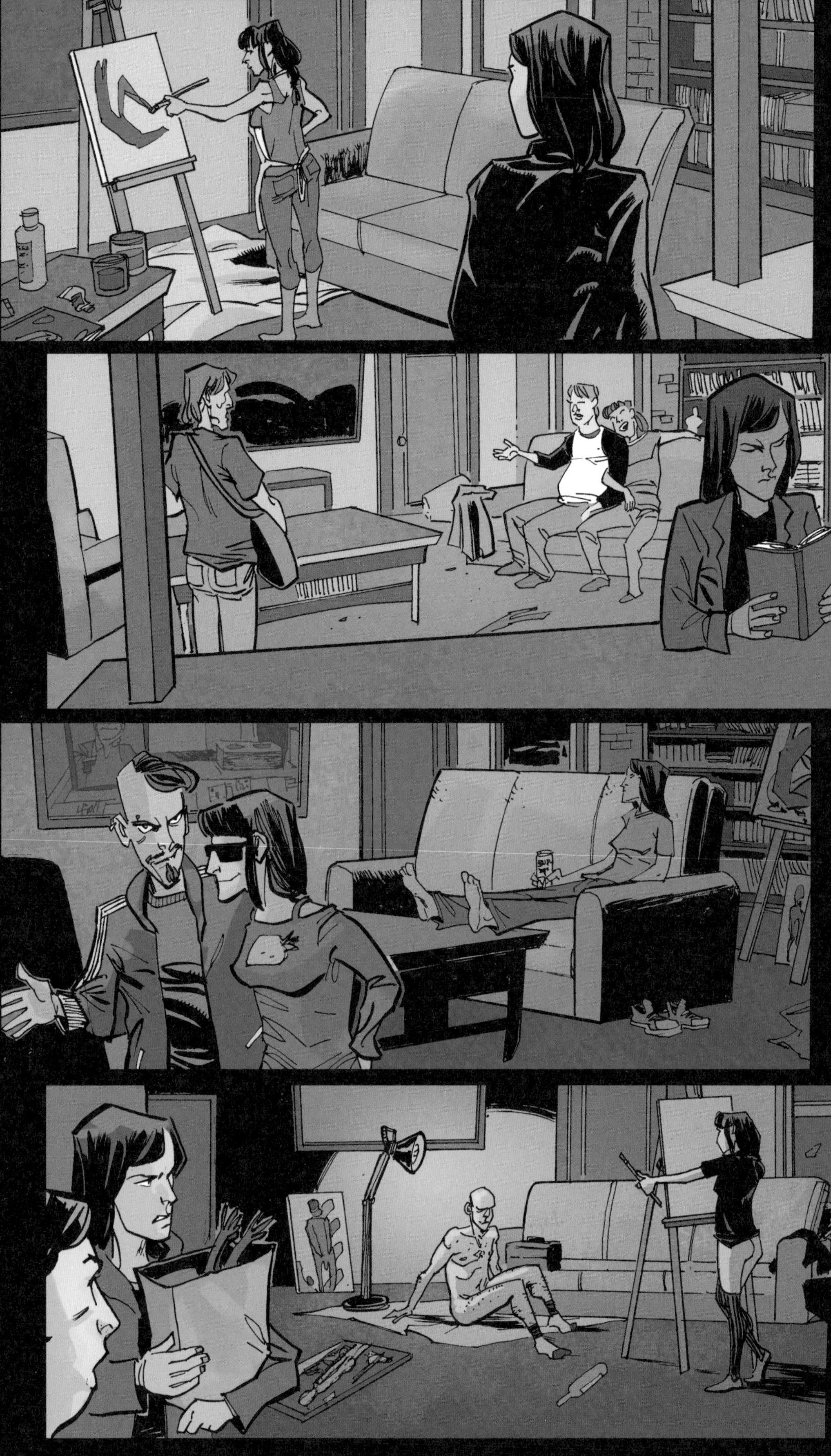

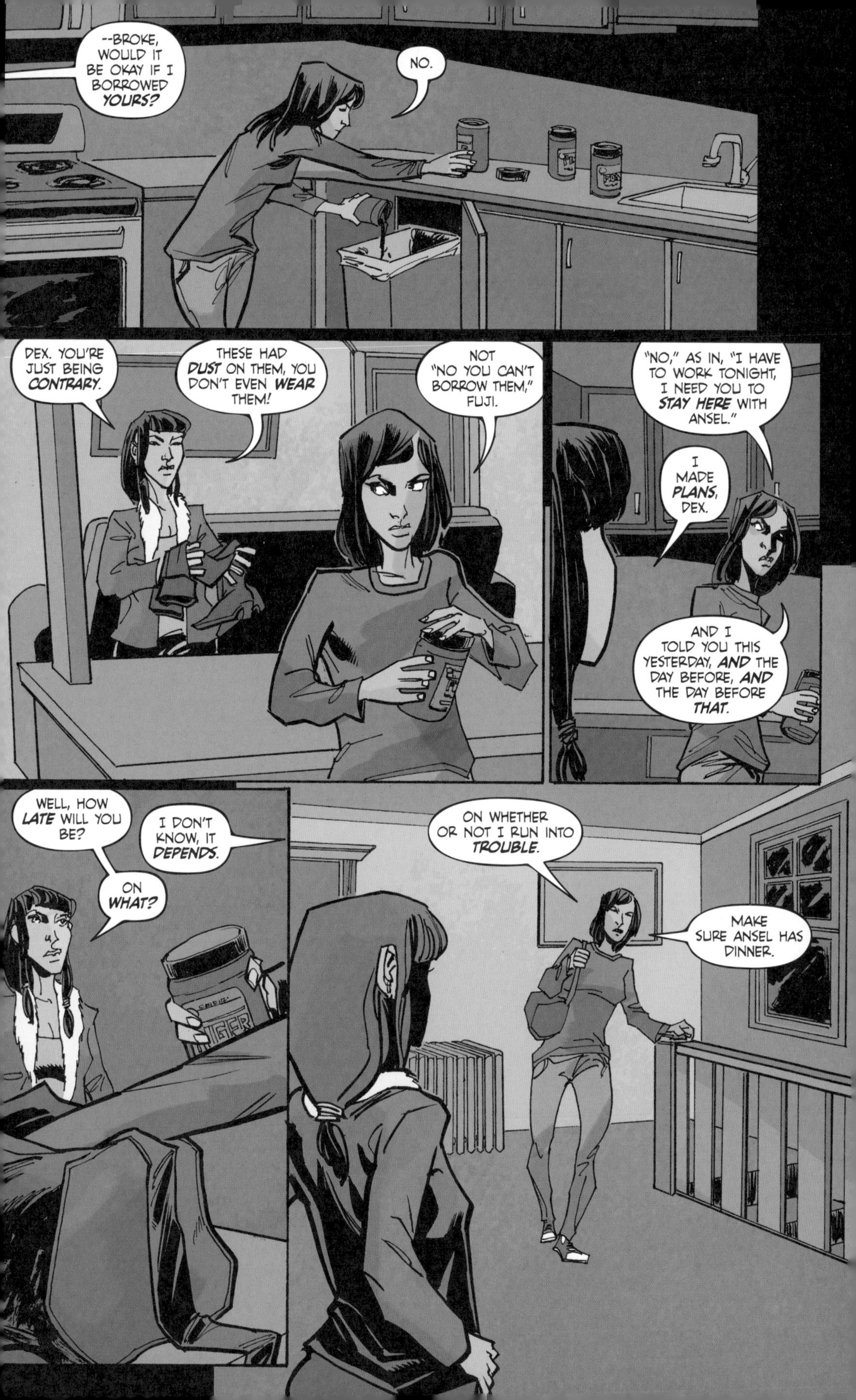

--BROKE, WOULD IT BE OKAY IF I BORROWED *YOURS?*
NO.
DEX. YOU'RE JUST BEING *CONTRARY*.
THESE HAD *DUST* ON THEM, YOU DON'T EVEN *WEAR* THEM!
NOT "NO YOU CAN'T BORROW THEM," FUJI.
"NO," AS IN, "I HAVE TO WORK TONIGHT, I NEED YOU TO *STAY HERE* WITH ANSEL."
I MADE *PLANS*, DEX.
AND I TOLD YOU THIS YESTERDAY, *AND* THE DAY BEFORE, *AND* THE DAY BEFORE *THAT*.
WELL, HOW *LATE* WILL YOU BE?
I DON'T KNOW, IT *DEPENDS*.
ON *WHAT?*
ON WHETHER OR NOT I RUN INTO *TROUBLE*.
MAKE SURE ANSEL HAS DINNER.

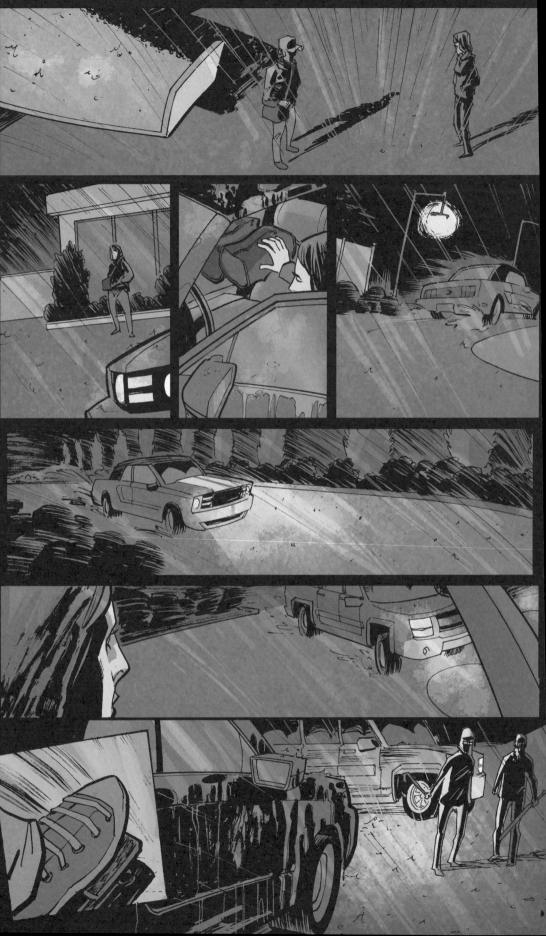

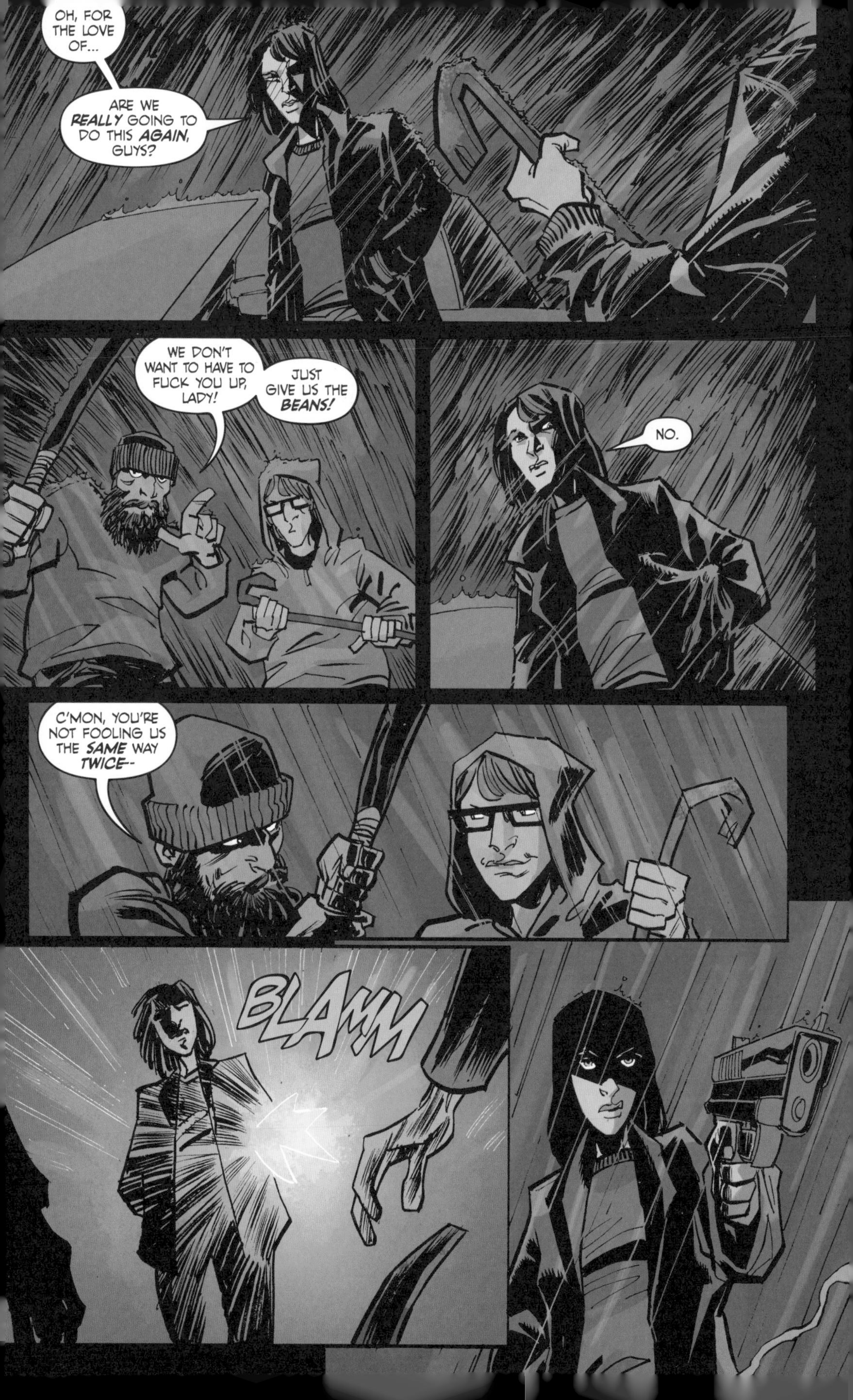
OH, FOR THE LOVE OF...
ARE WE *REALLY* GOING TO DO THIS *AGAIN*, GUYS?
WE DON'T WANT TO HAVE TO FUCK YOU UP, LADY!
JUST GIVE US THE *BEANS!*
NO.
C'MON, YOU'RE NOT FOOLING US THE *SAME* WAY *TWICE*--
BLAMM

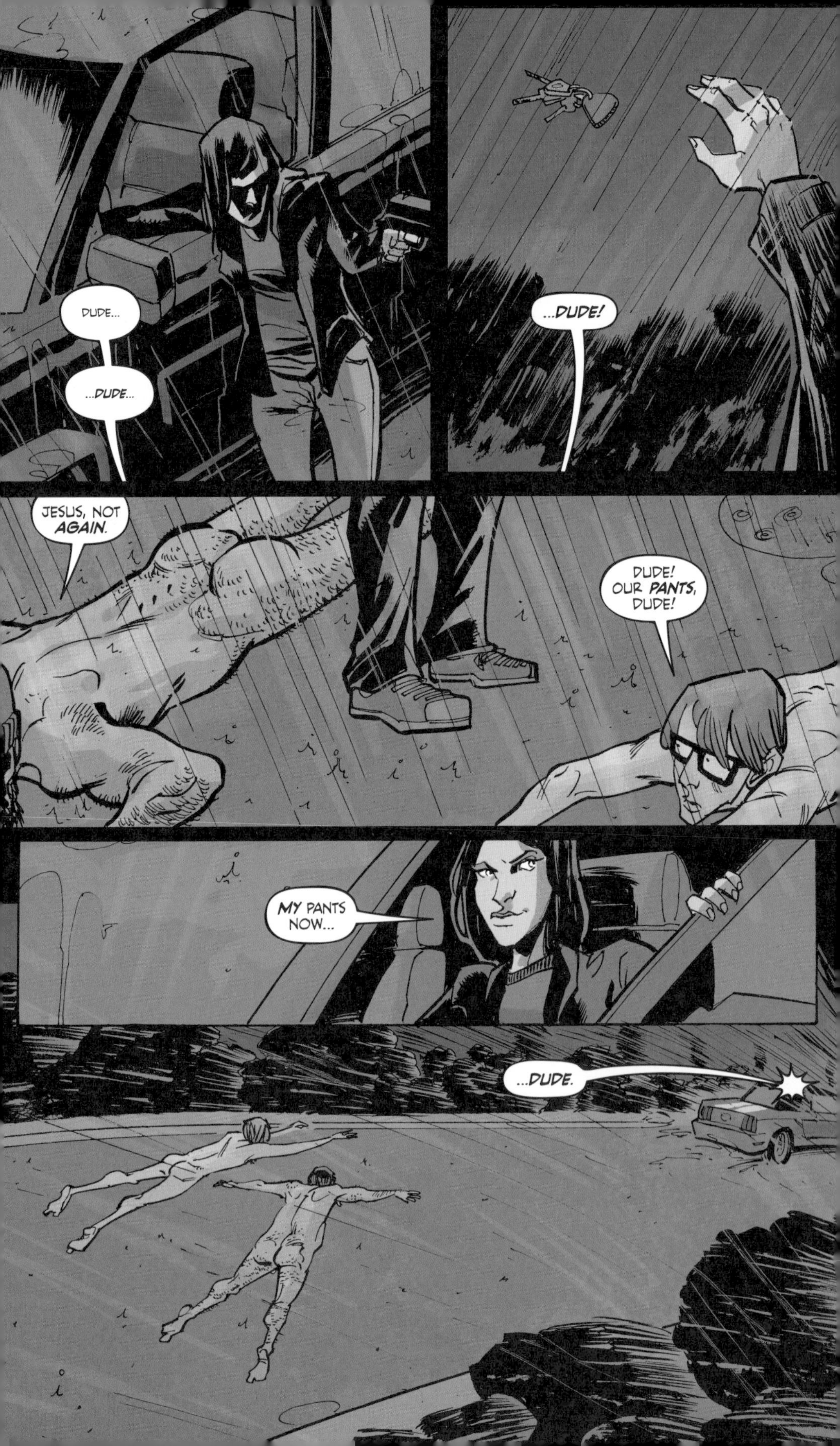
DUDE...
...DUDE...
...DUDE!
JESUS, NOT AGAIN.
DUDE! OUR PANTS, DUDE!
MY PANTS NOW...
...DUDE.

Chapter Three

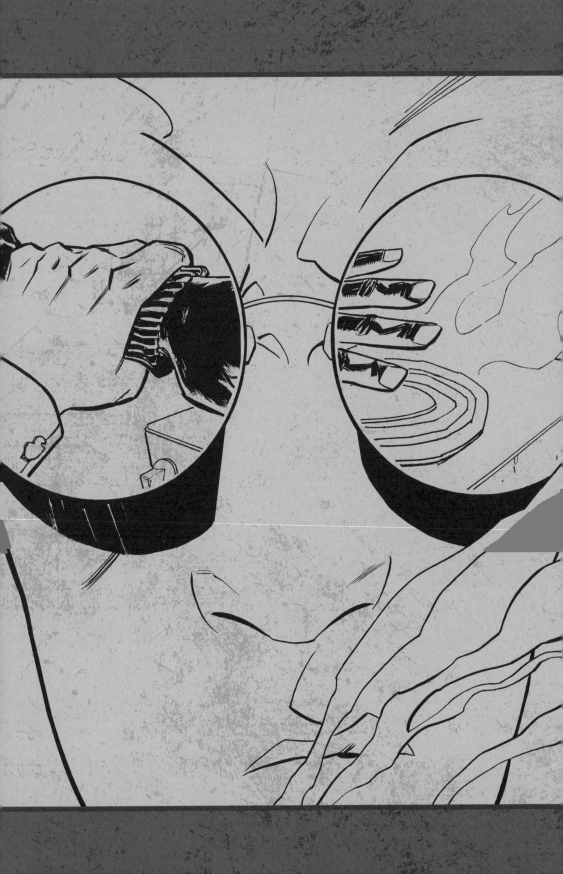

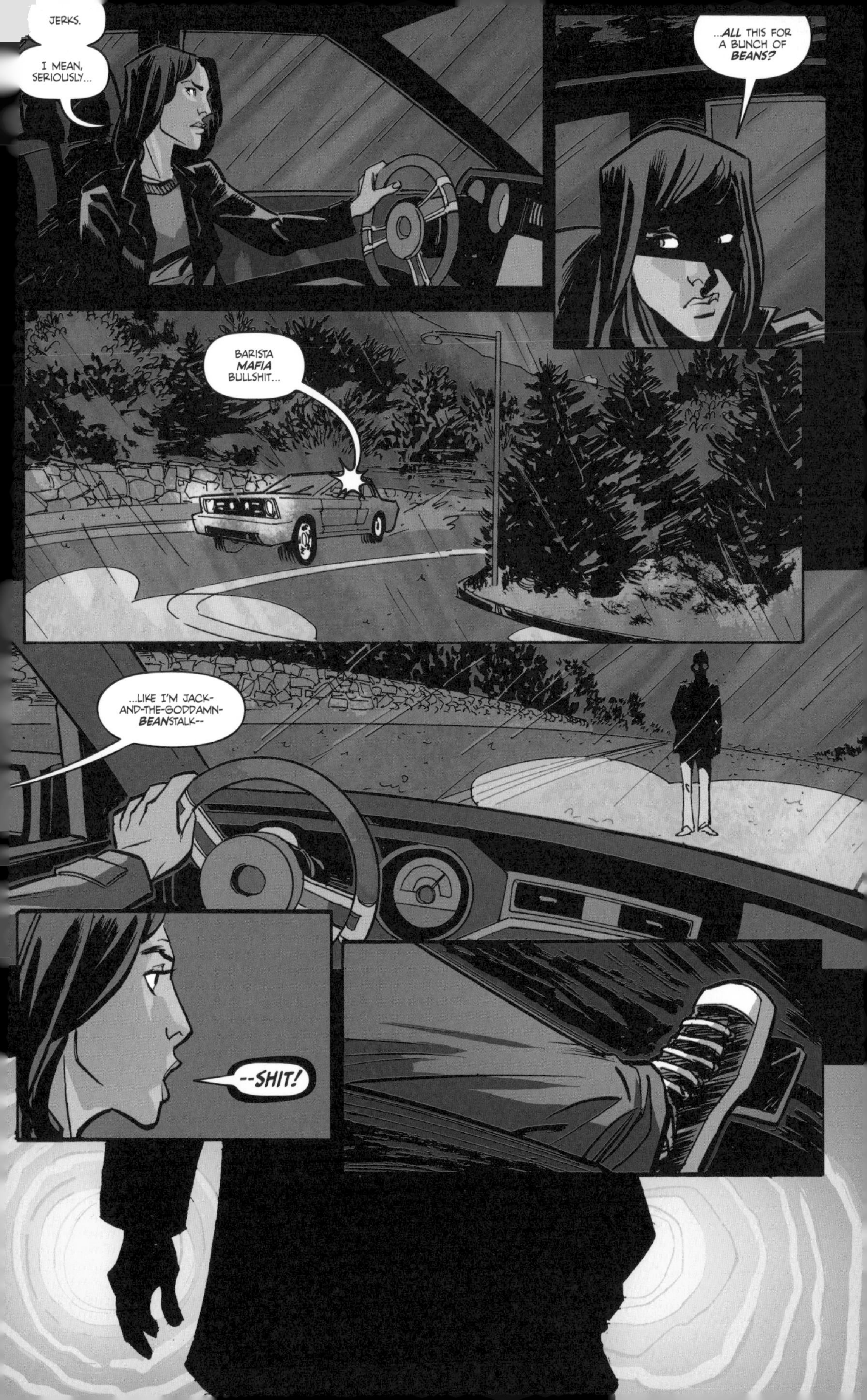
JERKS.
I MEAN, SERIOUSLY...
...ALL THIS FOR A BUNCH OF BEANS?
BARISTA MAFIA BULLSHIT...
...LIKE I'M JACK-AND-THE-GODDAMN-BEANSTALK--
--SHIT!

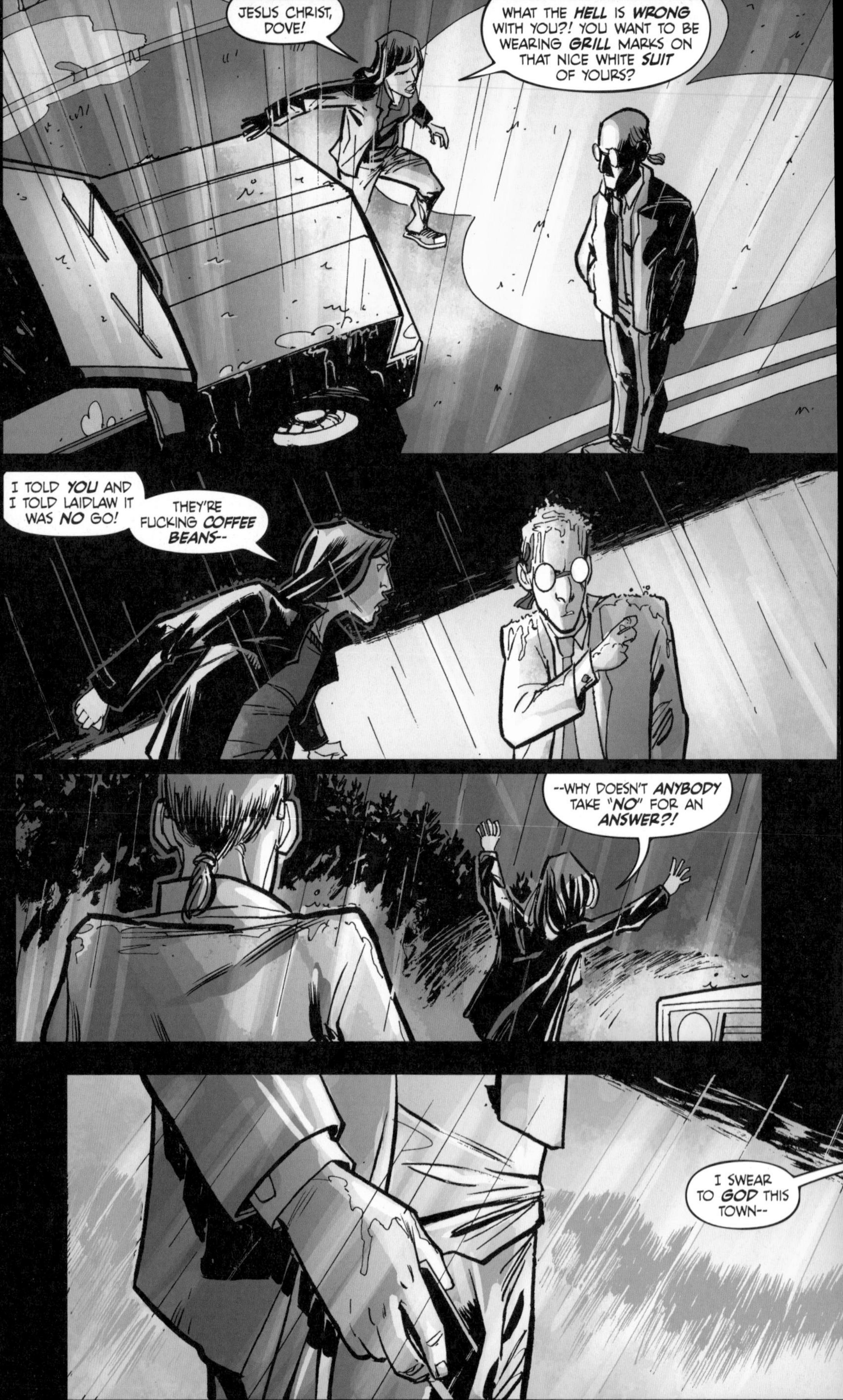
JESUS CHRIST, DOVE!
WHAT THE HELL IS WRONG WITH YOU?! YOU WANT TO BE WEARING GRILL MARKS ON THAT NICE WHITE SUIT OF YOURS?
I TOLD YOU AND I TOLD LAIDLAW IT WAS NO GO!
THEY'RE FUCKING COFFEE BEANS--
--WHY DOESN'T ANYBODY TAKE "NO" FOR AN ANSWER?!
I SWEAR TO GOD THIS TOWN--

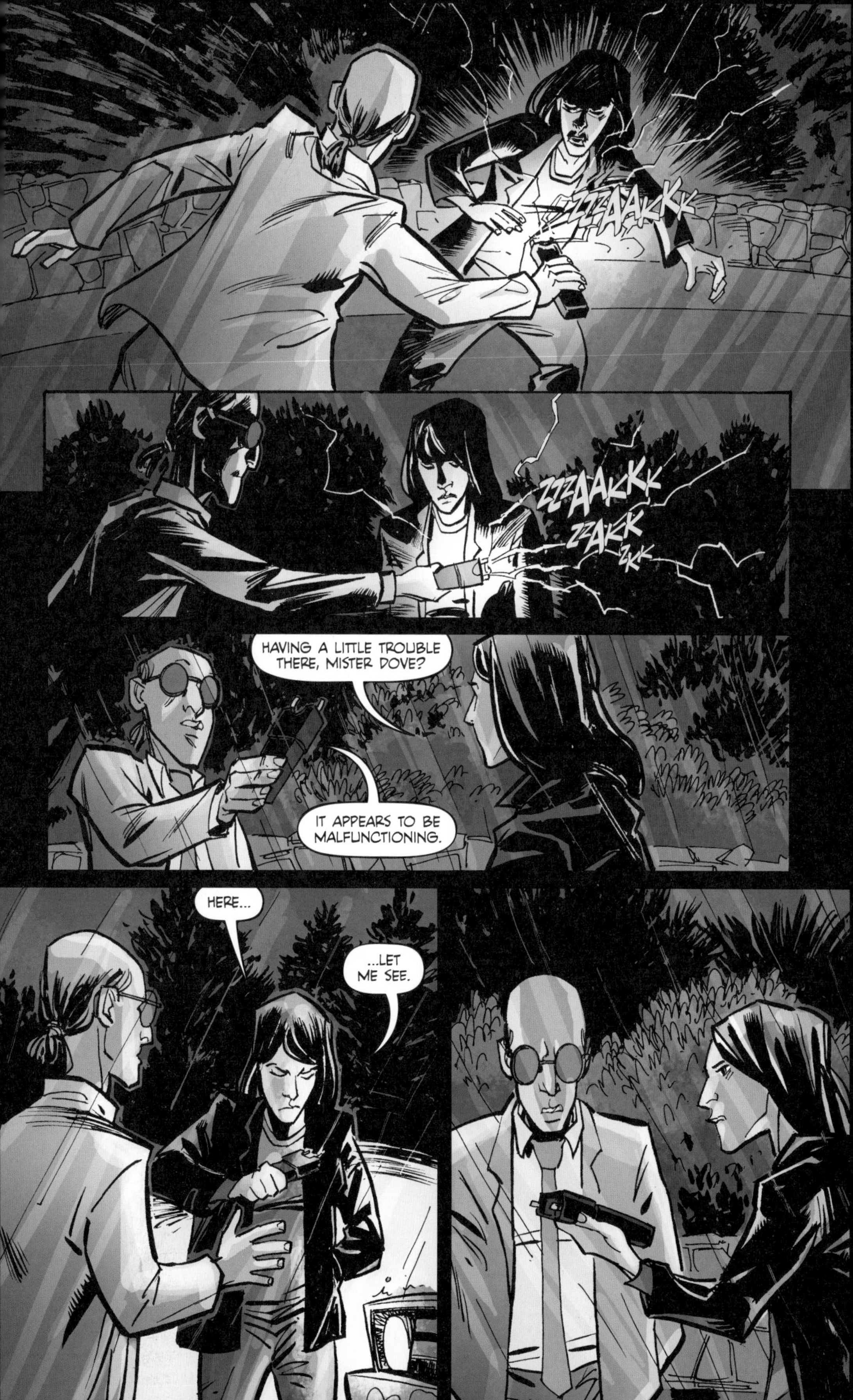
ZZZZAAKKK
ZZZAAKKK
ZZAKK
ZKK
HAVING A LITTLE TROUBLE THERE, MISTER DOVE?
IT APPEARS TO BE MALFUNCTIONING.
HERE...
...LET ME SEE.

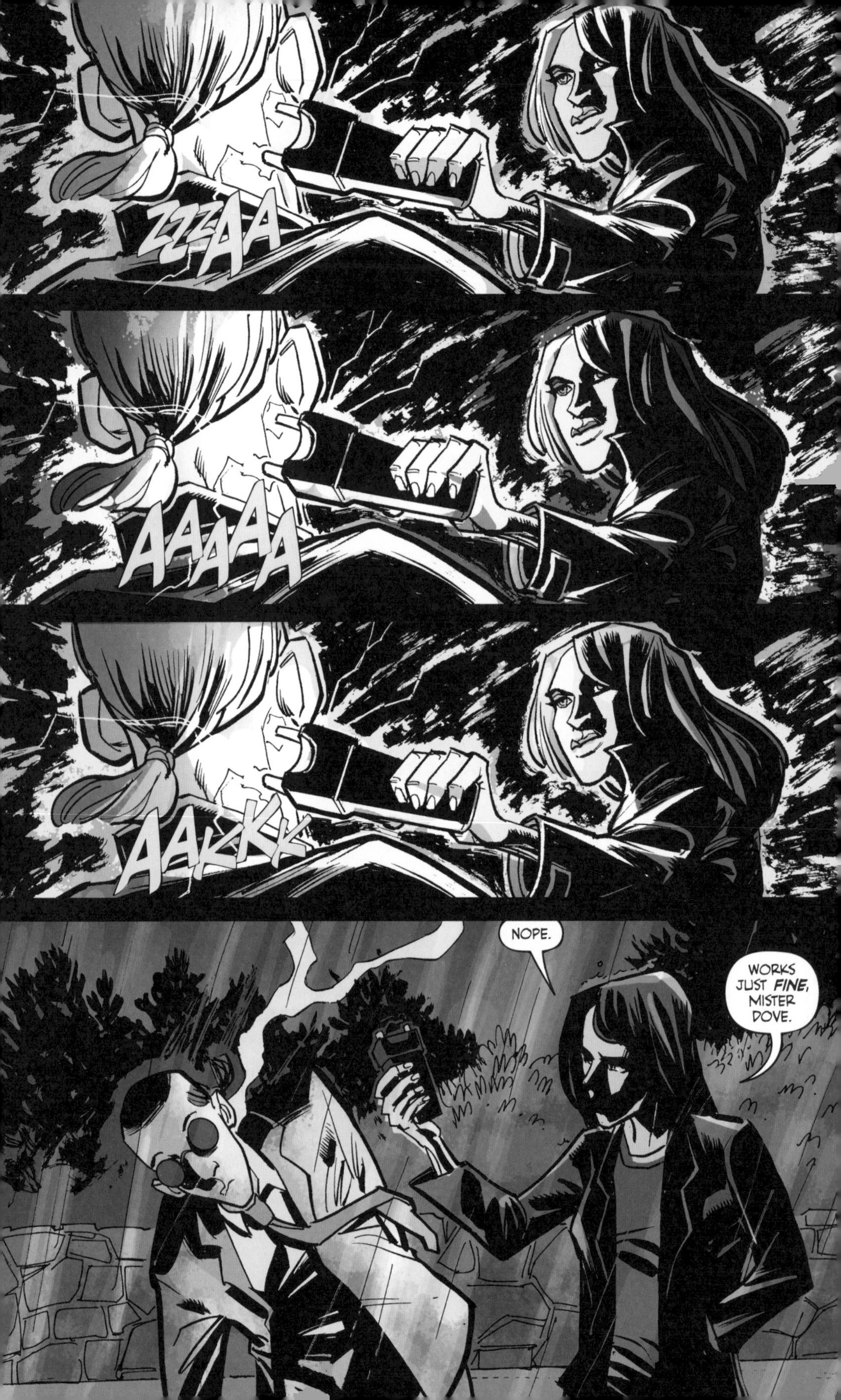
ZZZAA
AAAAA
AAKKK
NOPE.
WORKS JUST FINE, MISTER DOVE.

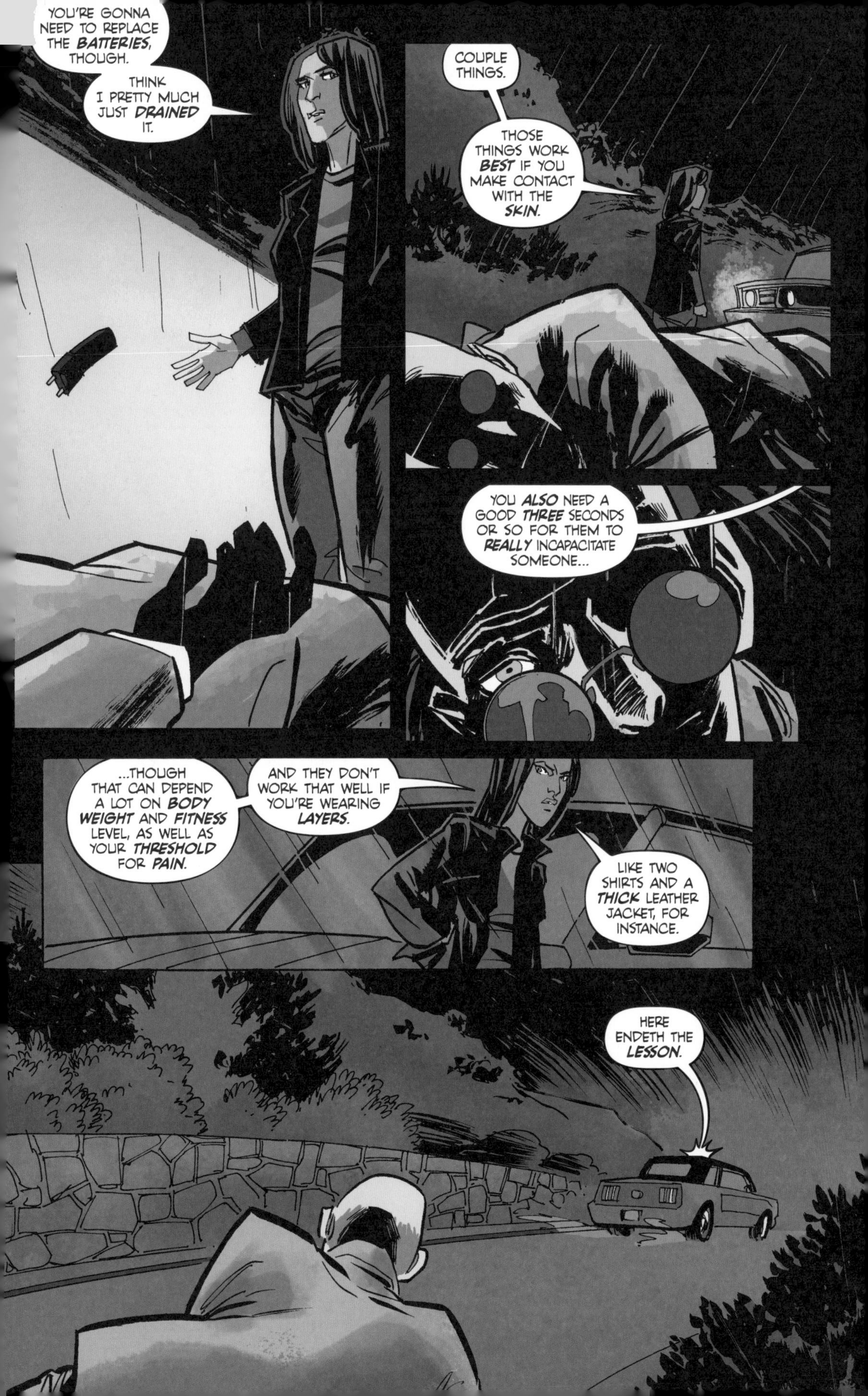
YOU'RE GONNA NEED TO REPLACE THE BATTERIES, THOUGH.
THINK I PRETTY MUCH JUST DRAINED IT.
COUPLE THINGS.
THOSE THINGS WORK BEST IF YOU MAKE CONTACT WITH THE SKIN.
YOU ALSO NEED A GOOD THREE SECONDS OR SO FOR THEM TO REALLY INCAPACITATE SOMEONE...
...THOUGH THAT CAN DEPEND A LOT ON BODY WEIGHT AND FITNESS LEVEL, AS WELL AS YOUR THRESHOLD FOR PAIN.
AND THEY DON'T WORK THAT WELL IF YOU'RE WEARING LAYERS.
LIKE TWO SHIRTS AND A THICK LEATHER JACKET, FOR INSTANCE.
HERE ENDETH THE LESSON.

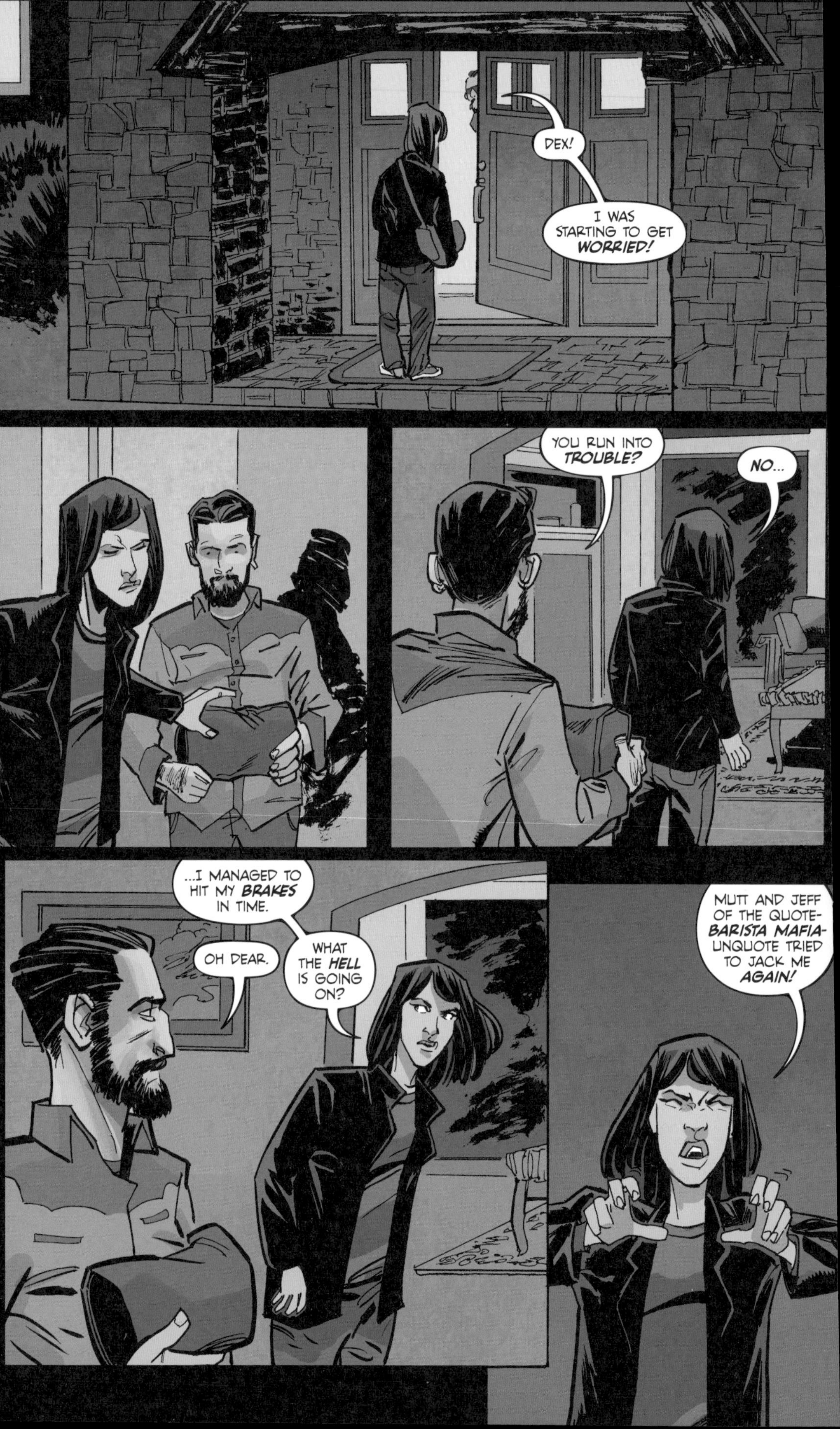

DEX!
I WAS STARTING TO GET WORRIED!
YOU RUN INTO TROUBLE?
NO...
...I MANAGED TO HIT MY BRAKES IN TIME.
OH DEAR.
WHAT THE HELL IS GOING ON?
MUTT AND JEFF OF THE QUOTE-BARISTA MAFIA-UNQUOTE TRIED TO JACK ME AGAIN!

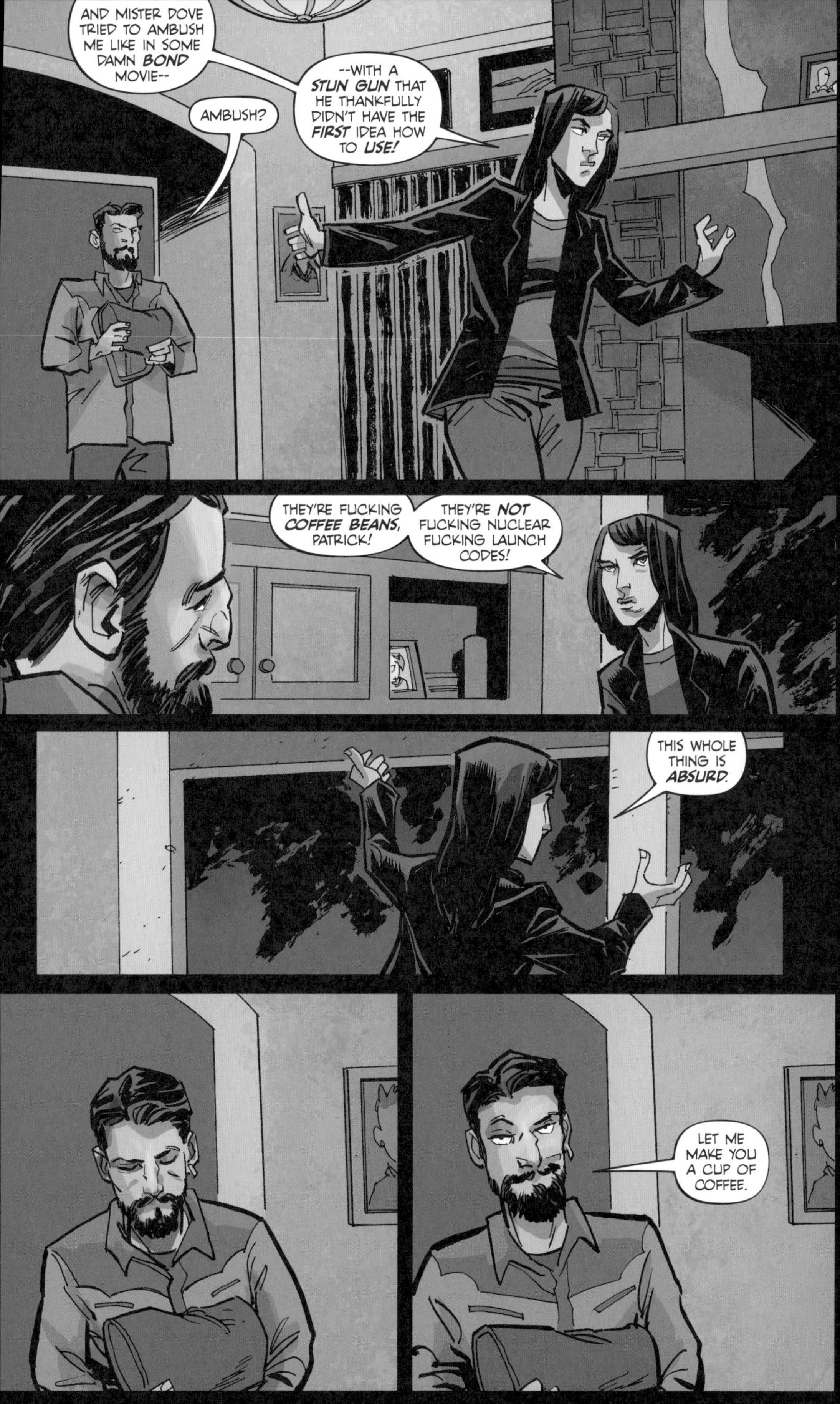
AND MISTER DOVE TRIED TO AMBUSH ME LIKE IN SOME DAMN BOND MOVIE--
AMBUSH?
--WITH A STUN GUN THAT HE THANKFULLY DIDN'T HAVE THE FIRST IDEA HOW TO USE!
THEY'RE FUCKING COFFEE BEANS, PATRICK!
THEY'RE NOT FUCKING NUCLEAR FUCKING LAUNCH CODES!
THIS WHOLE THING IS ABSURD.
LET ME MAKE YOU A CUP OF COFFEE.

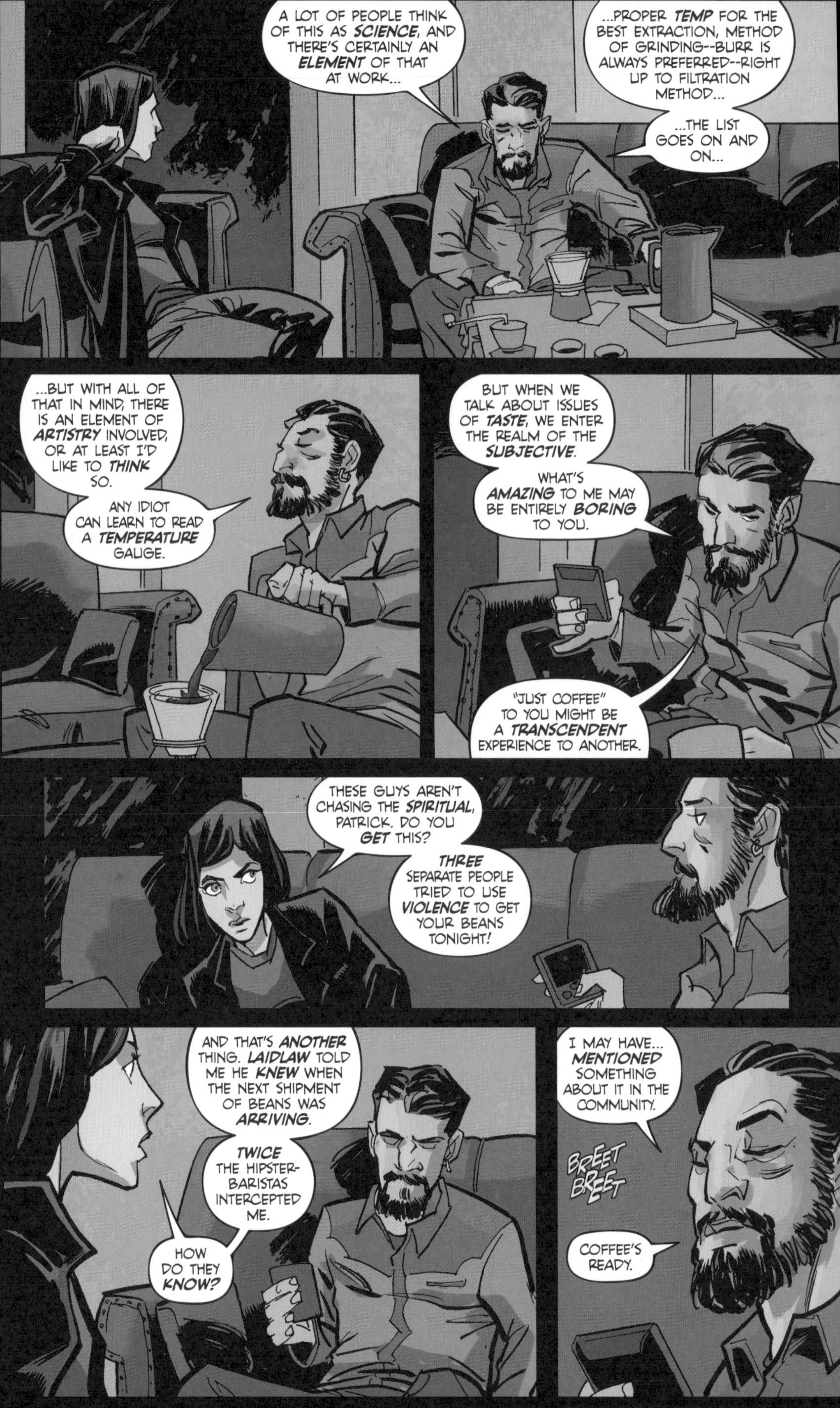

A LOT OF PEOPLE THINK OF THIS AS SCIENCE, AND THERE'S CERTAINLY AN ELEMENT OF THAT AT WORK...
...PROPER TEMP FOR THE BEST EXTRACTION, METHOD OF GRINDING--BURR IS ALWAYS PREFERRED--RIGHT UP TO FILTRATION METHOD...
...THE LIST GOES ON AND ON...
...BUT WITH ALL OF THAT IN MIND, THERE IS AN ELEMENT OF ARTISTRY INVOLVED, OR AT LEAST I'D LIKE TO THINK SO.
ANY IDIOT CAN LEARN TO READ A TEMPERATURE GAUGE.
BUT WHEN WE TALK ABOUT ISSUES OF TASTE, WE ENTER THE REALM OF THE SUBJECTIVE.
WHAT'S AMAZING TO ME MAY BE ENTIRELY BORING TO YOU.
"JUST COFFEE" TO YOU MIGHT BE A TRANSCENDENT EXPERIENCE TO ANOTHER.
THESE GUYS AREN'T CHASING THE SPIRITUAL, PATRICK. DO YOU GET THIS?
THREE SEPARATE PEOPLE TRIED TO USE VIOLENCE TO GET YOUR BEANS TONIGHT!
AND THAT'S ANOTHER THING. LAIDLAW TOLD ME HE KNEW WHEN THE NEXT SHIPMENT OF BEANS WAS ARRIVING.
TWICE THE HIPSTER-BARISTAS INTERCEPTED ME.
HOW DO THEY KNOW?
I MAY HAVE... MENTIONED SOMETHING ABOUT IT IN THE COMMUNITY.
BREET BREET
COFFEE'S READY.

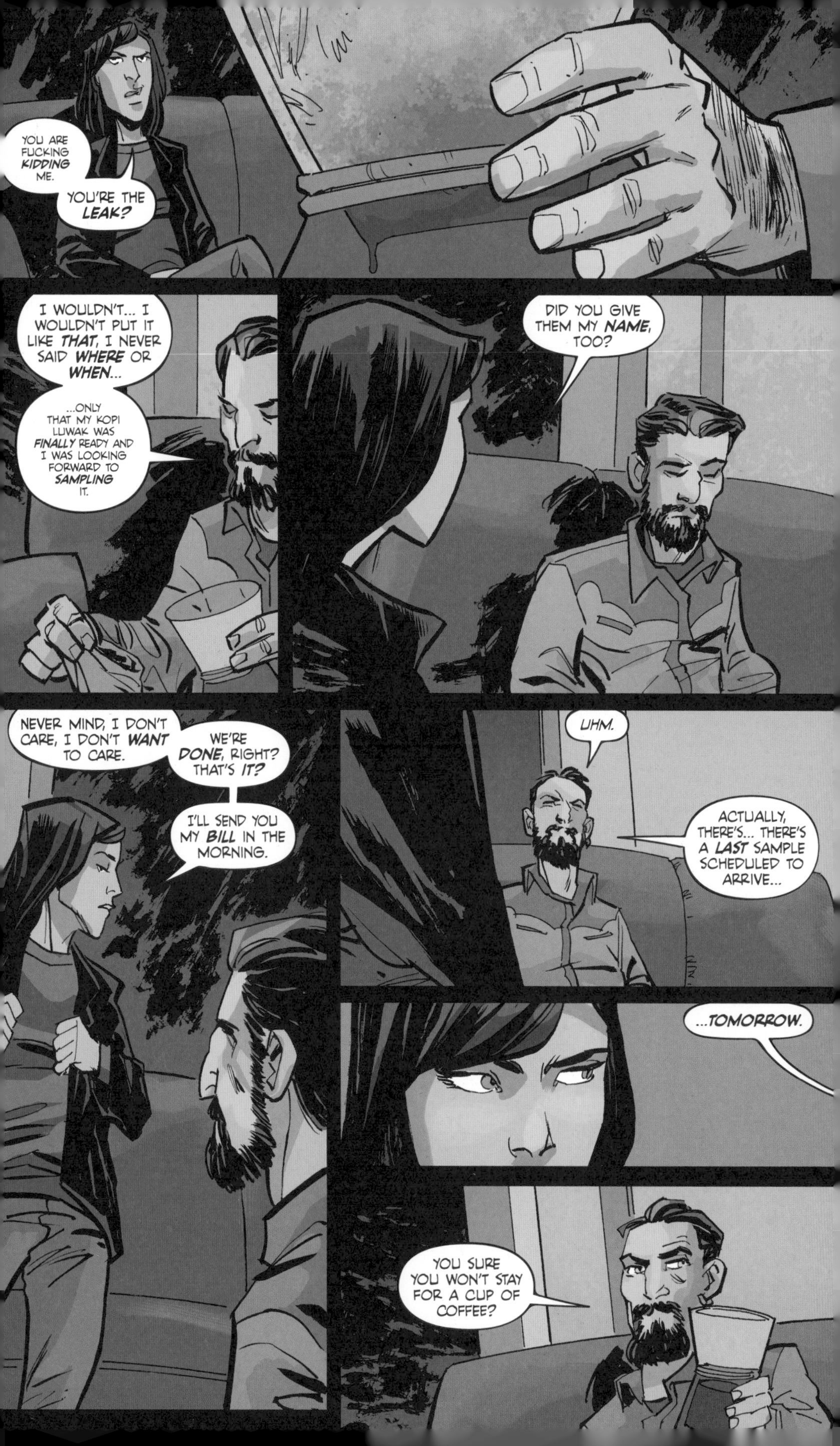
YOU ARE FUCKING KIDDING ME.
YOU'RE THE LEAK?
I WOULDN'T... I WOULDN'T PUT IT LIKE THAT, I NEVER SAID WHERE OR WHEN...
...ONLY THAT MY KOPI LUWAK WAS FINALLY READY AND I WAS LOOKING FORWARD TO SAMPLING IT.
DID YOU GIVE THEM MY NAME, TOO?
NEVER MIND, I DON'T CARE, I DON'T WANT TO CARE.
WE'RE DONE, RIGHT? THAT'S IT?
I'LL SEND YOU MY BILL IN THE MORNING.
UHM.
ACTUALLY, THERE'S... THERE'S A LAST SAMPLE SCHEDULED TO ARRIVE...
...TOMORROW.
YOU SURE YOU WON'T STAY FOR A CUP OF COFFEE?

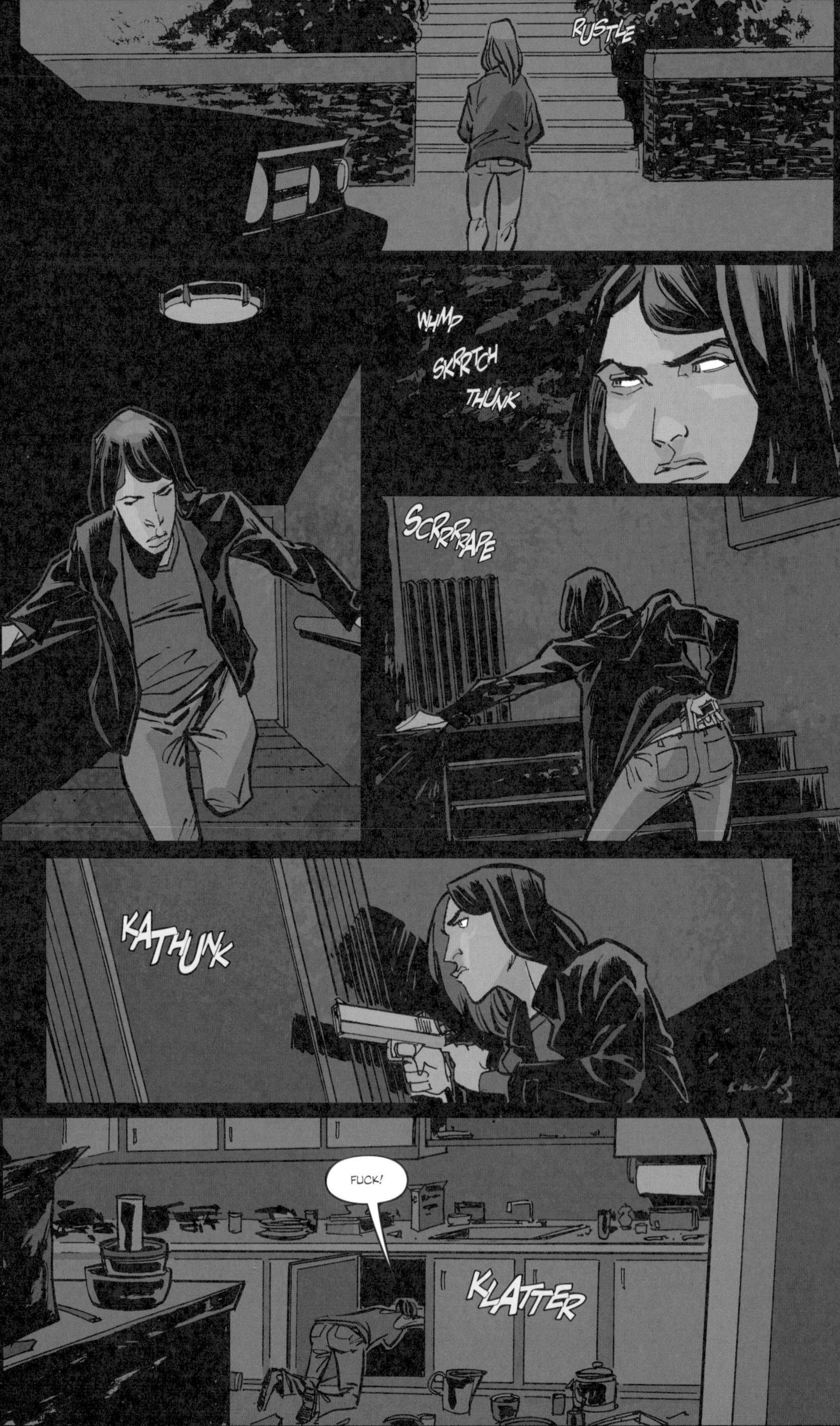

RUSTLE
WHMP
SKRRTCH
THUNK
SCRRRRAPE
KATHUNK
FUCK!
KLATTER

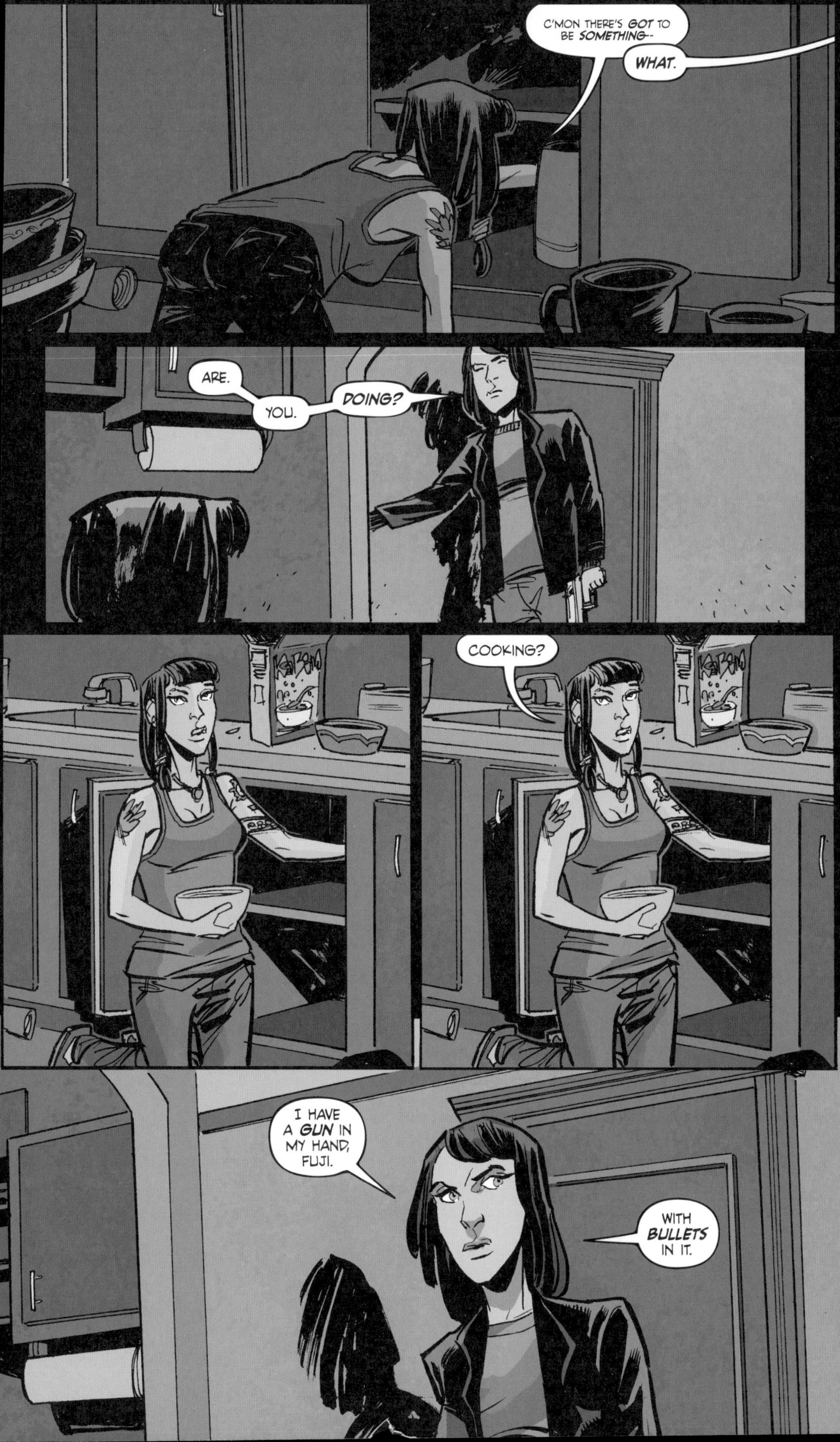
C'MON THERE'S GOT TO BE SOMETHING--
WHAT.
ARE.
YOU.
DOING?
COOKING?
I HAVE A GUN IN MY HAND, FUJI.
WITH BULLETS IN IT.

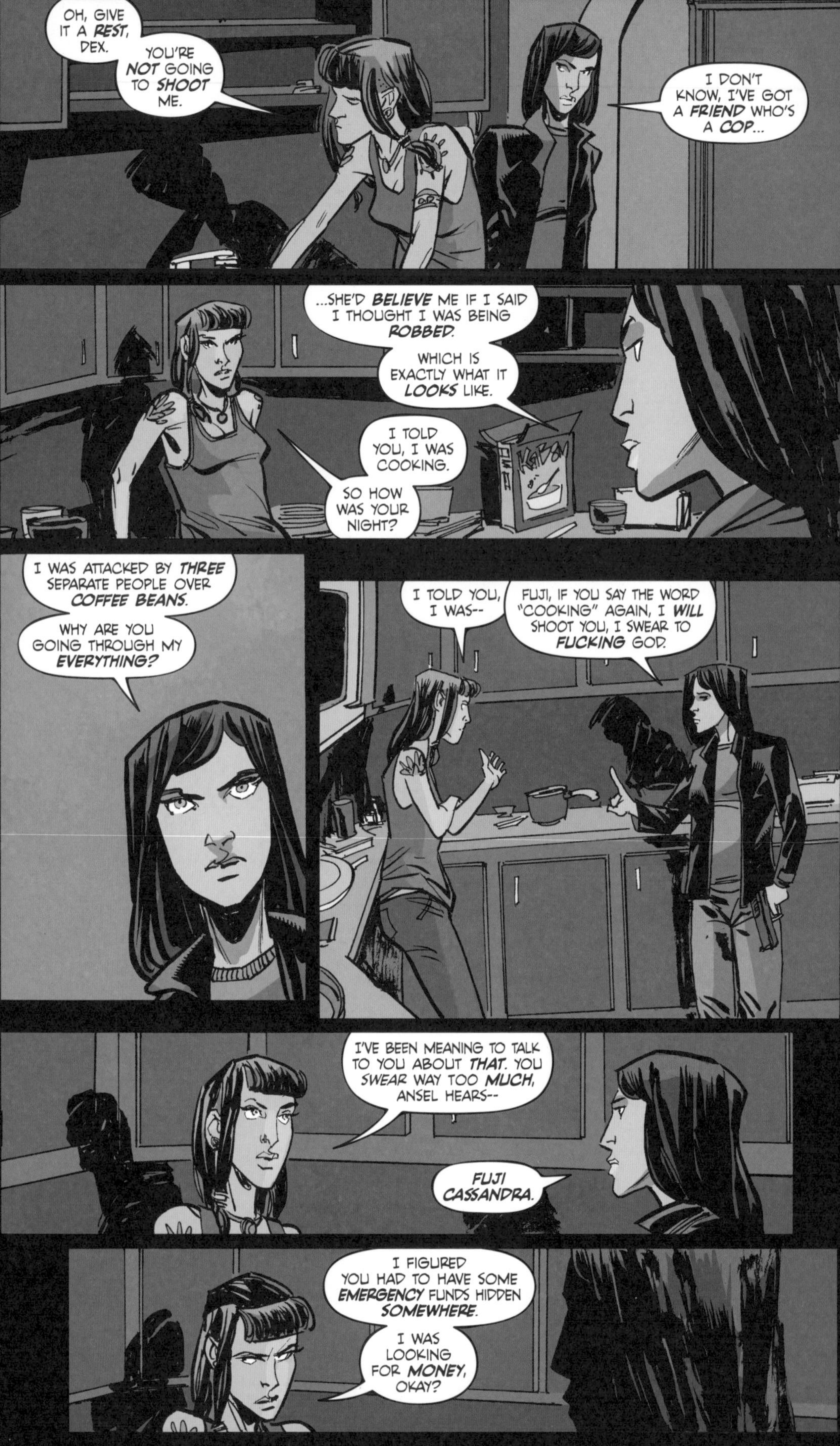

OH, GIVE IT A REST, DEX.
YOU'RE NOT GOING TO SHOOT ME.
I DON'T KNOW, I'VE GOT A FRIEND WHO'S A COP...
...SHE'D BELIEVE ME IF I SAID I THOUGHT I WAS BEING ROBBED.
WHICH IS EXACTLY WHAT IT LOOKS LIKE.
I TOLD YOU, I WAS COOKING.
SO HOW WAS YOUR NIGHT?
I WAS ATTACKED BY THREE SEPARATE PEOPLE OVER COFFEE BEANS.
WHY ARE YOU GOING THROUGH MY EVERYTHING?
I TOLD YOU, I WAS--
FUJI, IF YOU SAY THE WORD "COOKING" AGAIN, I WILL SHOOT YOU, I SWEAR TO FUCKING GOD.
I'VE BEEN MEANING TO TALK TO YOU ABOUT THAT. YOU SWEAR WAY TOO MUCH, ANSEL HEARS--
FUJI CASSANDRA.
I FIGURED YOU HAD TO HAVE SOME EMERGENCY FUNDS HIDDEN SOMEWHERE.
I WAS LOOKING FOR MONEY, OKAY?

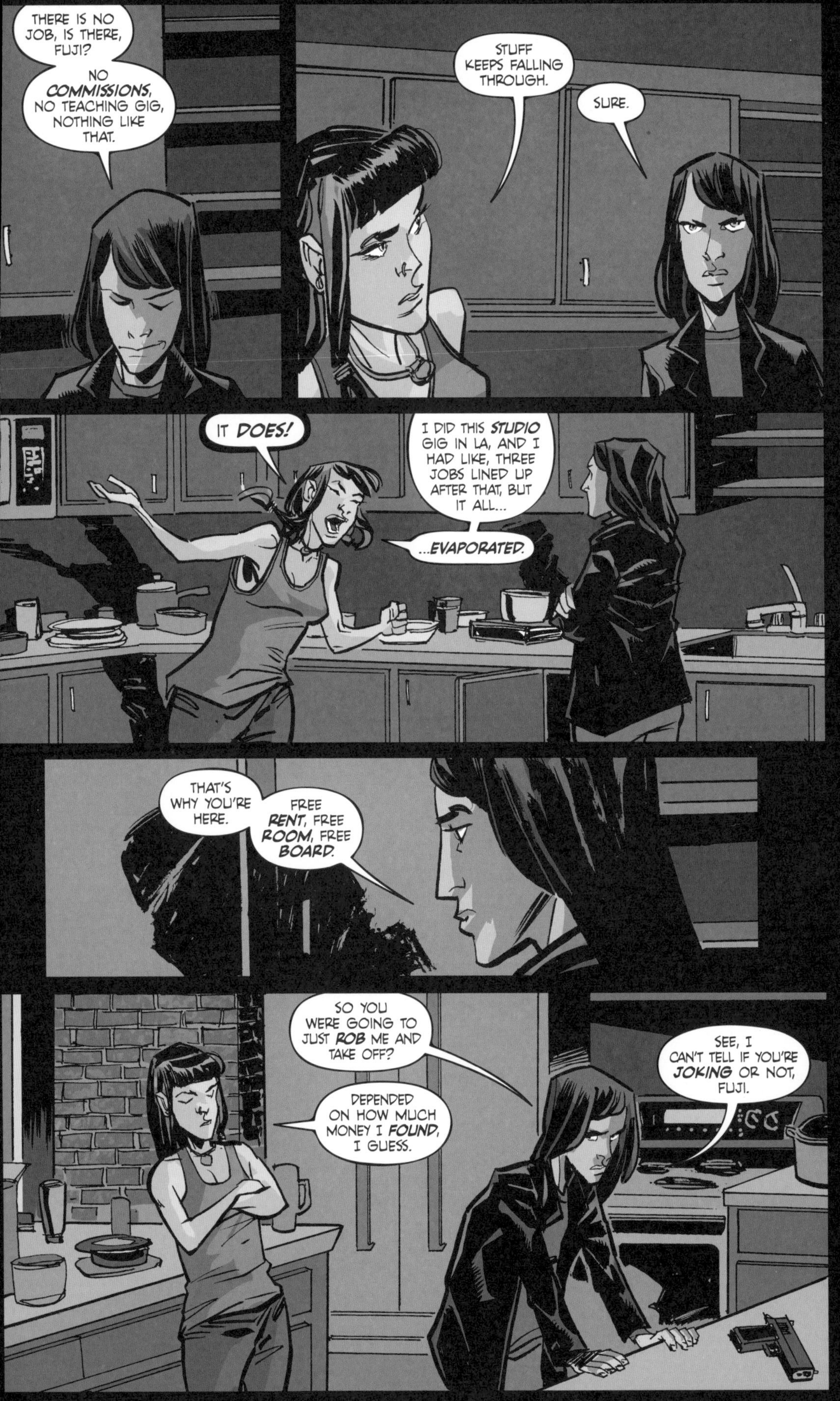
THERE IS NO JOB, IS THERE, FUJI?
NO COMMISSIONS, NO TEACHING GIG, NOTHING LIKE THAT.
STUFF KEEPS FALLING THROUGH.
SURE.
IT DOES!
I DID THIS STUDIO GIG IN LA, AND I HAD LIKE, THREE JOBS LINED UP AFTER THAT, BUT IT ALL...
...EVAPORATED.
THAT'S WHY YOU'RE HERE.
FREE RENT, FREE ROOM, FREE BOARD.
SO YOU WERE GOING TO JUST ROB ME AND TAKE OFF?
DEPENDED ON HOW MUCH MONEY I FOUND, I GUESS.
SEE, I CAN'T TELL IF YOU'RE JOKING OR NOT, FUJI.

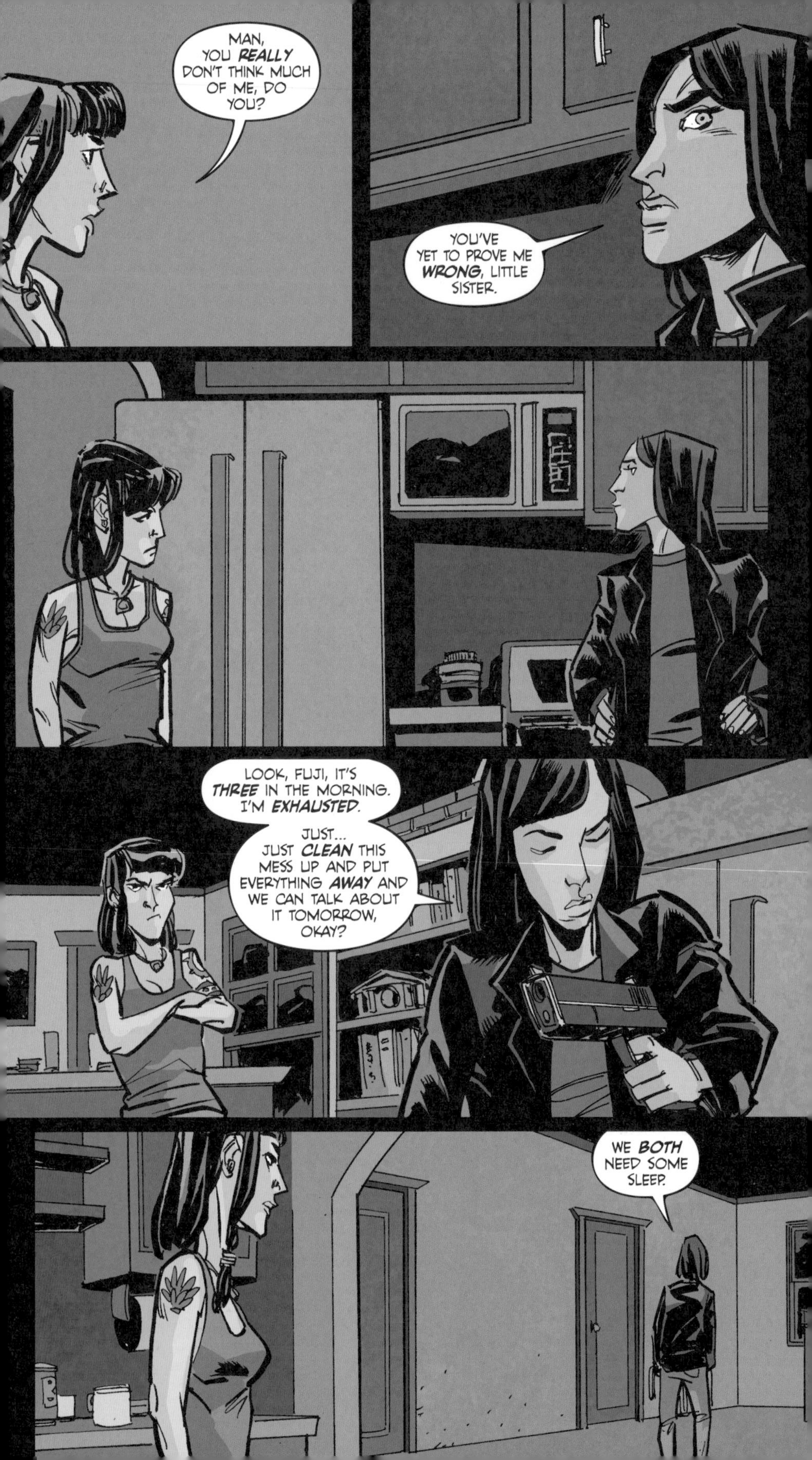
MAN, YOU REALLY DON'T THINK MUCH OF ME, DO YOU?
YOU'VE YET TO PROVE ME WRONG, LITTLE SISTER.
LOOK, FUJI, IT'S THREE IN THE MORNING. I'M EXHAUSTED.
JUST... JUST CLEAN THIS MESS UP AND PUT EVERYTHING AWAY AND WE CAN TALK ABOUT IT TOMORROW, OKAY?
WE BOTH NEED SOME SLEEP.

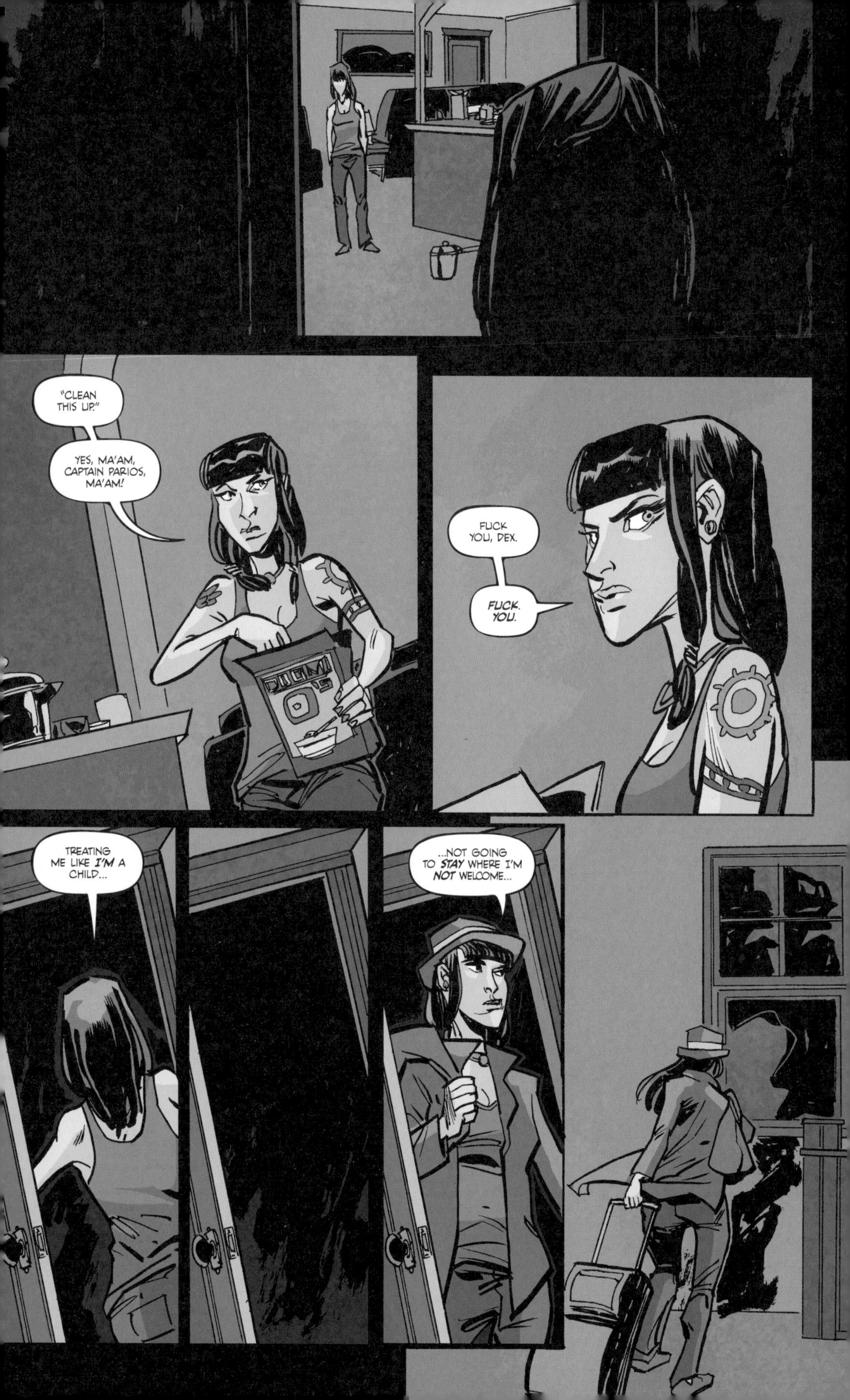
"CLEAN THIS UP."
YES, MA'AM, CAPTAIN PARIOS, MA'AM!
FUCK YOU, DEX.
FUCK. YOU.
TREATING ME LIKE *I'M* A CHILD...
...NOT GOING TO *STAY* WHERE I'M *NOT* WELCOME...

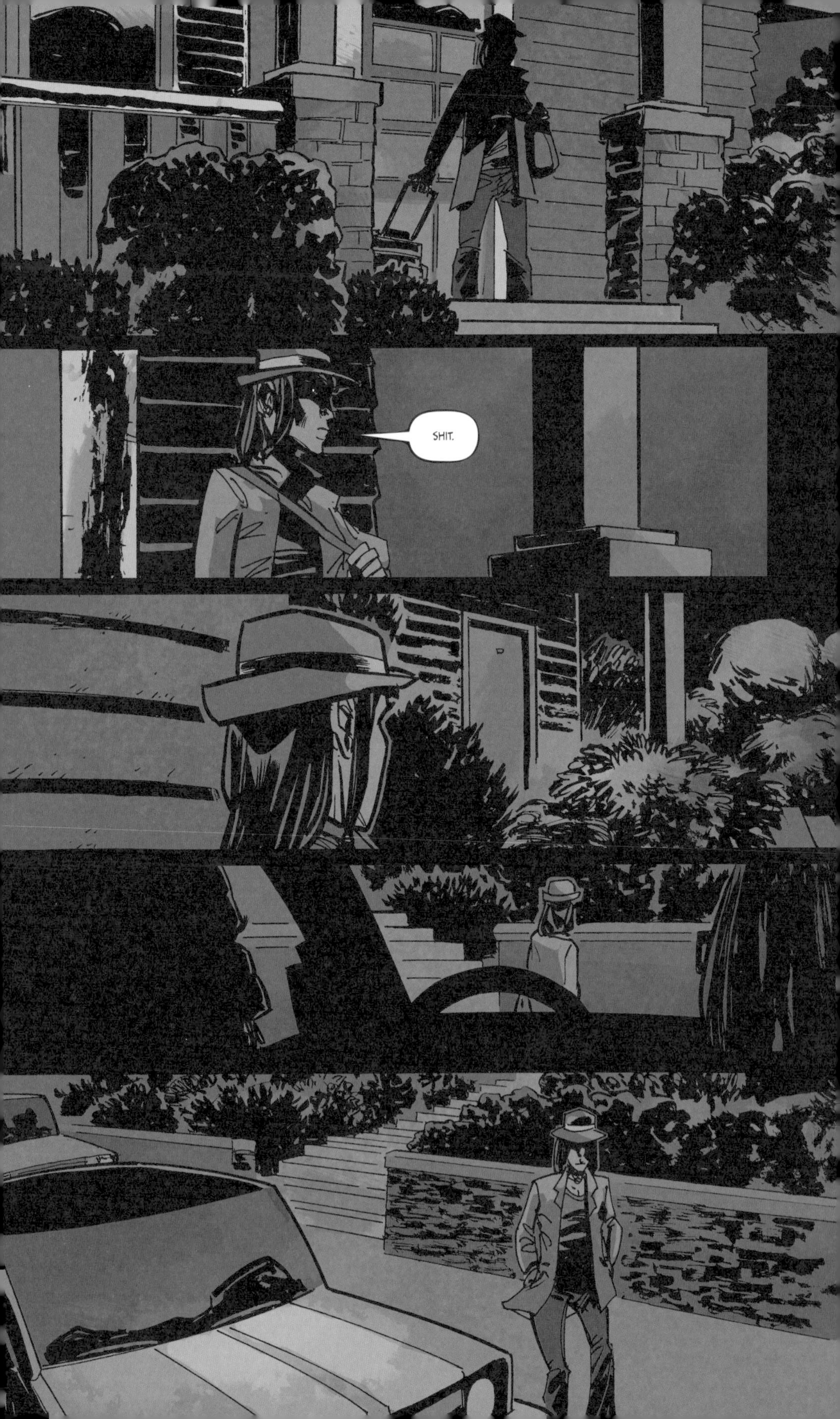
SHIT.

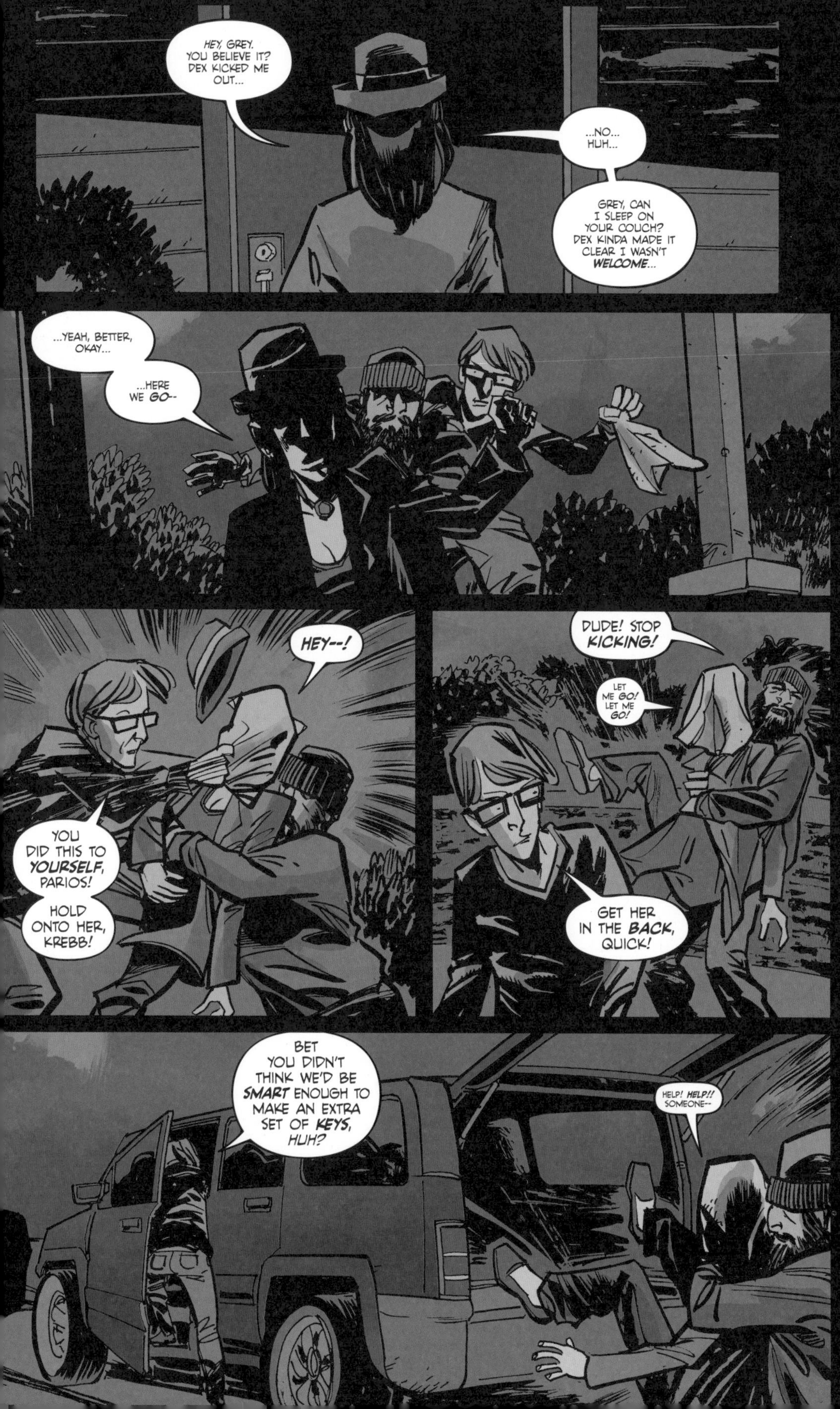
HEY, GREY. YOU BELIEVE IT? DEX KICKED ME OUT...
...NO... HUH...
GREY, CAN I SLEEP ON YOUR COUCH? DEX KINDA MADE IT CLEAR I WASN'T WELCOME...
...YEAH, BETTER, OKAY...
...HERE WE GO--
HEY--!
YOU DID THIS TO YOURSELF, PARIOS!
HOLD ONTO HER, KREBB!
DUDE! STOP KICKING!
LET ME GO! LET ME GO!
GET HER IN THE BACK, QUICK!
BET YOU DIDN'T THINK WE'D BE SMART ENOUGH TO MAKE AN EXTRA SET OF KEYS, HUH?
HELP! HELP!! SOMEONE--

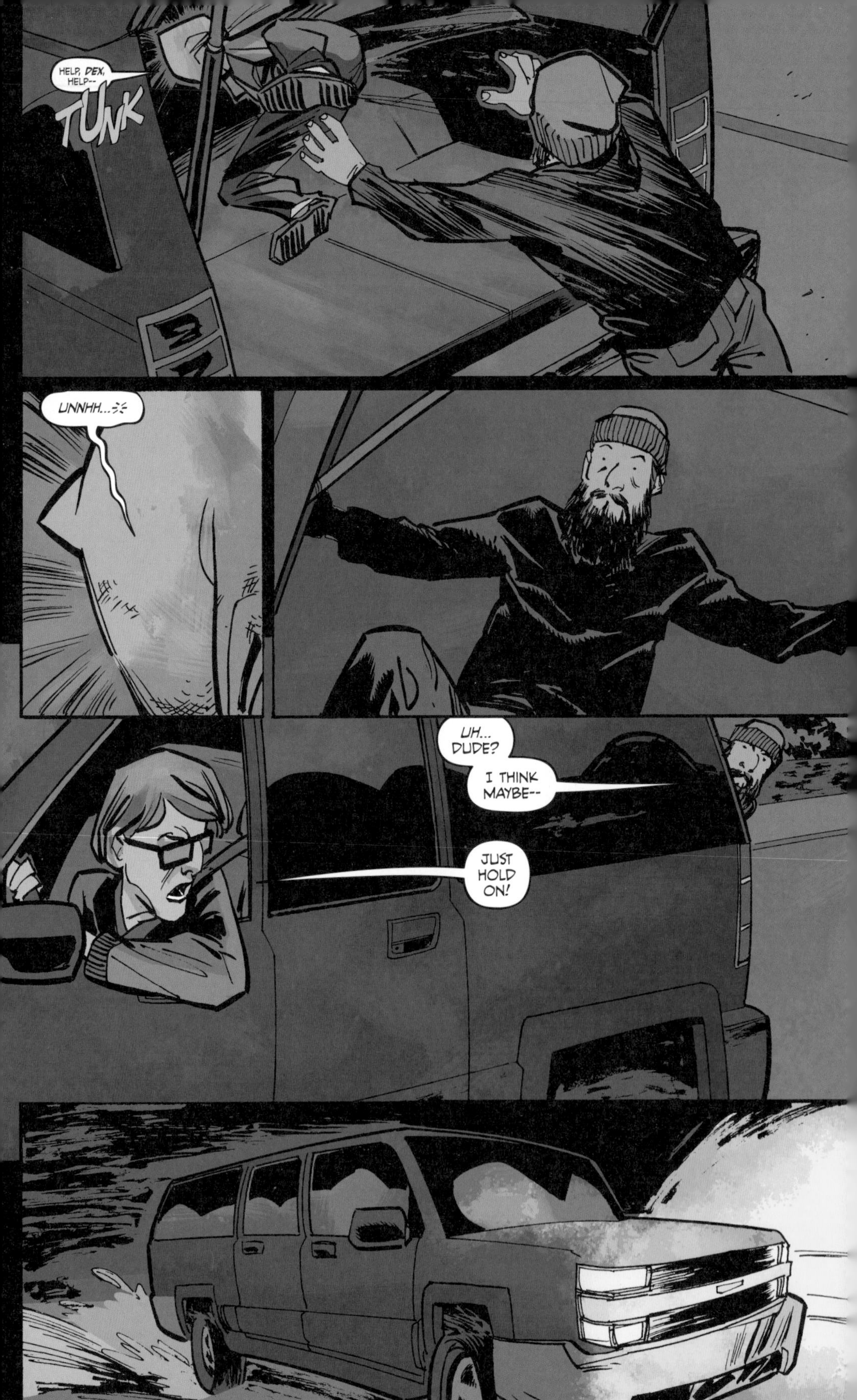

HELP, DEX, HELP--
TUNK
UNNHH...
UH... DUDE?
I THINK MAYBE--
JUST HOLD ON!

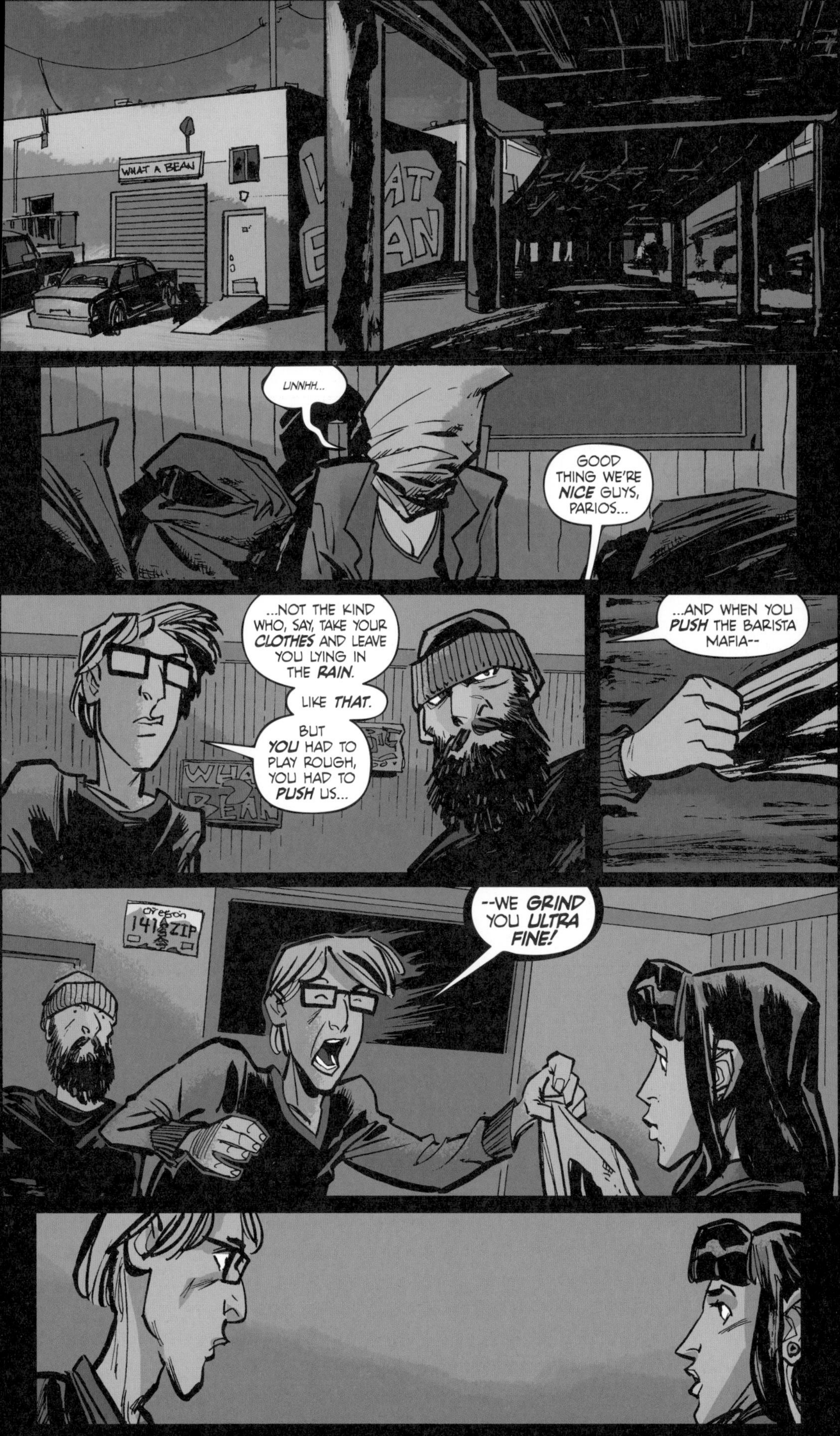

WHAT A BEAN
UNNHH...
GOOD THING WE'RE NICE GUYS, PARIOS...
...NOT THE KIND WHO, SAY, TAKE YOUR CLOTHES AND LEAVE YOU LYING IN THE RAIN.
LIKE THAT.
BUT YOU HAD TO PLAY ROUGH, YOU HAD TO PUSH US...
...AND WHEN YOU PUSH THE BARISTA MAFIA--
--WE GRIND YOU ULTRA FINE!

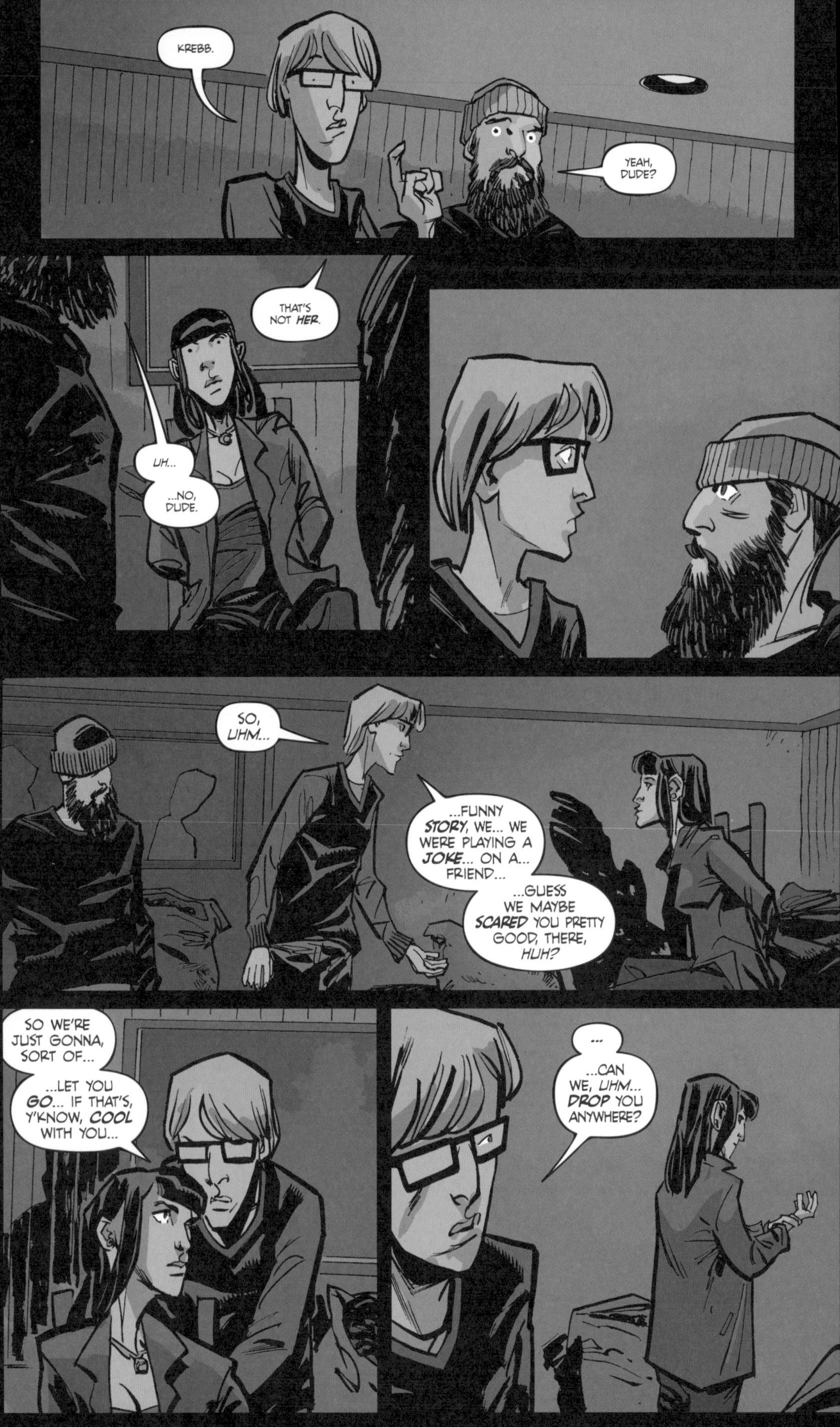
KREBB.
YEAH, DUDE?
THAT'S NOT HER.
UH...
...NO, DUDE.
SO, UHM...
...FUNNY STORY, WE... WE WERE PLAYING A JOKE... ON A... FRIEND...
...GUESS WE MAYBE SCARED YOU PRETTY GOOD, THERE, HUH?
SO WE'RE JUST GONNA, SORT OF...
...LET YOU GO... IF THAT'S, Y'KNOW, COOL WITH YOU...
...
...CAN WE, UHM... DROP YOU ANYWHERE?

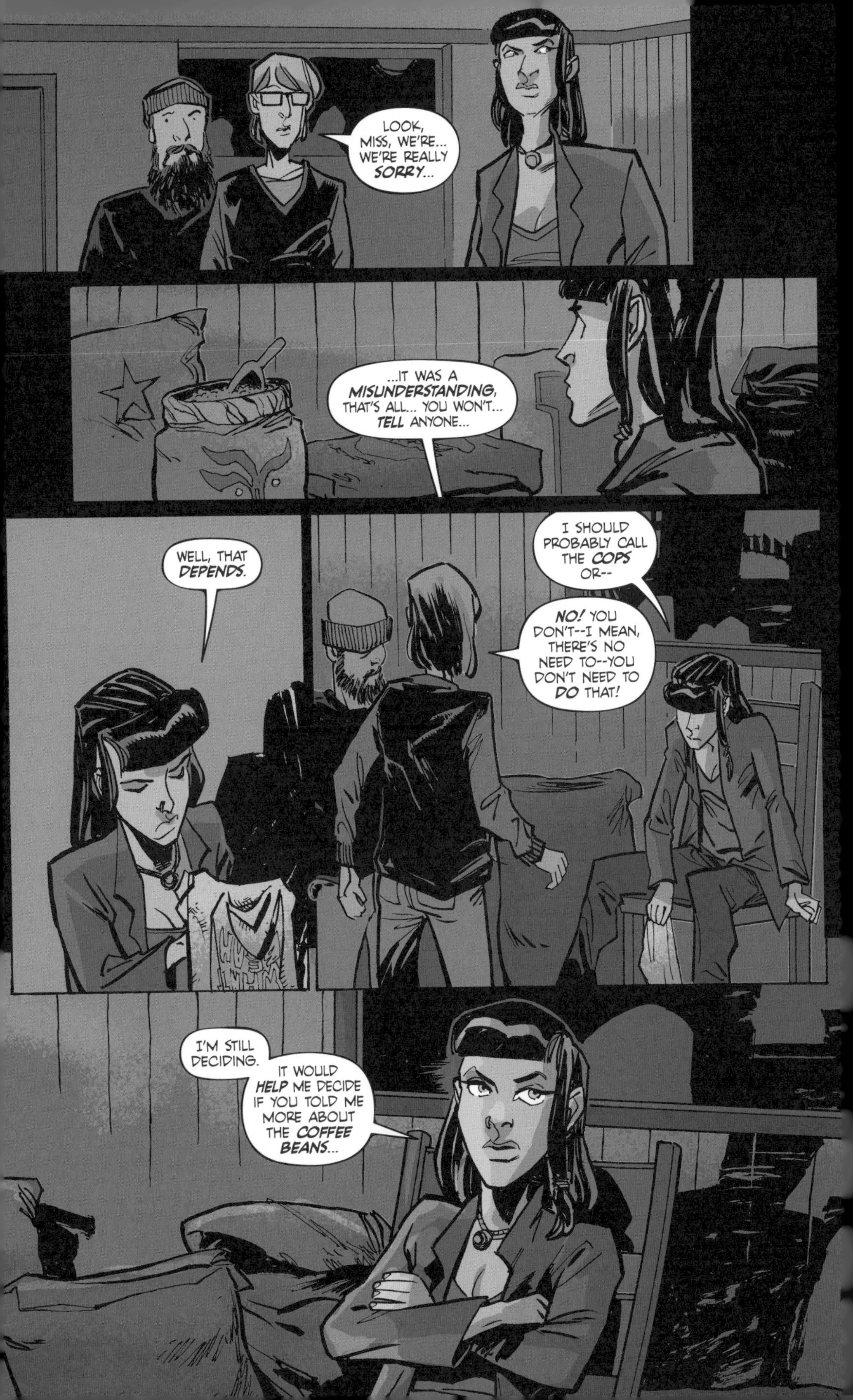

LOOK, MISS, WE'RE... WE'RE REALLY SORRY...
...IT WAS A MISUNDERSTANDING, THAT'S ALL... YOU WON'T... TELL ANYONE...
WELL, THAT DEPENDS.
I SHOULD PROBABLY CALL THE COPS OR--
NO! YOU DON'T--I MEAN, THERE'S NO NEED TO--YOU DON'T NEED TO DO THAT!
I'M STILL DECIDING.
IT WOULD HELP ME DECIDE IF YOU TOLD ME MORE ABOUT THE COFFEE BEANS...

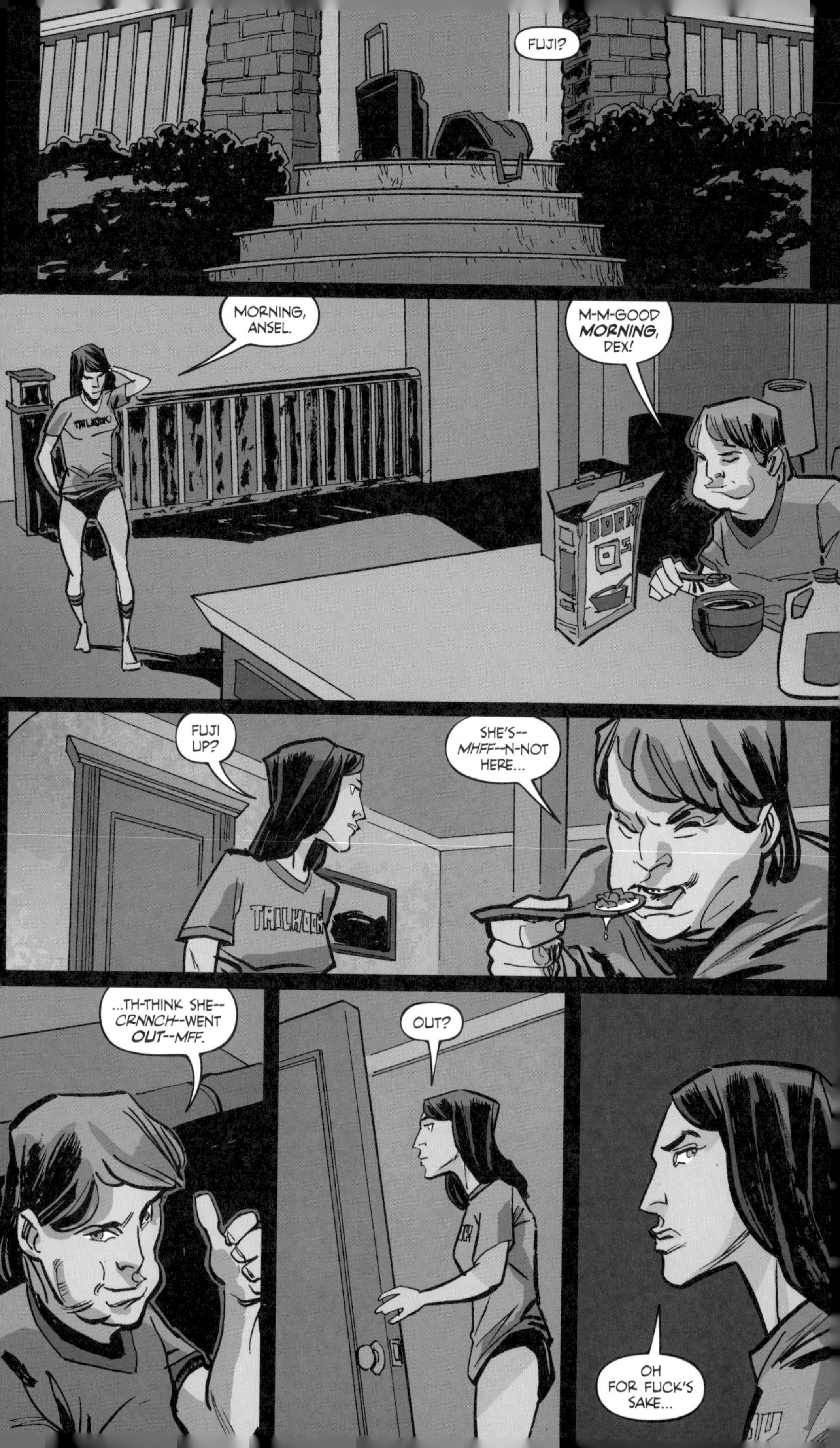
FUJI?
MORNING, ANSEL.
M-M-GOOD MORNING, DEX!
FUJI UP?
SHE'S-- MHFF--N-NOT HERE...
...TH-THINK SHE-- CRNNCH--WENT OUT--MFF.
OUT?
OH FOR FUCK'S SAKE...

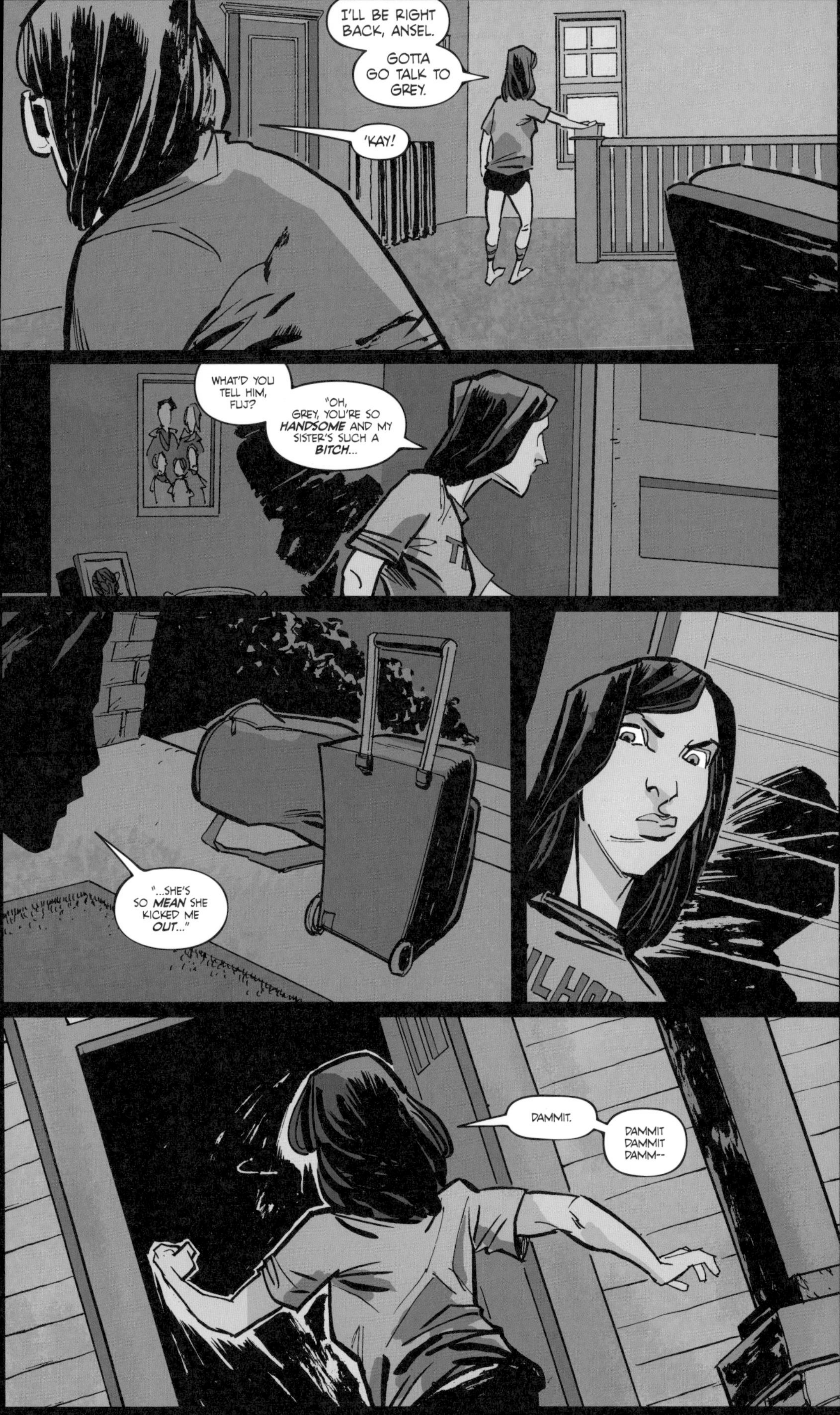
I'LL BE RIGHT BACK, ANSEL.
GOTTA GO TALK TO GREY.
'KAY!
WHAT'D YOU TELL HIM, FUJ?
"OH, GREY, YOU'RE SO HANDSOME AND MY SISTER'S SUCH A BITCH...
"...SHE'S SO MEAN SHE KICKED ME OUT..."
DAMMIT.
DAMMIT DAMMIT DAMM--

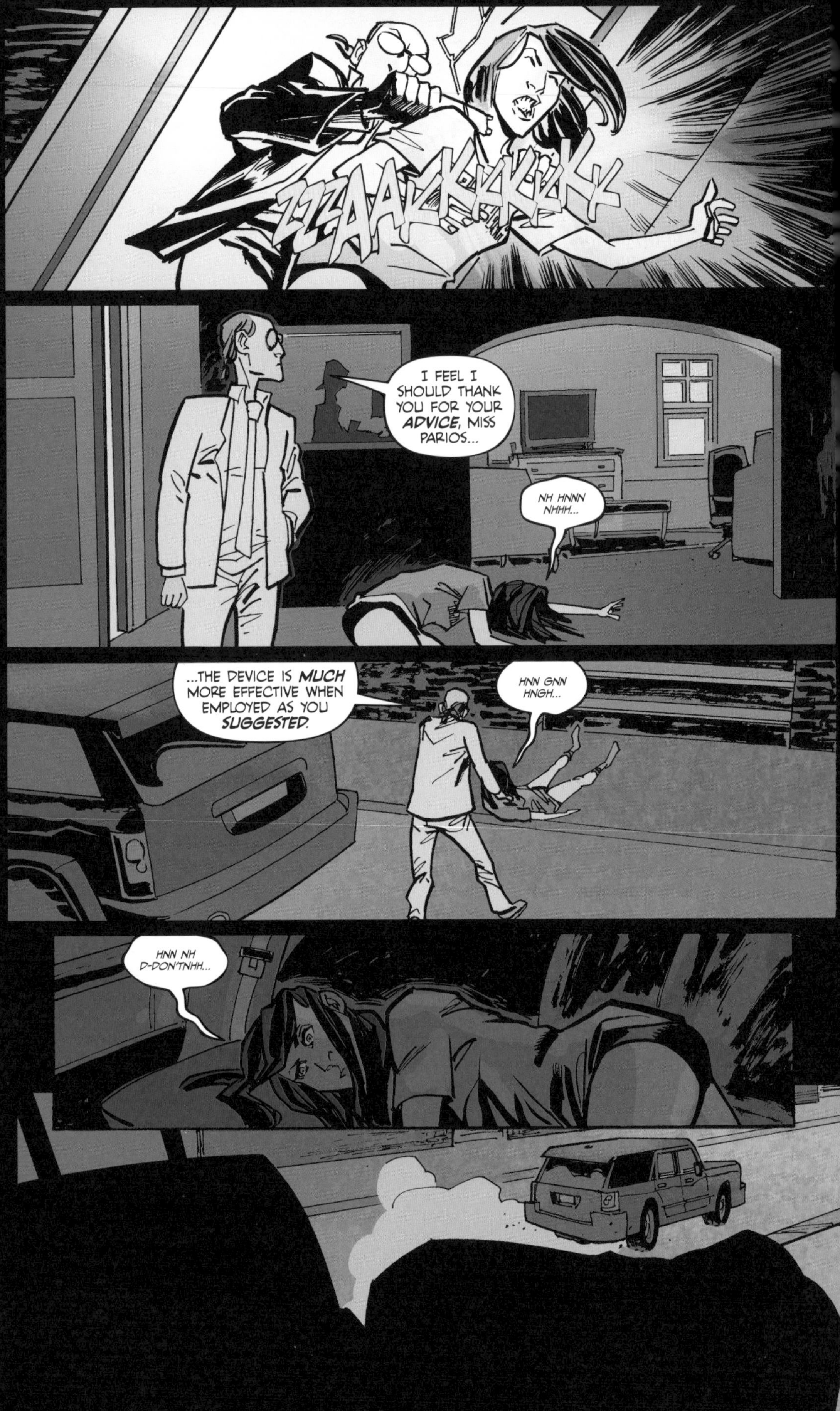
ZZZAAKKKKKK
I FEEL I SHOULD THANK YOU FOR YOUR ADVICE, MISS PARIOS...
NH HNNN NHHH...
...THE DEVICE IS MUCH MORE EFFECTIVE WHEN EMPLOYED AS YOU SUGGESTED.
HNN GNN HNGH...
HNN NH D-DON'TNHH...

Chapter Four

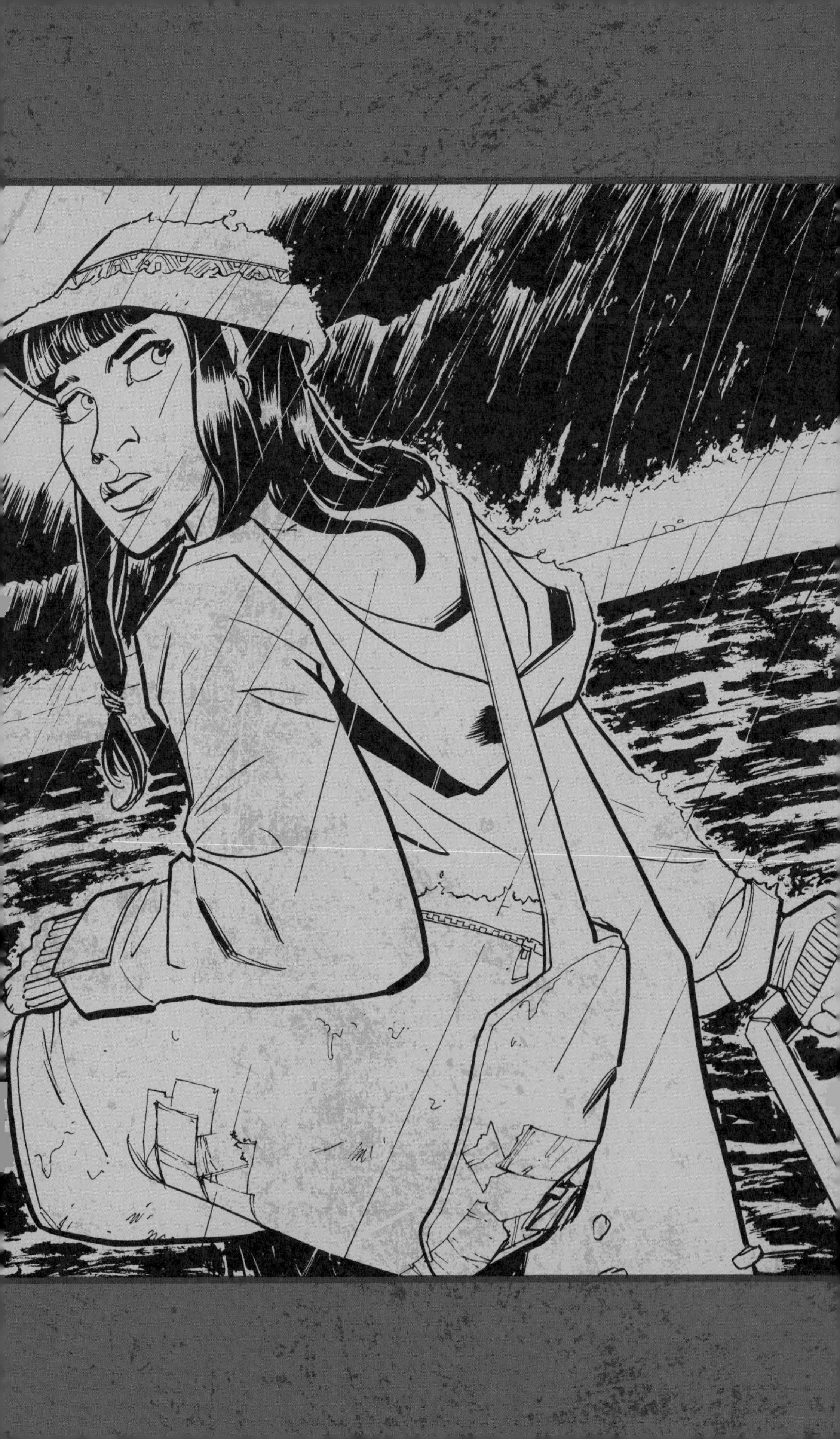

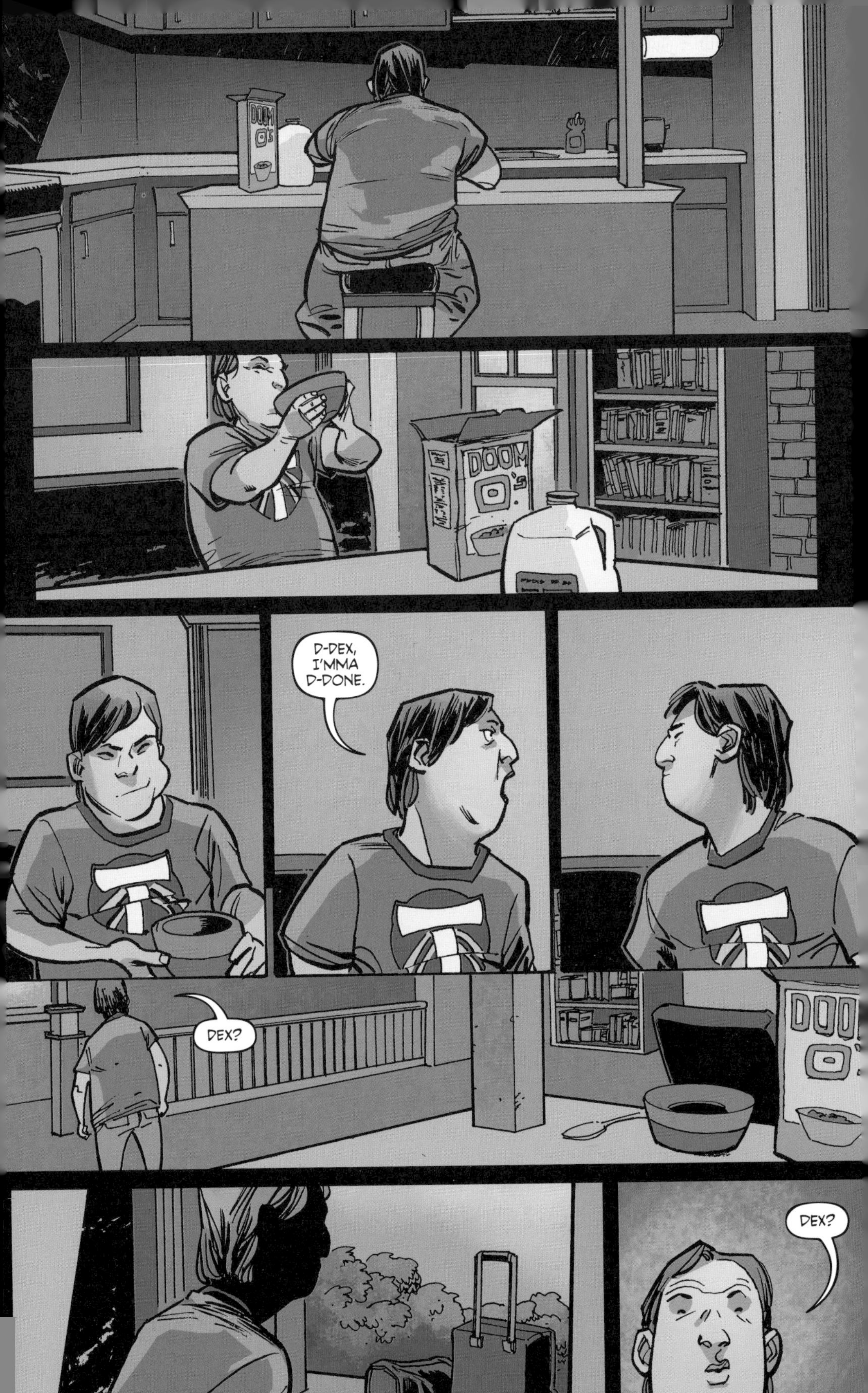
DOOM O's
DOOM O's
D-DEX, I'MMA D-DONE.
DEX?
DEX?

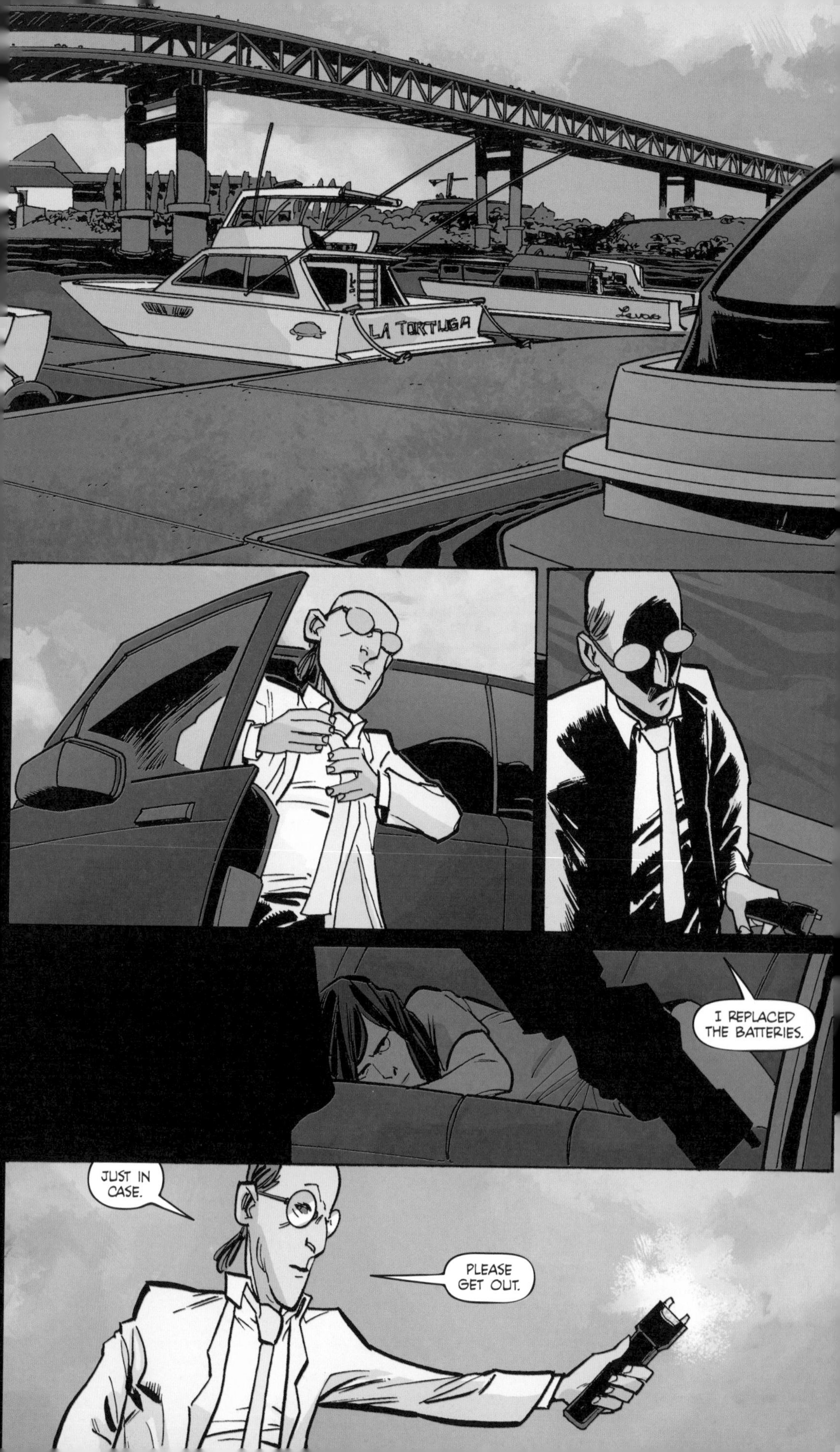
LA TORTUGA
I REPLACED THE BATTERIES.
JUST IN CASE.
PLEASE GET OUT.

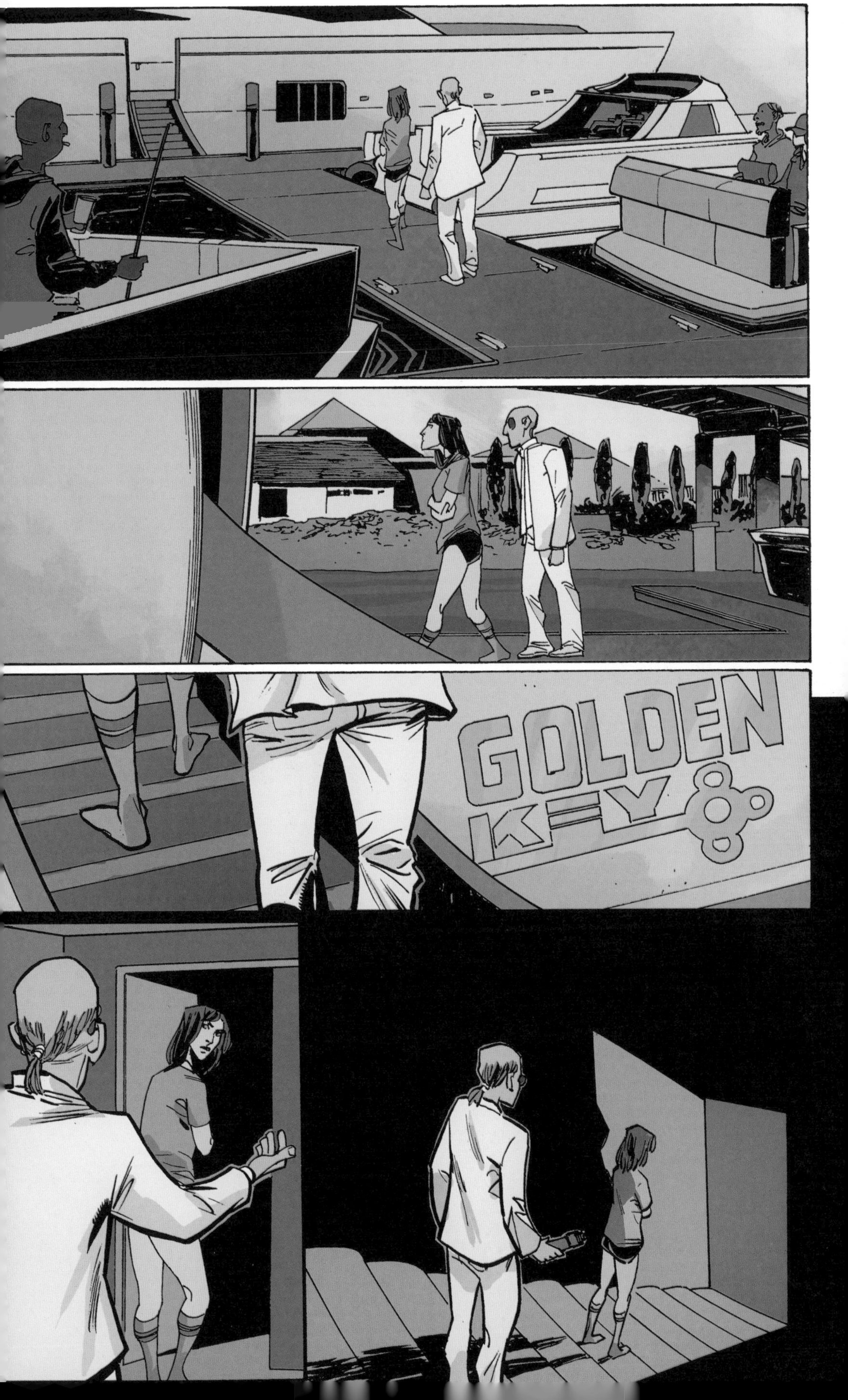
GOLDEN
KEY

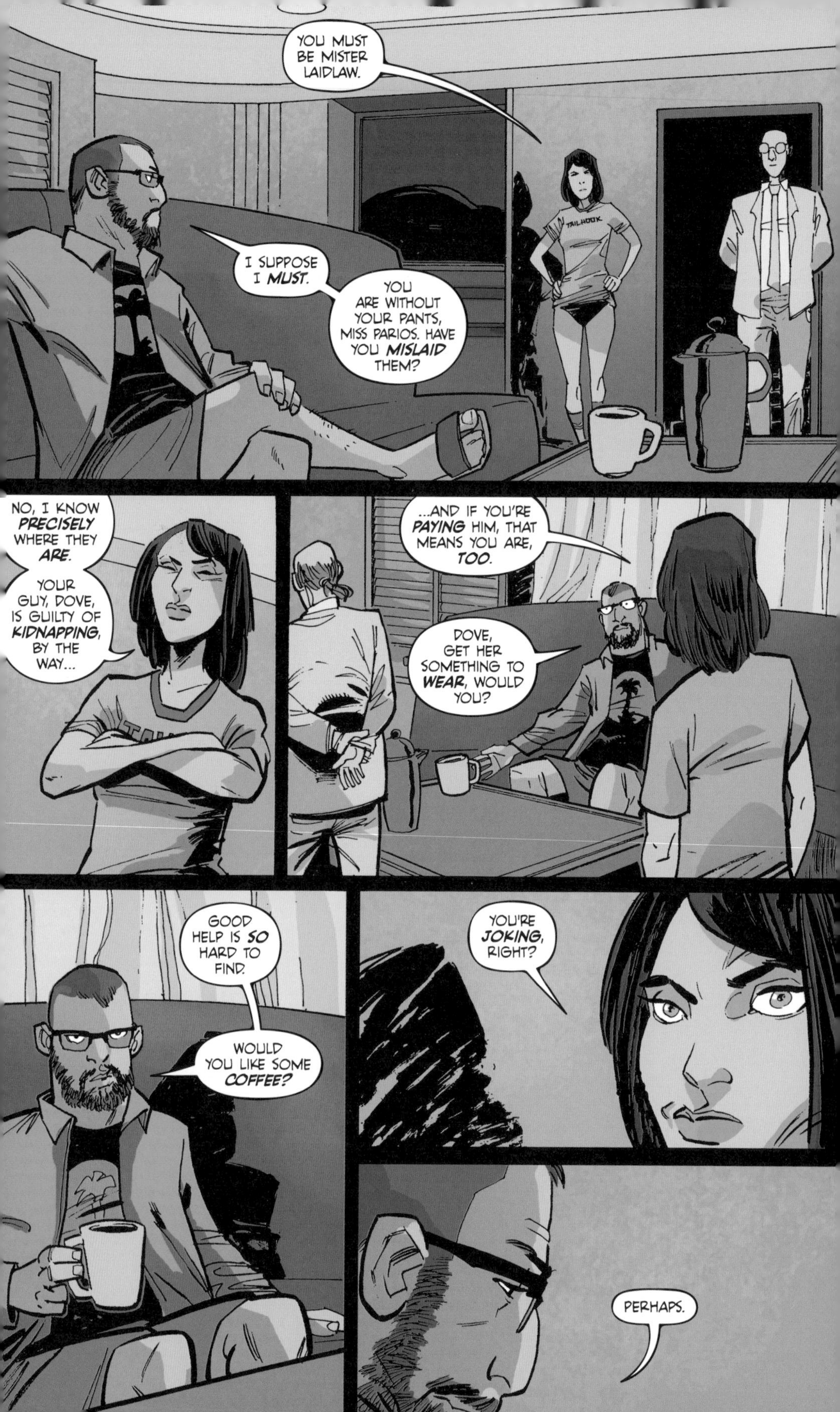

YOU MUST BE MISTER LAIDLAW.
I SUPPOSE I *MUST.*
YOU ARE WITHOUT YOUR PANTS, MISS PARIOS. HAVE YOU *MISLAID* THEM?
TAILHOOK
NO, I KNOW *PRECISELY* WHERE THEY *ARE.*
YOUR GUY, DOVE, IS GUILTY OF *KIDNAPPING,* BY THE WAY...
...AND IF YOU'RE *PAYING* HIM, THAT MEANS YOU ARE, *TOO.*
DOVE, GET HER SOMETHING TO *WEAR,* WOULD YOU?
GOOD HELP IS *SO* HARD TO FIND.
WOULD YOU LIKE SOME *COFFEE?*
YOU'RE *JOKING,* RIGHT?
PERHAPS.

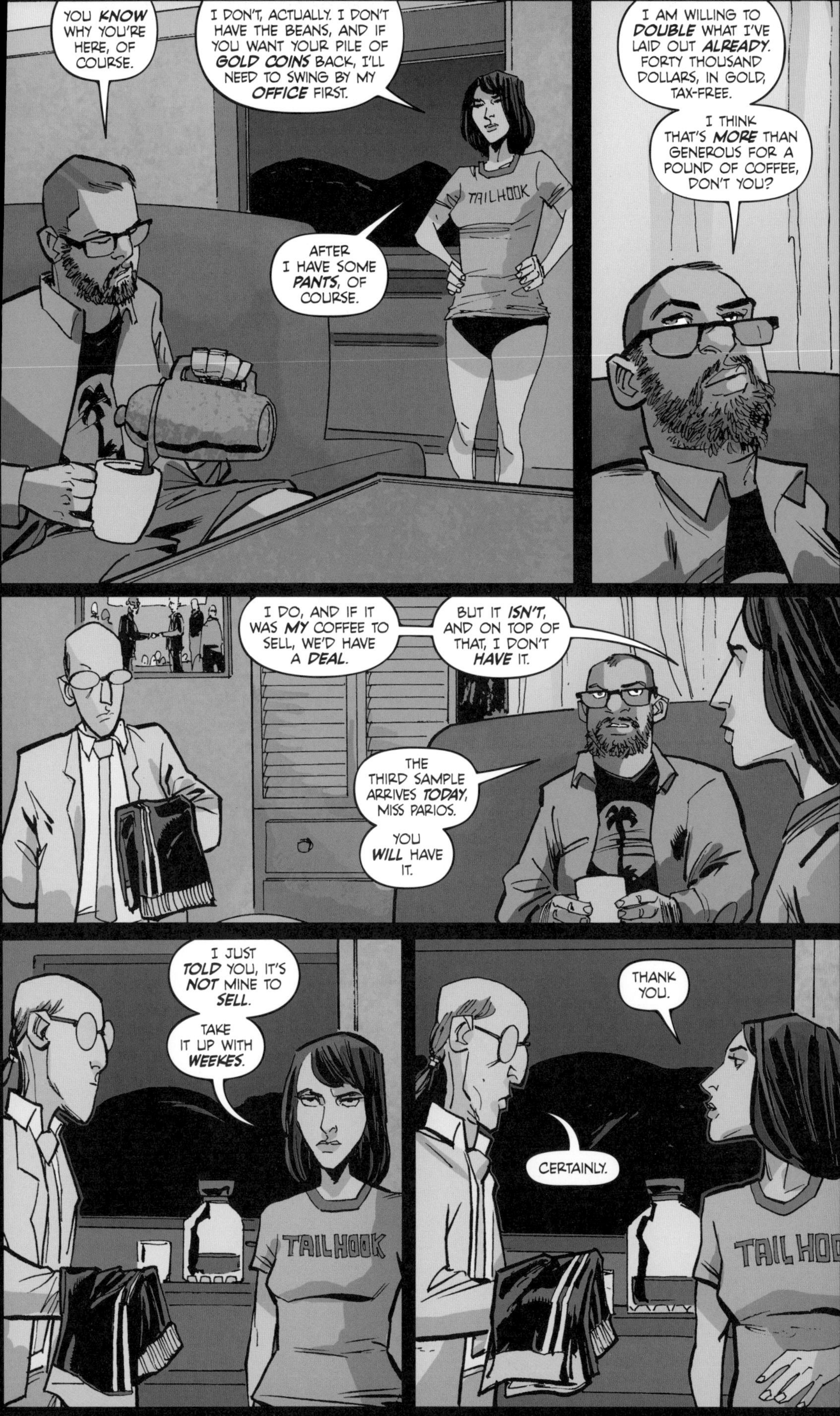
YOU KNOW WHY YOU'RE HERE, OF COURSE.
I DON'T, ACTUALLY. I DON'T HAVE THE BEANS, AND IF YOU WANT YOUR PILE OF GOLD COINS BACK, I'LL NEED TO SWING BY MY OFFICE FIRST.
AFTER I HAVE SOME PANTS, OF COURSE.
TAILHOOK
I AM WILLING TO DOUBLE WHAT I'VE LAID OUT ALREADY. FORTY THOUSAND DOLLARS, IN GOLD, TAX-FREE.
I THINK THAT'S MORE THAN GENEROUS FOR A POUND OF COFFEE, DON'T YOU?
I DO, AND IF IT WAS MY COFFEE TO SELL, WE'D HAVE A DEAL.
BUT IT ISN'T, AND ON TOP OF THAT, I DON'T HAVE IT.
THE THIRD SAMPLE ARRIVES TODAY, MISS PARIOS.
YOU WILL HAVE IT.
I JUST TOLD YOU, IT'S NOT MINE TO SELL.
TAKE IT UP WITH WEEKES.
TAILHOOK
THANK YOU.
CERTAINLY.

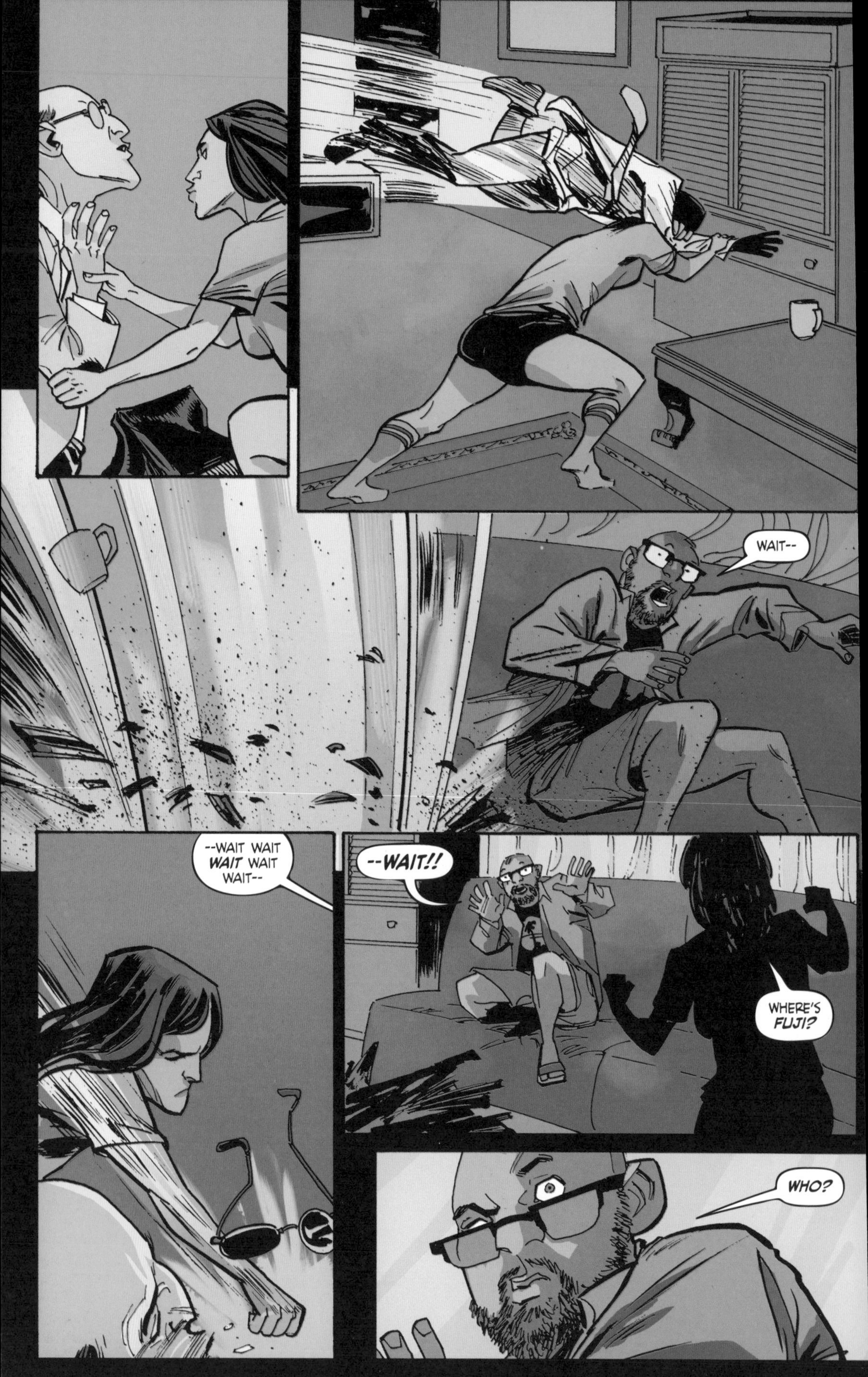
WAIT--
--WAIT WAIT
WAIT WAIT
WAIT--
--WAIT!!
WHERE'S FUJI?
WHO?

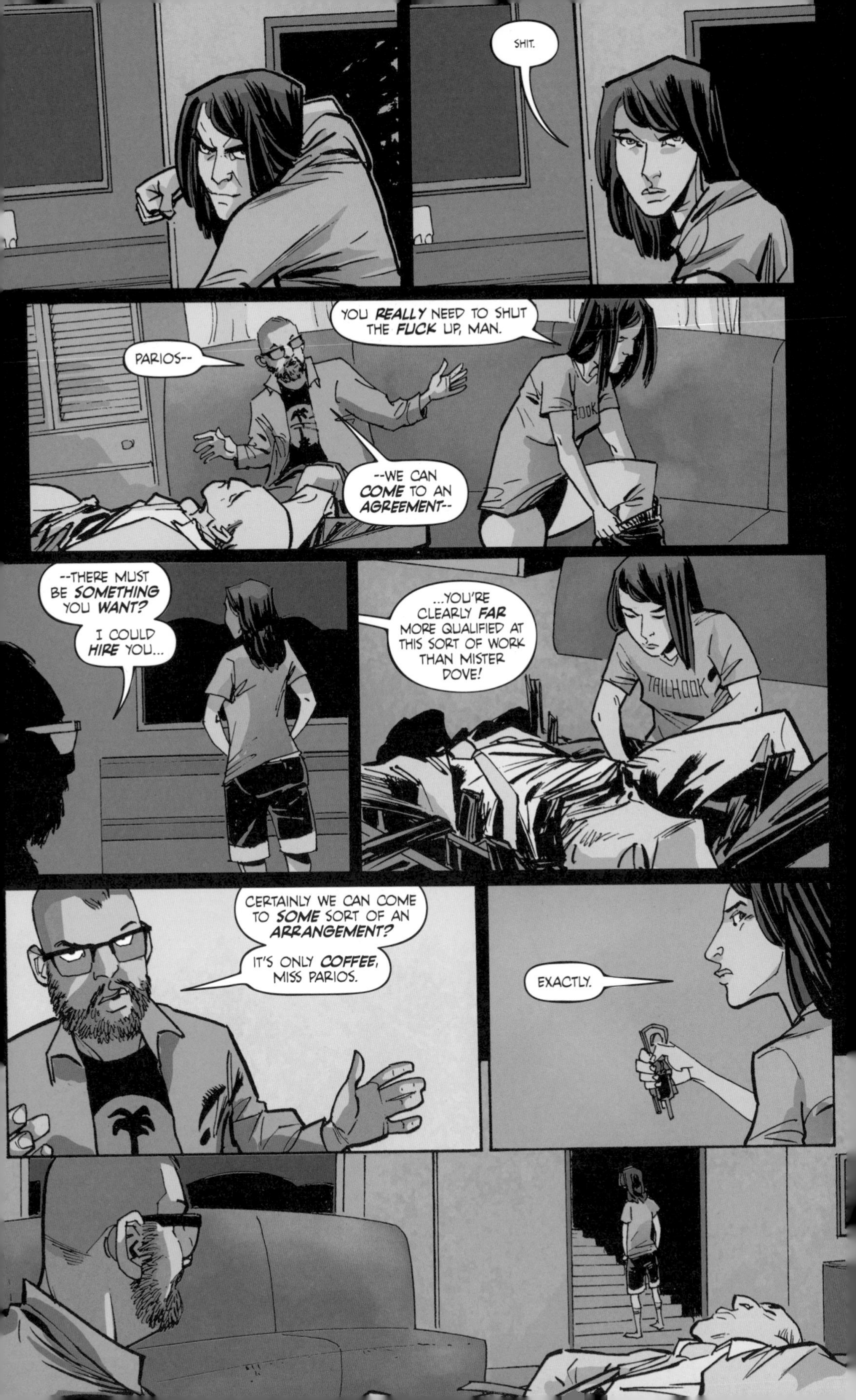

SHIT.
YOU REALLY NEED TO SHUT THE FUCK UP, MAN.
PARIOS--
--WE CAN COME TO AN AGREEMENT--
HOOK
--THERE MUST BE SOMETHING YOU WANT?
I COULD HIRE YOU...
...YOU'RE CLEARLY FAR MORE QUALIFIED AT THIS SORT OF WORK THAN MISTER DOVE!
TAILHOOK
CERTAINLY WE CAN COME TO SOME SORT OF AN ARRANGEMENT?
IT'S ONLY COFFEE, MISS PARIOS.
EXACTLY.

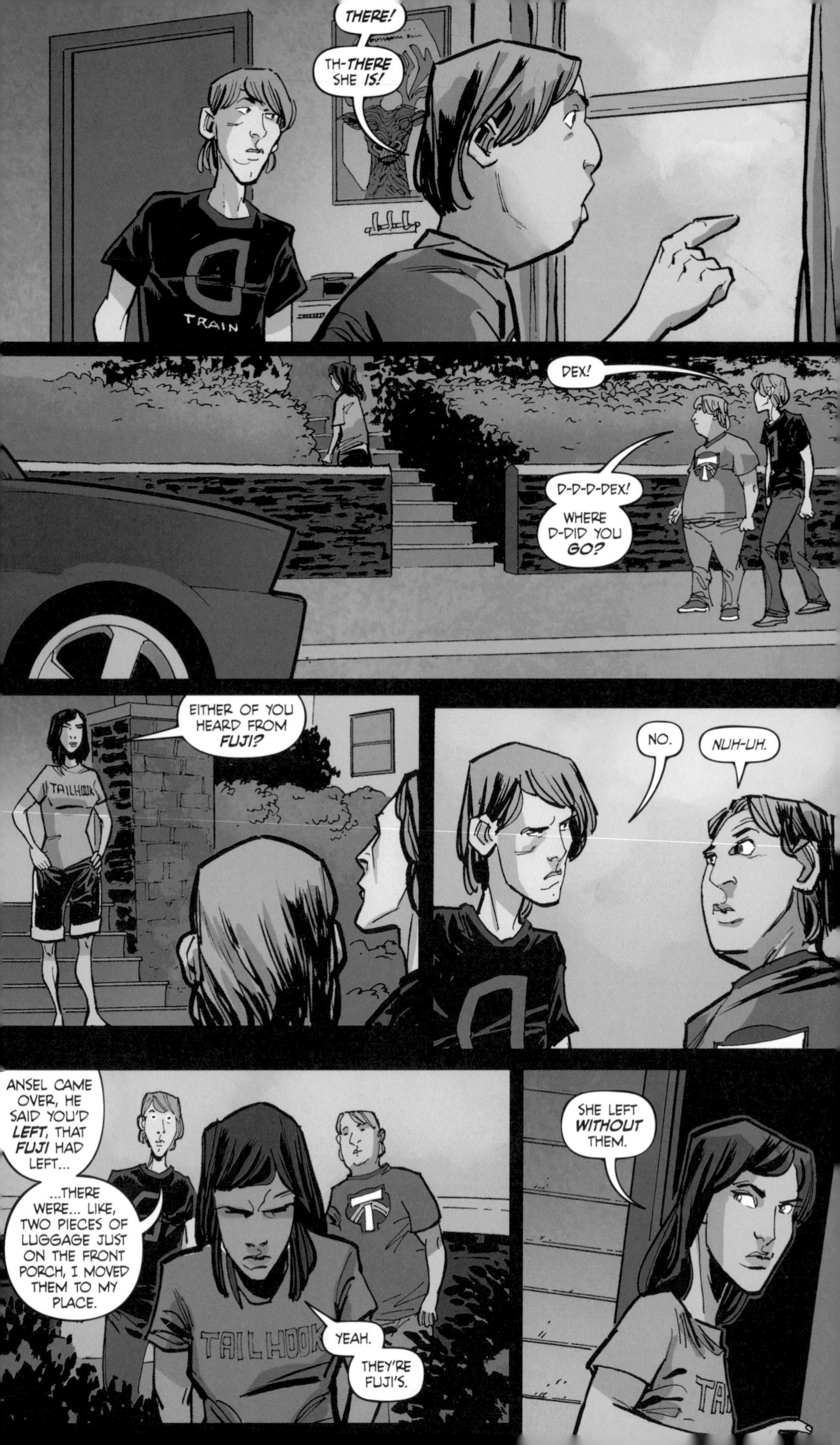
THERE!
TH-THERE SHE IS!
TRAIN
DEX!
D-D-D-DEX!
WHERE D-DID YOU GO?
EITHER OF YOU HEARD FROM FUJI?
TAILHOOK
NO.
NUH-UH.
ANSEL CAME OVER, HE SAID YOU'D LEFT, THAT FUJI HAD LEFT...
...THERE WERE... LIKE, TWO PIECES OF LUGGAGE JUST ON THE FRONT PORCH, I MOVED THEM TO MY PLACE.
TAILHOOK
YEAH.
THEY'RE FUJI'S.
SHE LEFT WITHOUT THEM.

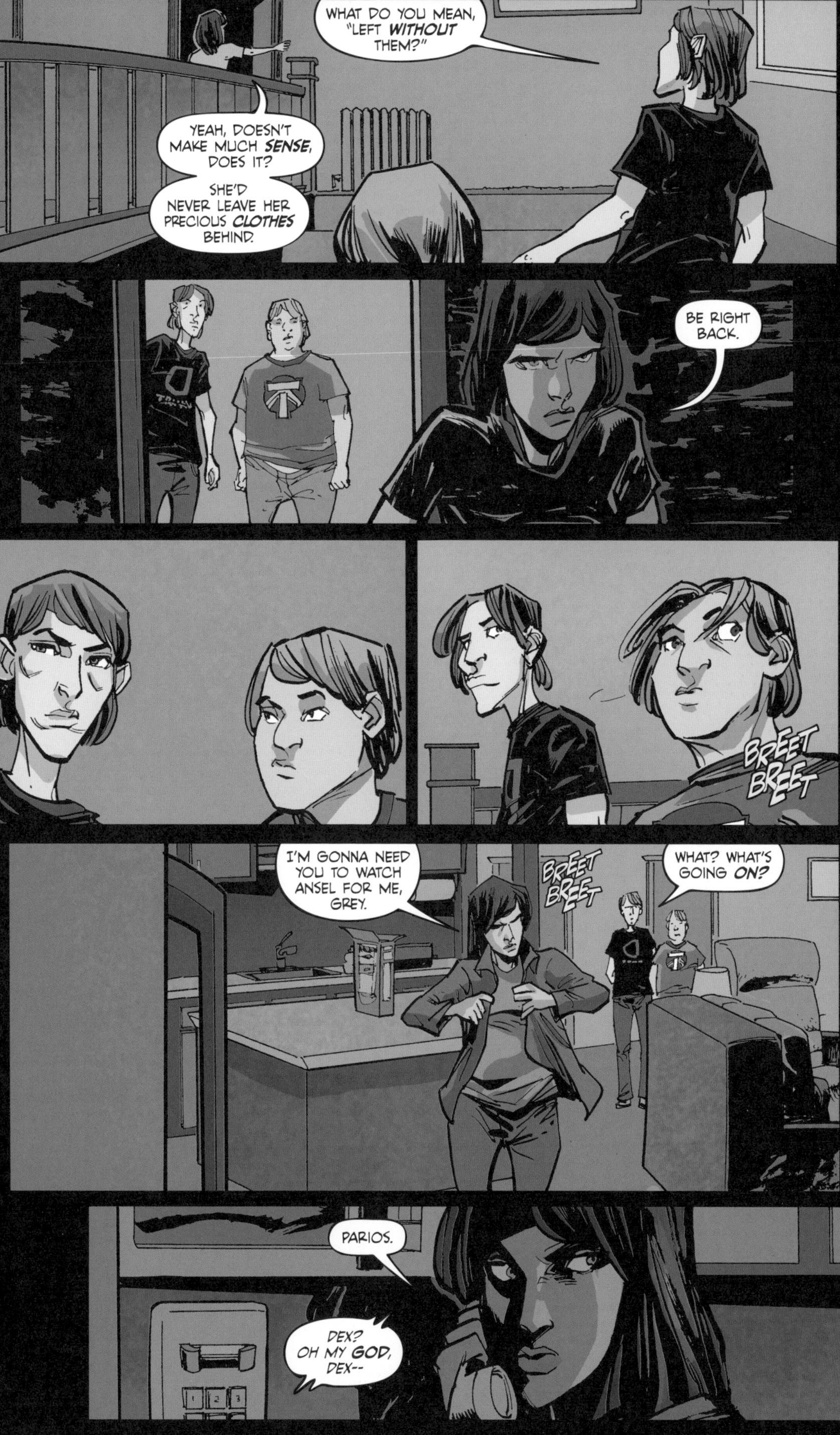
WHAT DO YOU MEAN, "LEFT WITHOUT THEM?"
YEAH, DOESN'T MAKE MUCH SENSE, DOES IT?
SHE'D NEVER LEAVE HER PRECIOUS CLOTHES BEHIND.
BE RIGHT BACK.
BREET BREET
I'M GONNA NEED YOU TO WATCH ANSEL FOR ME, GREY.
BREET BREET
WHAT? WHAT'S GOING ON?
PARIOS.
DEX? OH MY GOD, DEX--

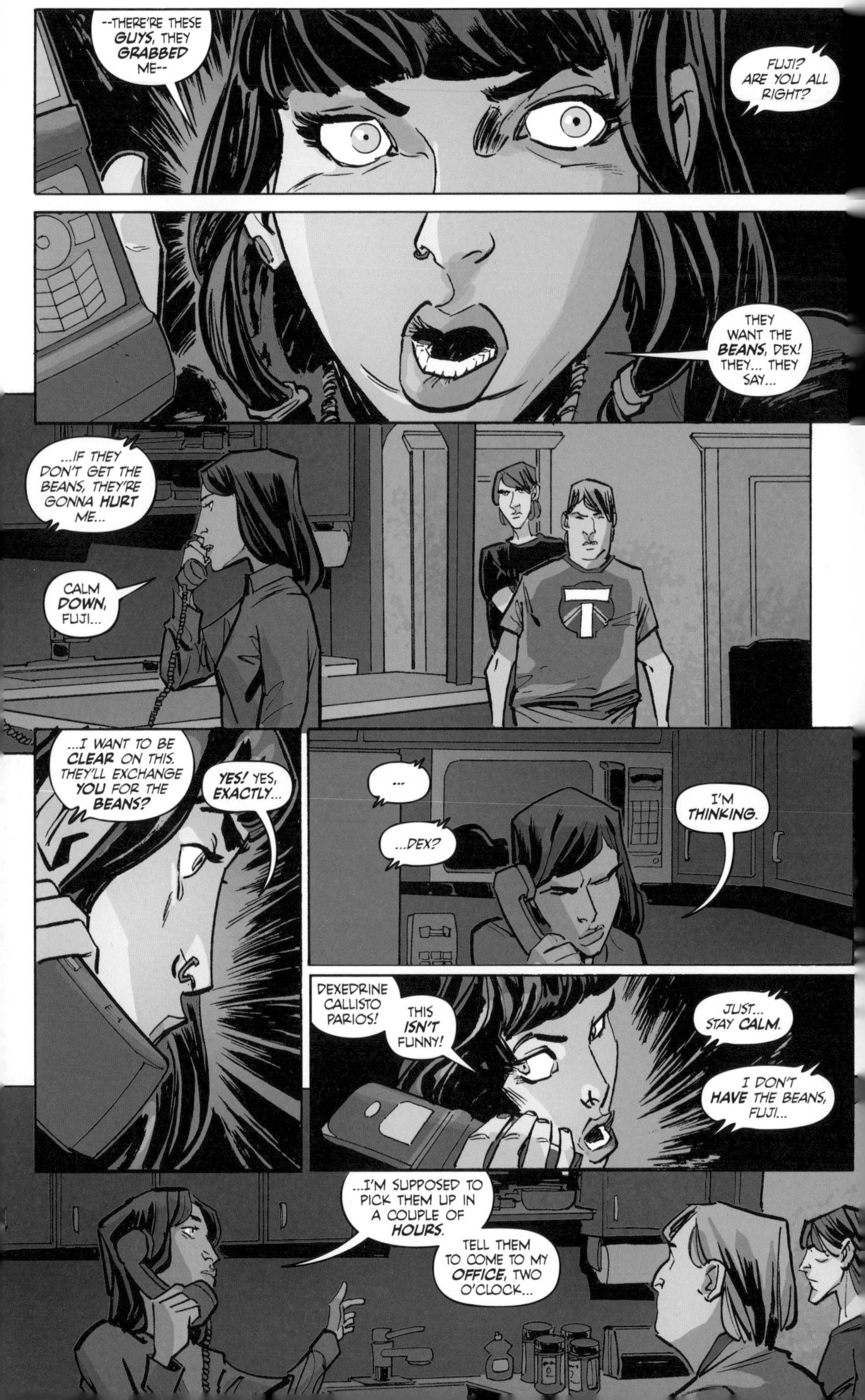
--THERE'RE THESE GUYS, THEY GRABBED ME--
FUJI? ARE YOU ALL RIGHT?
THEY WANT THE BEANS, DEX! THEY... THEY SAY...
...IF THEY DON'T GET THE BEANS, THEY'RE GONNA HURT ME...
CALM DOWN, FUJI...
...I WANT TO BE CLEAR ON THIS. THEY'LL EXCHANGE YOU FOR THE BEANS?
YES! YES, EXACTLY...
...
...DEX?
I'M THINKING.
DEXEDRINE CALLISTO PARIOS!
THIS ISN'T FUNNY!
JUST... STAY CALM.
I DON'T HAVE THE BEANS, FUJI...
...I'M SUPPOSED TO PICK THEM UP IN A COUPLE OF HOURS.
TELL THEM TO COME TO MY OFFICE, TWO O'CLOCK...

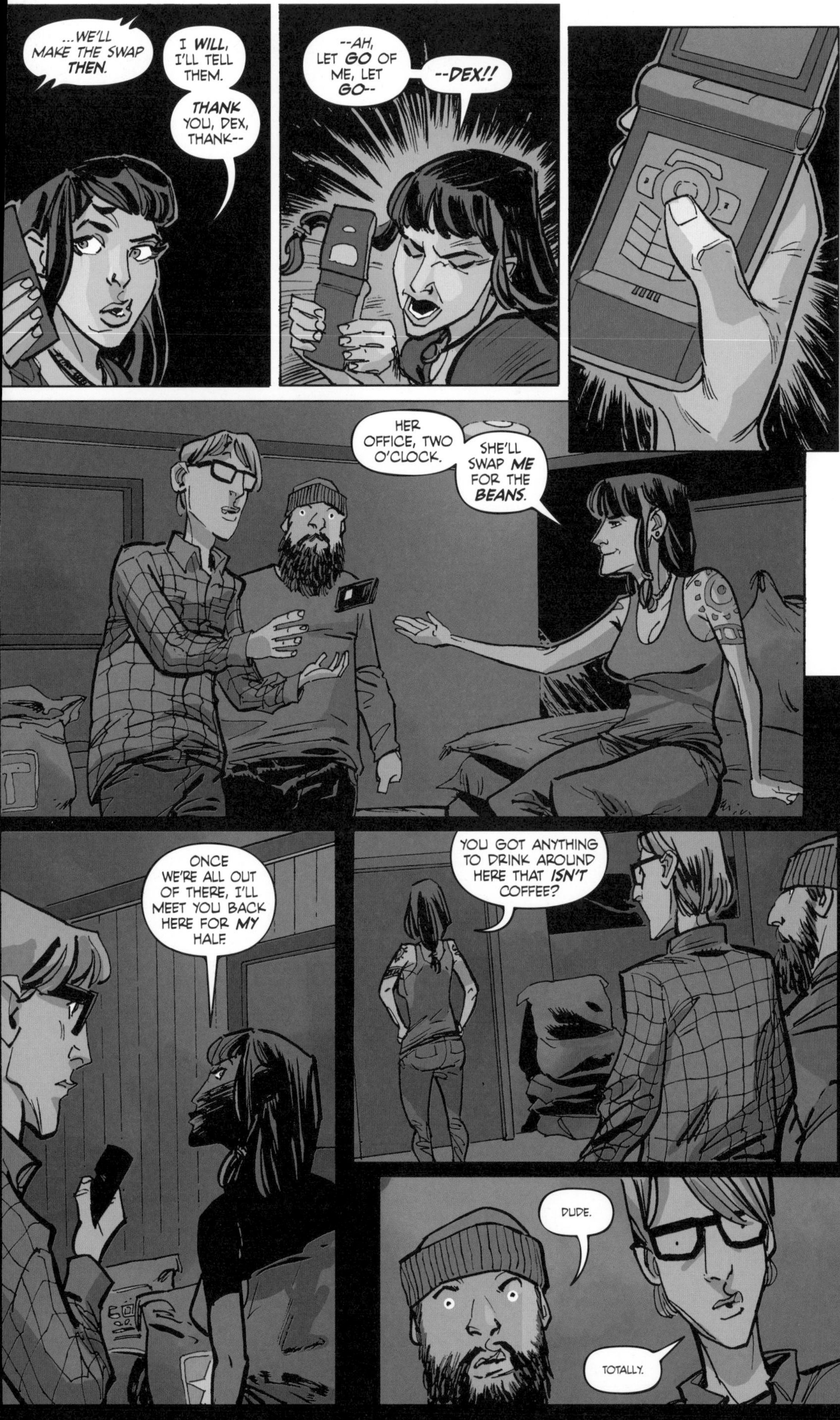
...WE'LL MAKE THE SWAP THEN.
I WILL, I'LL TELL THEM.
THANK YOU, DEX, THANK--
--AH, LET GO OF ME, LET GO--
--DEX!!
HER OFFICE, TWO O'CLOCK.
SHE'LL SWAP ME FOR THE BEANS.
ONCE WE'RE ALL OUT OF THERE, I'LL MEET YOU BACK HERE FOR MY HALF.
YOU GOT ANYTHING TO DRINK AROUND HERE THAT ISN'T COFFEE?
DUDE.
TOTALLY.

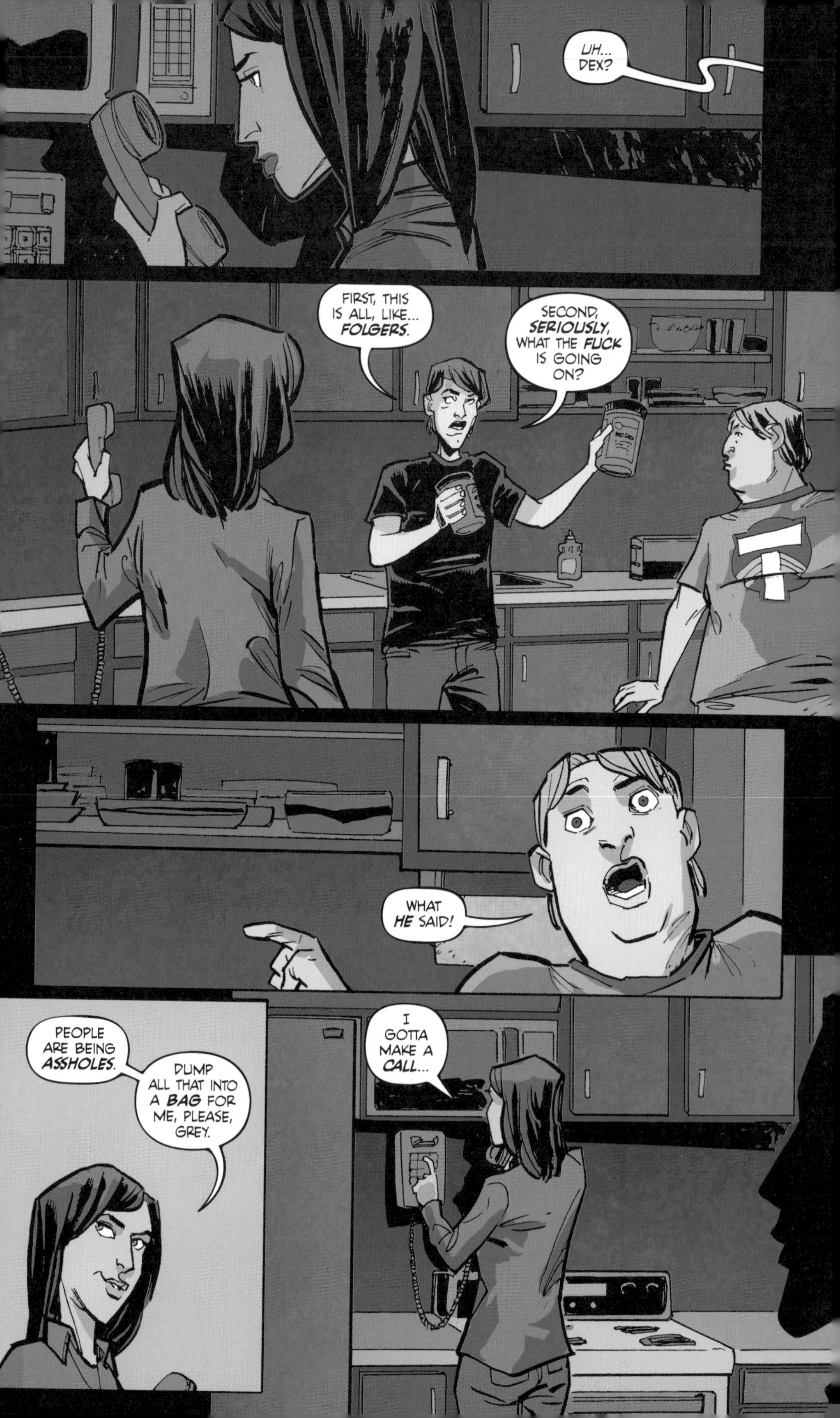
UH... DEX?
FIRST, THIS IS ALL, LIKE... FOLGERS.
SECOND, SERIOUSLY, WHAT THE FUCK IS GOING ON?
WHAT HE SAID!
PEOPLE ARE BEING ASSHOLES.
DUMP ALL THAT INTO A BAG FOR ME, PLEASE, GREY.
I GOTTA MAKE A CALL...

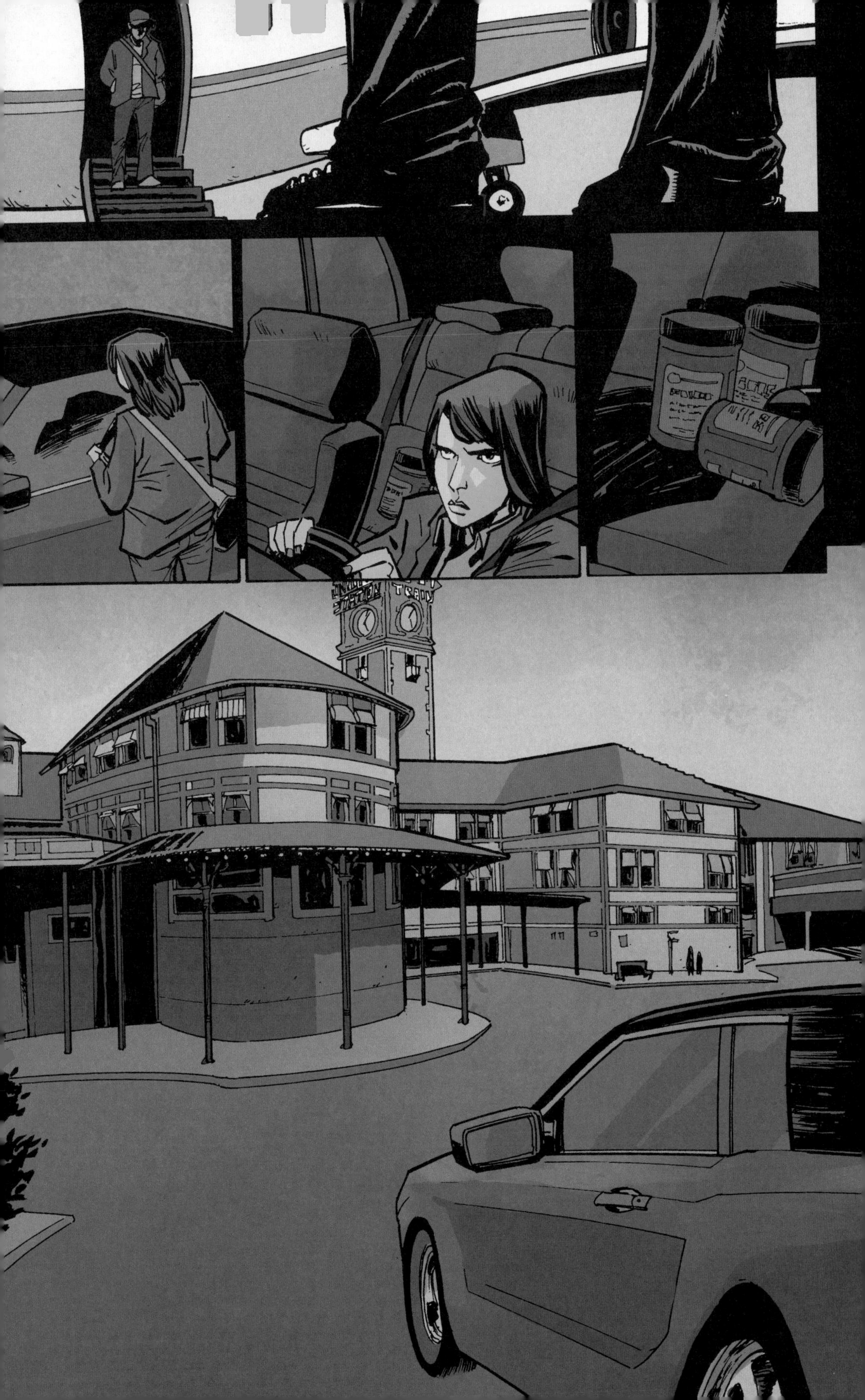

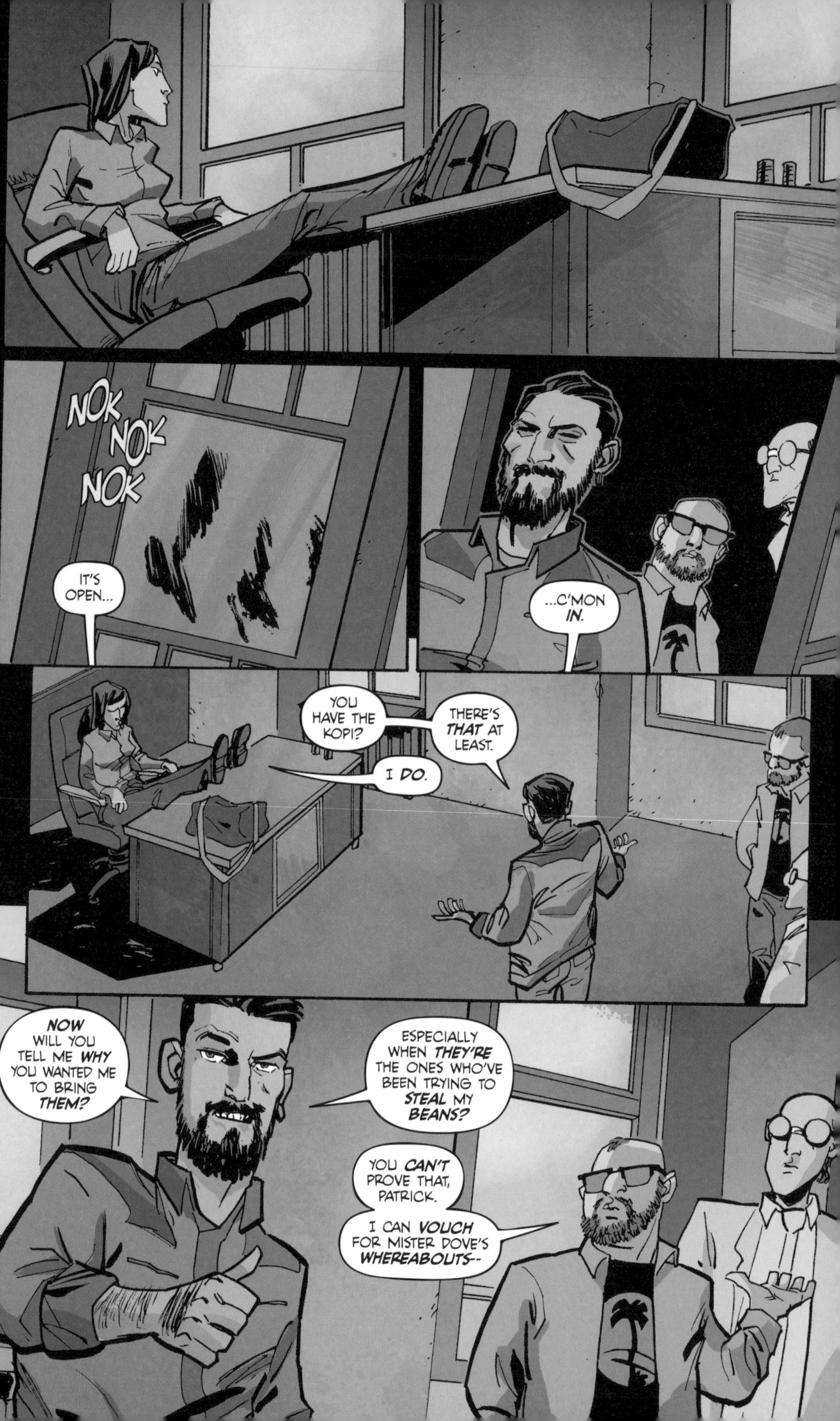

NOK NOK NOK
IT'S OPEN...
...C'MON IN.
YOU HAVE THE KOPI?
I DO.
THERE'S THAT AT LEAST.
NOW WILL YOU TELL ME WHY YOU WANTED ME TO BRING THEM?
ESPECIALLY WHEN THEY'RE THE ONES WHO'VE BEEN TRYING TO STEAL MY BEANS?
YOU CAN'T PROVE THAT, PATRICK.
I CAN VOUCH FOR MISTER DOVE'S WHEREABOUTS--

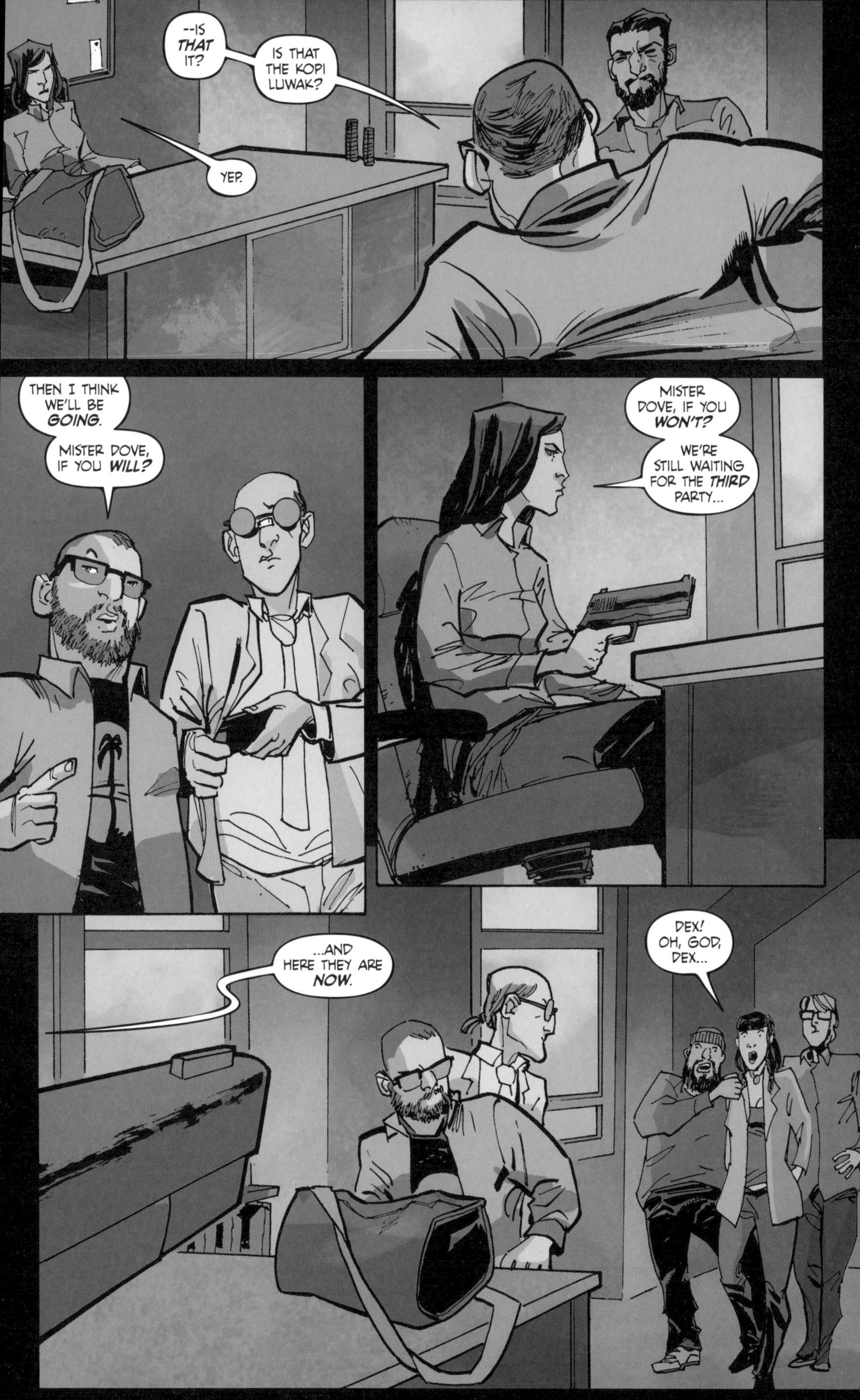
--IS THAT IT?
IS THAT THE KOPI LUWAK?
YEP.
THEN I THINK WE'LL BE GOING.
MISTER DOVE, IF YOU WILL?
MISTER DOVE, IF YOU WON'T?
WE'RE STILL WAITING FOR THE THIRD PARTY...
...AND HERE THEY ARE NOW.
DEX! OH, GOD, DEX...

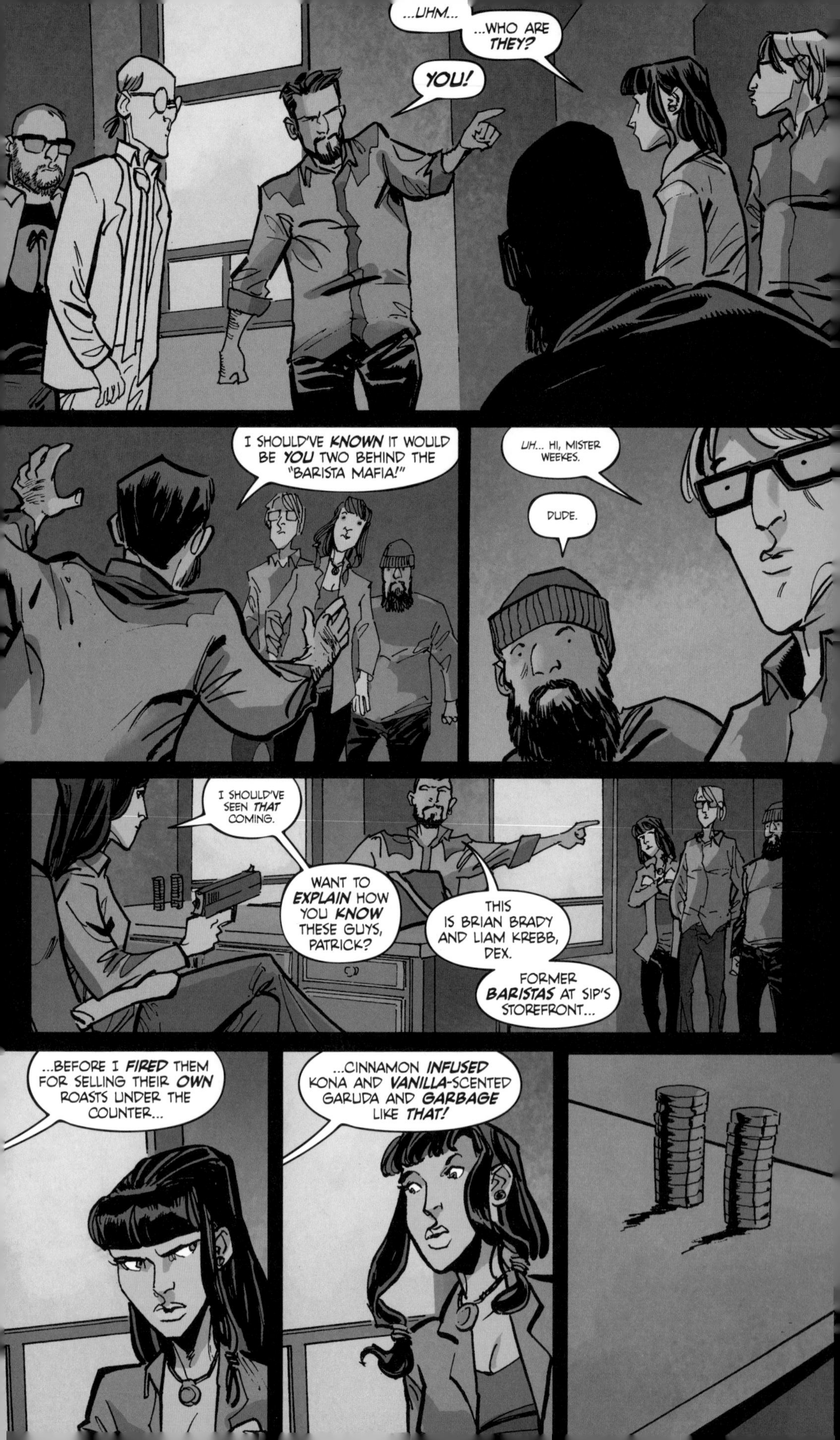

...UHM...
...WHO ARE THEY?
YOU!
I SHOULD'VE KNOWN IT WOULD BE YOU TWO BEHIND THE "BARISTA MAFIA!"
UH... HI, MISTER WEEKES.
DUDE.
I SHOULD'VE SEEN THAT COMING.
WANT TO EXPLAIN HOW YOU KNOW THESE GUYS, PATRICK?
THIS IS BRIAN BRADY AND LIAM KREBB, DEX.
FORMER BARISTAS AT SIP'S STOREFRONT...
...BEFORE I FIRED THEM FOR SELLING THEIR OWN ROASTS UNDER THE COUNTER...
...CINNAMON INFUSED KONA AND VANILLA-SCENTED GARUDA AND GARBAGE LIKE THAT!

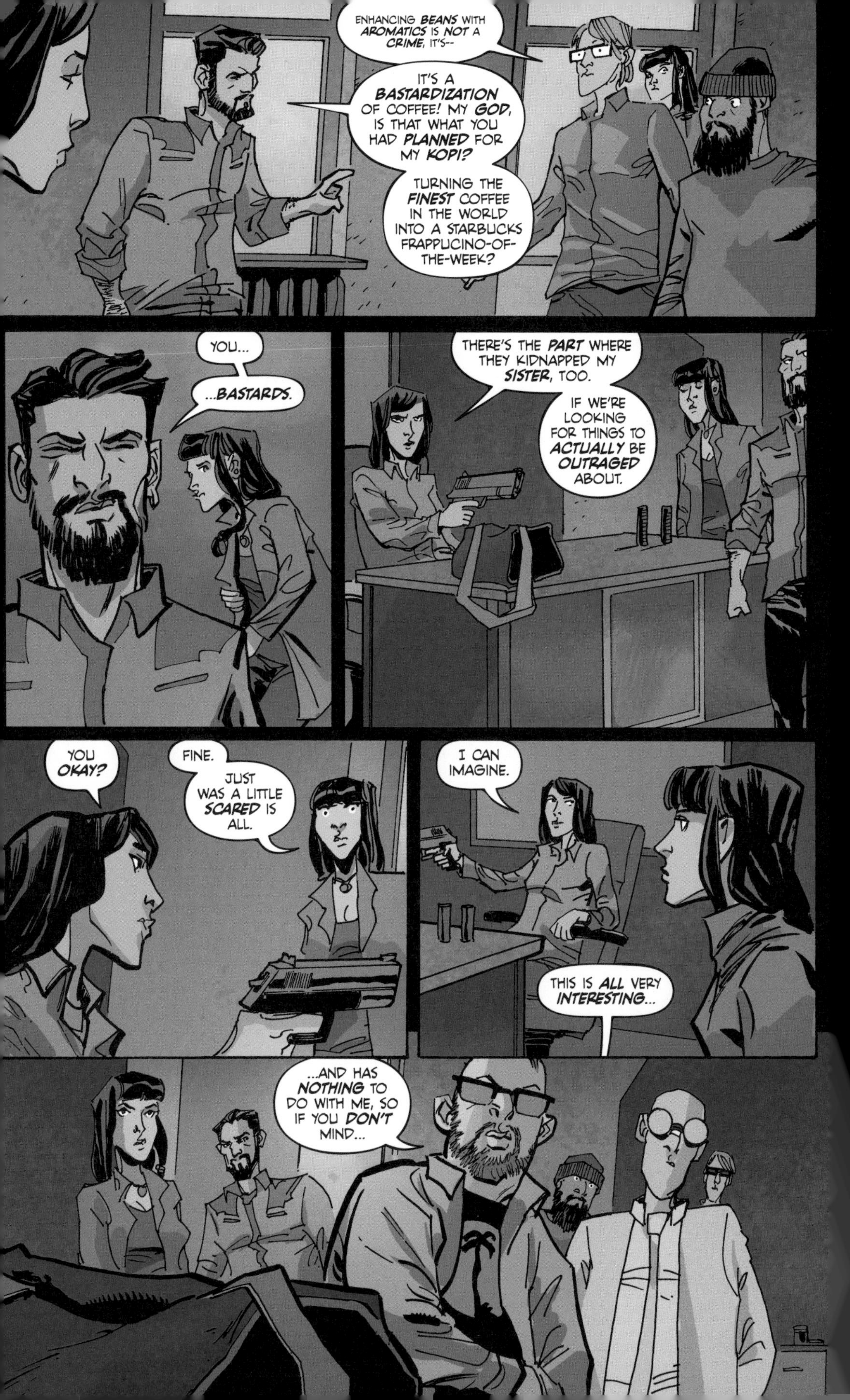
ENHANCING BEANS WITH AROMATICS IS NOT A CRIME, IT'S--
IT'S A BASTARDIZATION OF COFFEE! MY GOD, IS THAT WHAT YOU HAD PLANNED FOR MY KOPI?
TURNING THE FINEST COFFEE IN THE WORLD INTO A STARBUCKS FRAPPUCINO-OF-THE-WEEK?
YOU...
...BASTARDS.
THERE'S THE PART WHERE THEY KIDNAPPED MY SISTER, TOO.
IF WE'RE LOOKING FOR THINGS TO ACTUALLY BE OUTRAGED ABOUT.
YOU OKAY?
FINE.
JUST WAS A LITTLE SCARED IS ALL.
I CAN IMAGINE.
THIS IS ALL VERY INTERESTING...
...AND HAS NOTHING TO DO WITH ME, SO IF YOU DON'T MIND...

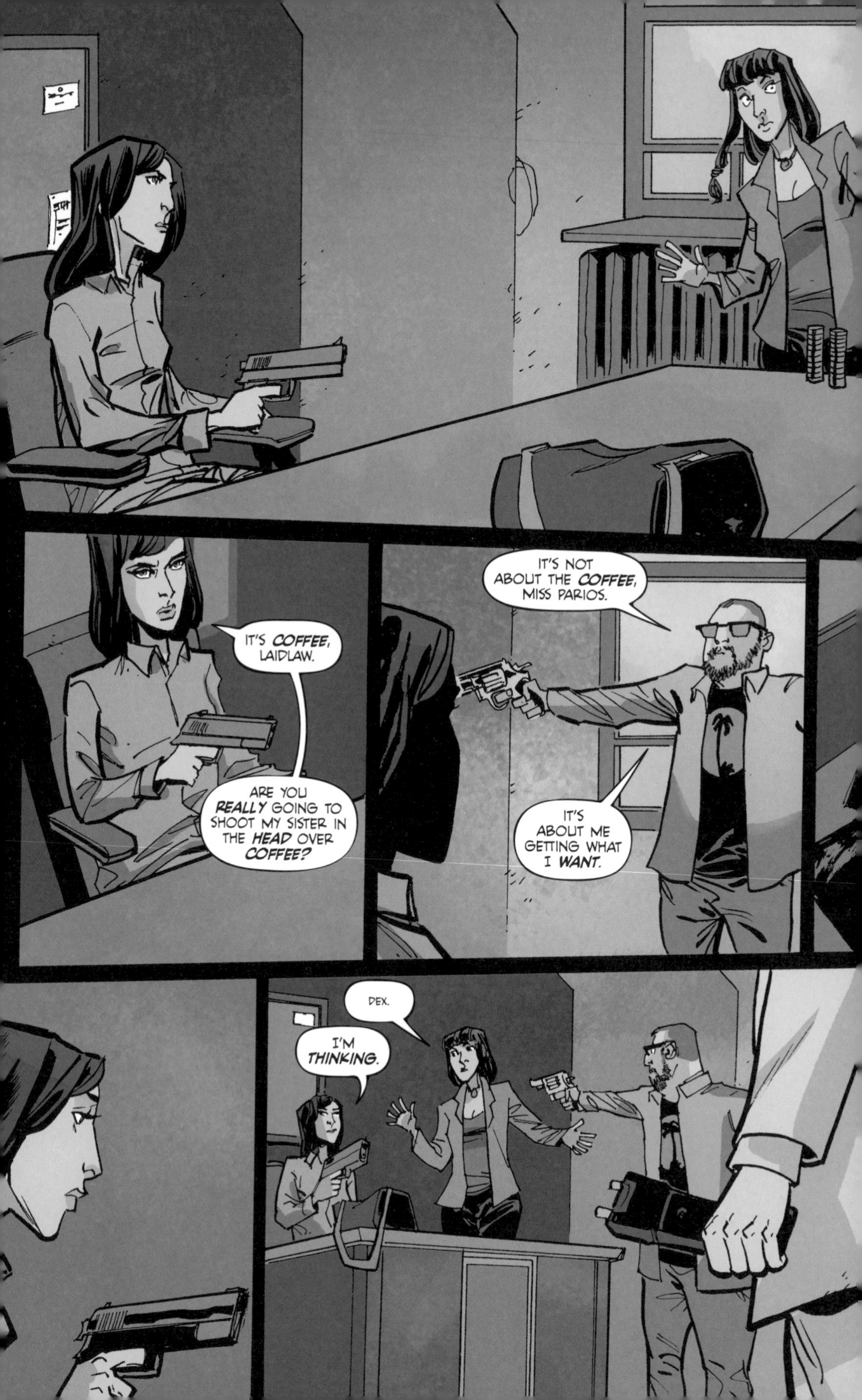

IT'S COFFEE, LAIDLAW.
ARE YOU REALLY GOING TO SHOOT MY SISTER IN THE HEAD OVER COFFEE?
IT'S NOT ABOUT THE COFFEE, MISS PARIOS.
IT'S ABOUT ME GETTING WHAT I WANT.
DEX.
I'M THINKING.

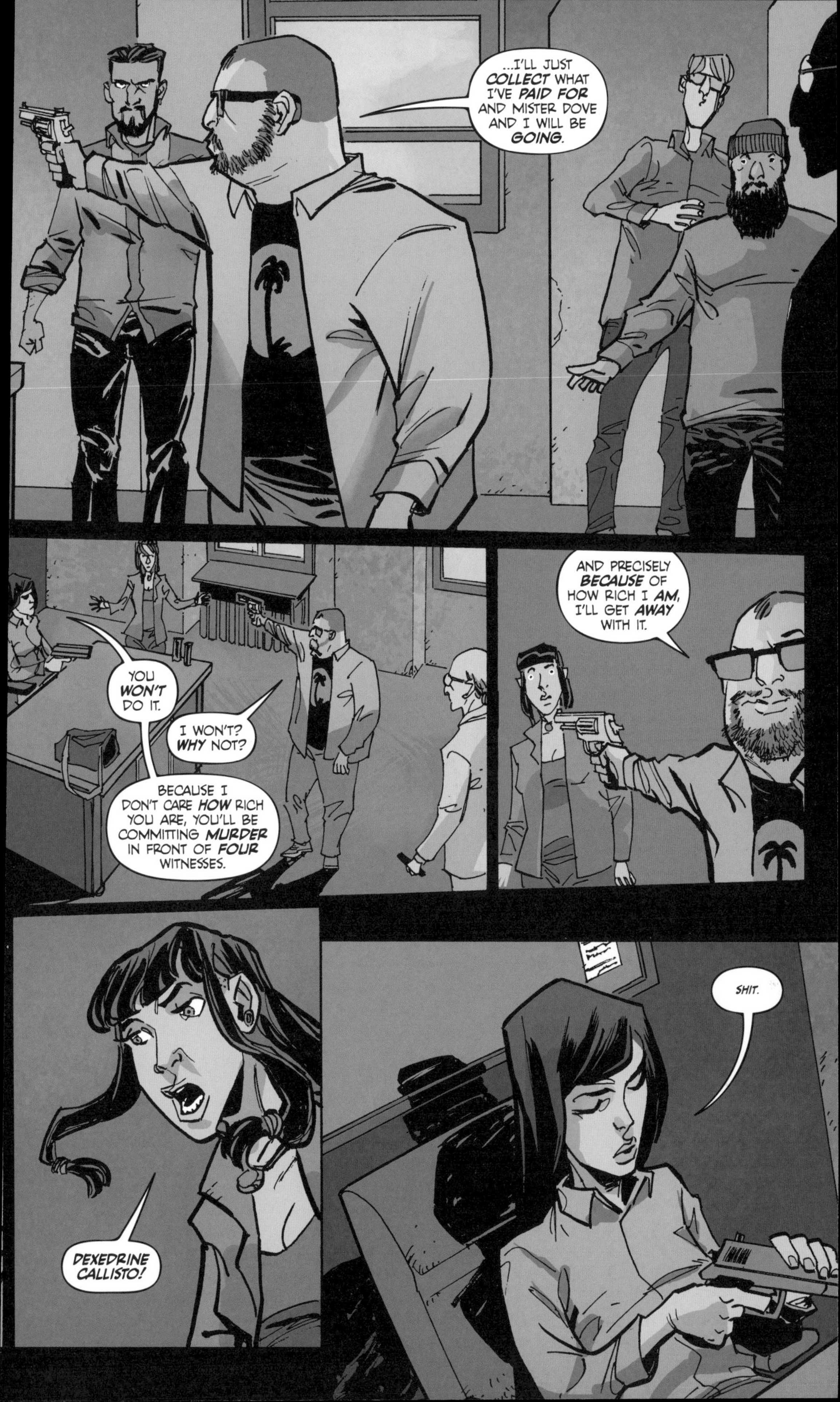
...I'LL JUST COLLECT WHAT I'VE PAID FOR AND MISTER DOVE AND I WILL BE GOING.
YOU WON'T DO IT.
I WON'T? WHY NOT?
BECAUSE I DON'T CARE HOW RICH YOU ARE, YOU'LL BE COMMITTING MURDER IN FRONT OF FOUR WITNESSES.
AND PRECISELY BECAUSE OF HOW RICH I AM, I'LL GET AWAY WITH IT.
DEXEDRINE CALLISTO!
SHIT.

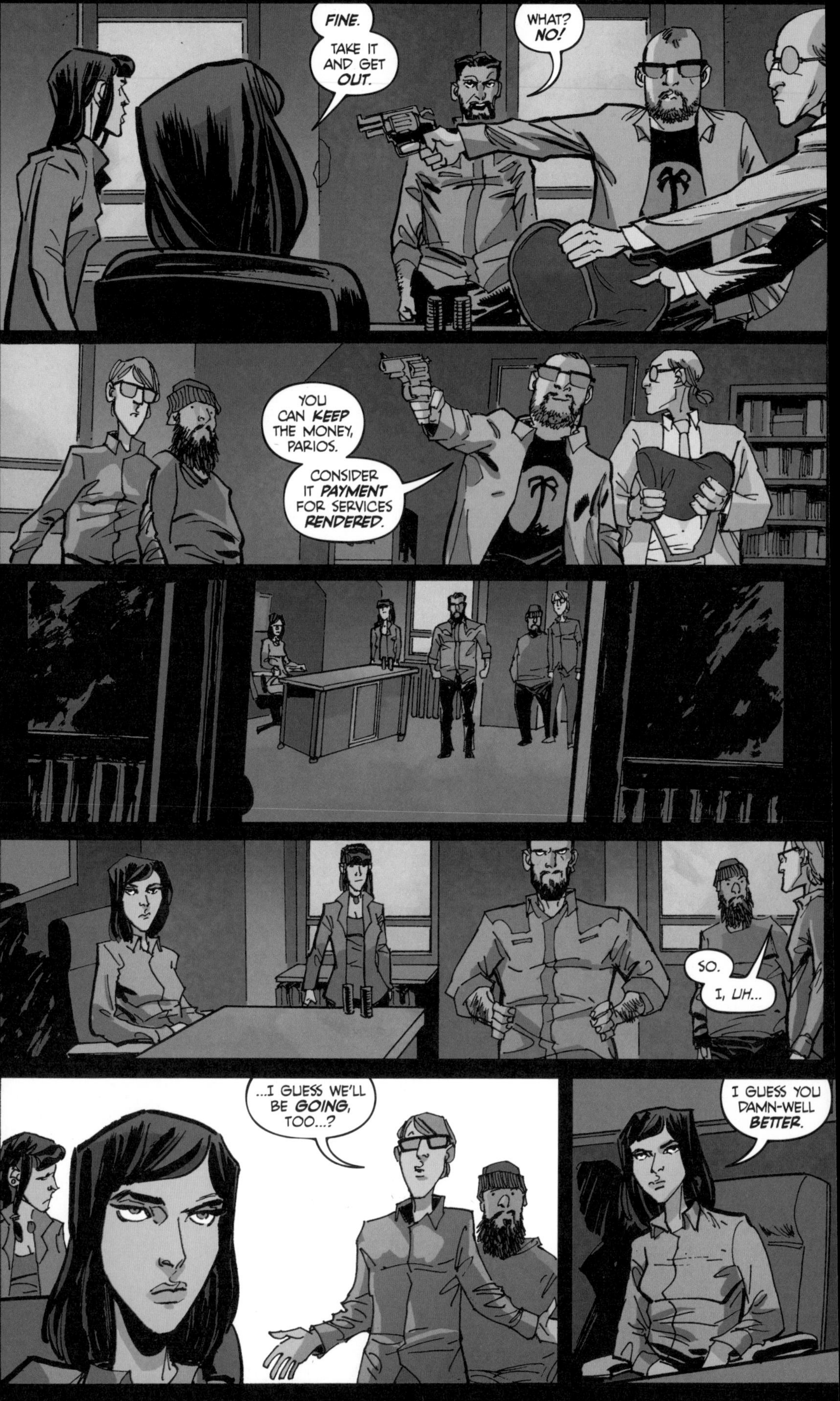
FINE.
TAKE IT AND GET OUT.
WHAT? NO!
YOU CAN KEEP THE MONEY, PARIOS.
CONSIDER IT PAYMENT FOR SERVICES RENDERED.
SO.
I, UH...
...I GUESS WE'LL BE GOING, TOO...?
I GUESS YOU DAMN-WELL BETTER.

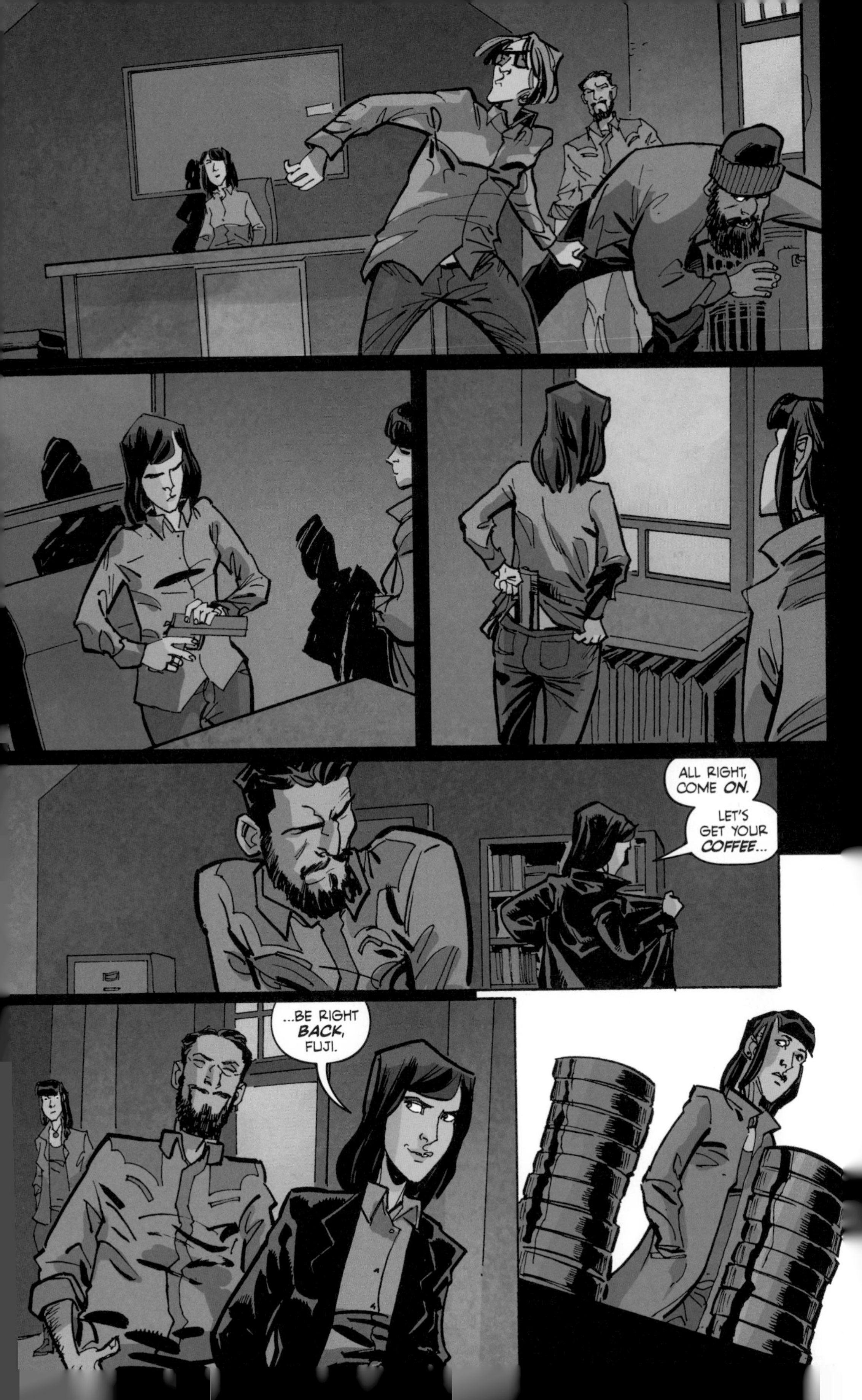
ALL RIGHT, COME ON.
LET'S GET YOUR COFFEE...
...BE RIGHT BACK, FUJI.

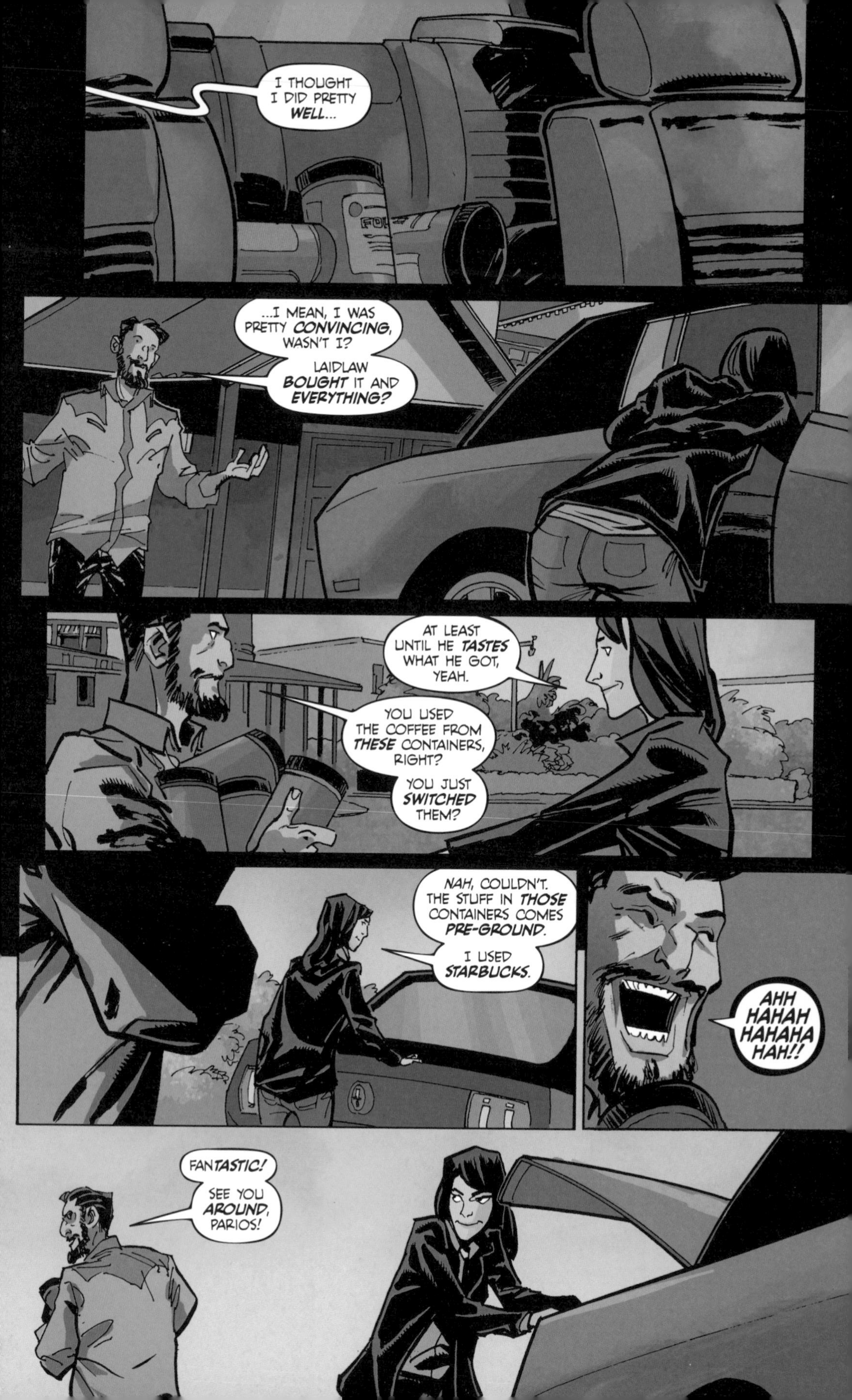
I THOUGHT I DID PRETTY *WELL*...
...I MEAN, I WAS PRETTY *CONVINCING*, WASN'T I?
LAIDLAW *BOUGHT* IT AND *EVERYTHING?*
AT LEAST UNTIL HE *TASTES* WHAT HE GOT, YEAH.
YOU USED THE COFFEE FROM *THESE* CONTAINERS, RIGHT?
YOU JUST *SWITCHED* THEM?
NAH, COULDN'T. THE STUFF IN *THOSE* CONTAINERS COMES *PRE-GROUND*.
I USED *STARBUCKS*.
AHH HAHAH HAHAHA HAH!!
FAN*TASTIC!*
SEE YOU *AROUND*, PARIOS!

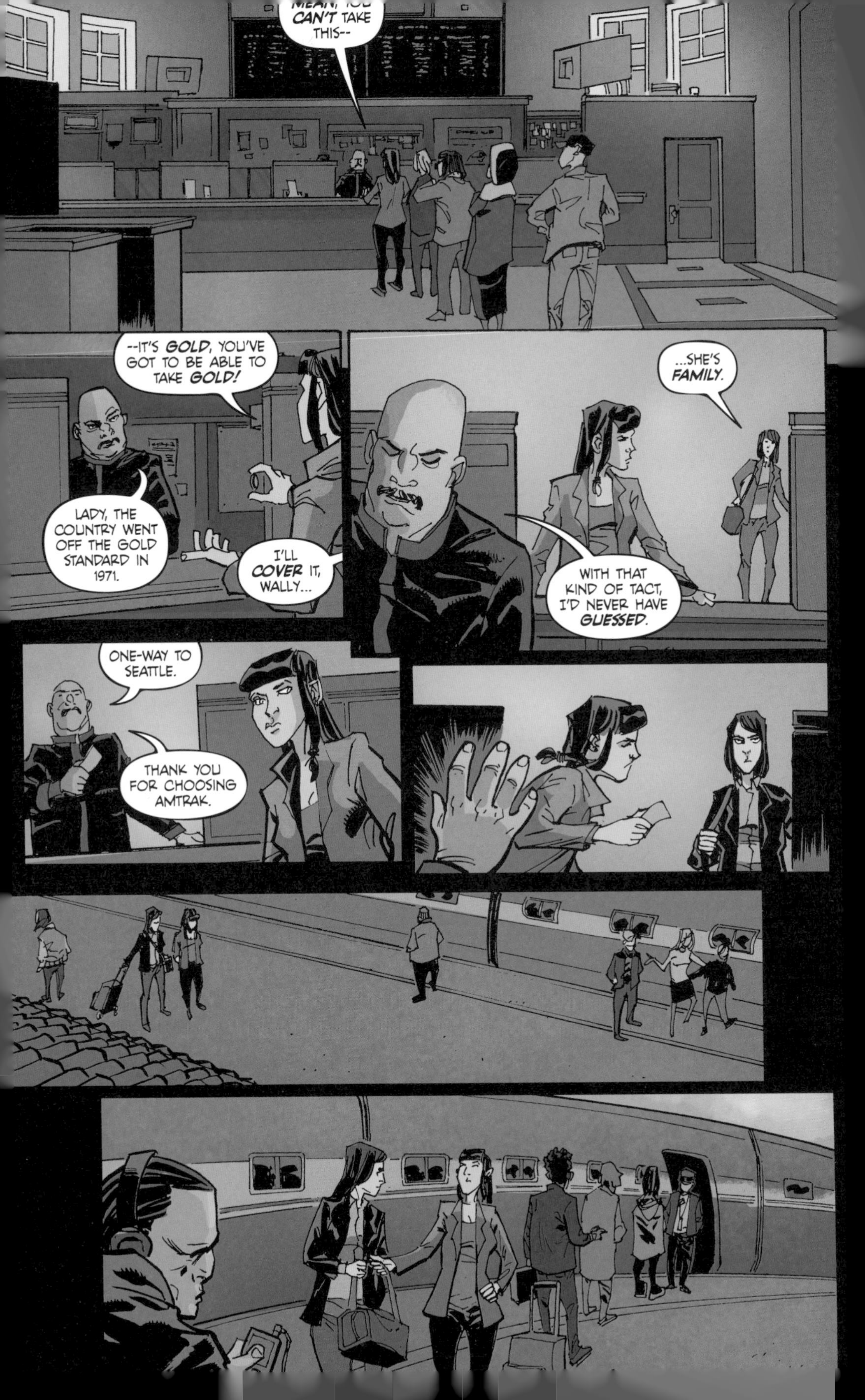
CAN'T TAKE THIS--
--IT'S GOLD, YOU'VE GOT TO BE ABLE TO TAKE GOLD!
LADY, THE COUNTRY WENT OFF THE GOLD STANDARD IN 1971.
I'LL COVER IT, WALLY...
...SHE'S FAMILY.
WITH THAT KIND OF TACT, I'D NEVER HAVE GUESSED.
ONE-WAY TO SEATTLE.
THANK YOU FOR CHOOSING AMTRAK.

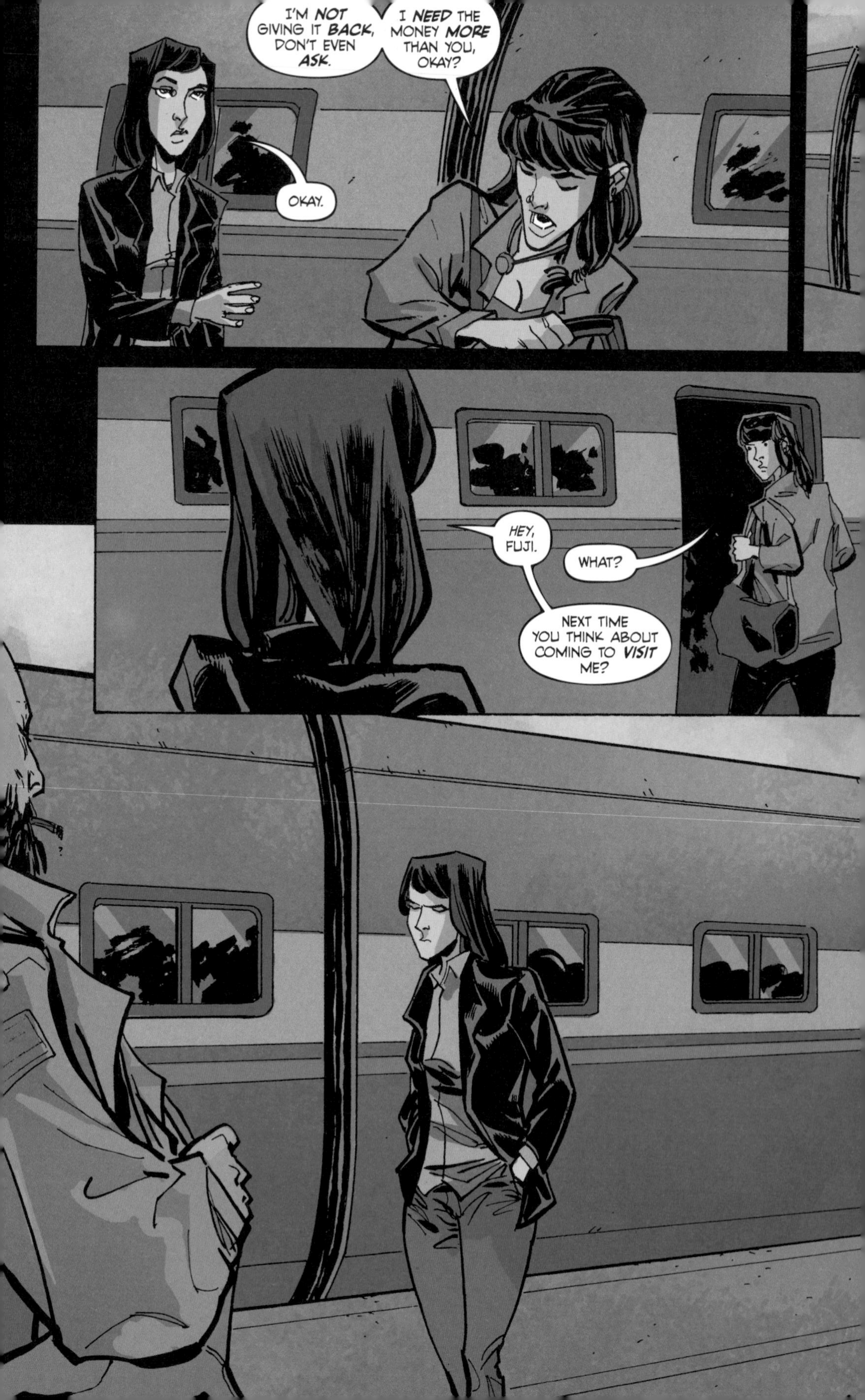
I'M NOT GIVING IT BACK, DON'T EVEN ASK.
I NEED THE MONEY MORE THAN YOU, OKAY?
OKAY.
HEY, FUJI.
WHAT?
NEXT TIME YOU THINK ABOUT COMING TO VISIT ME?

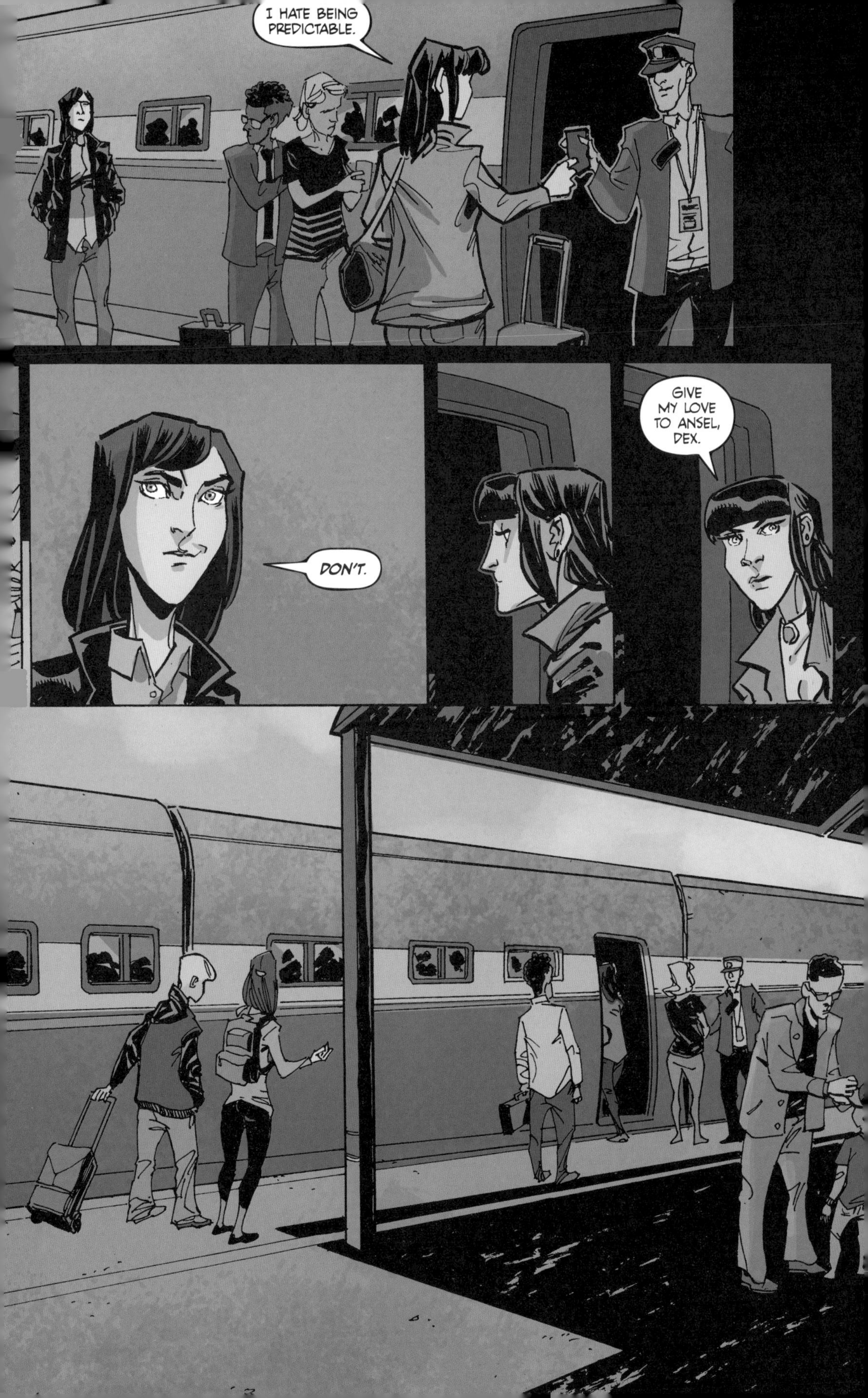
I HATE BEING PREDICTABLE.
DON'T.
GIVE MY LOVE TO ANSEL, DEX.

Chapter Five

The Case of the Night That Wouldn't End

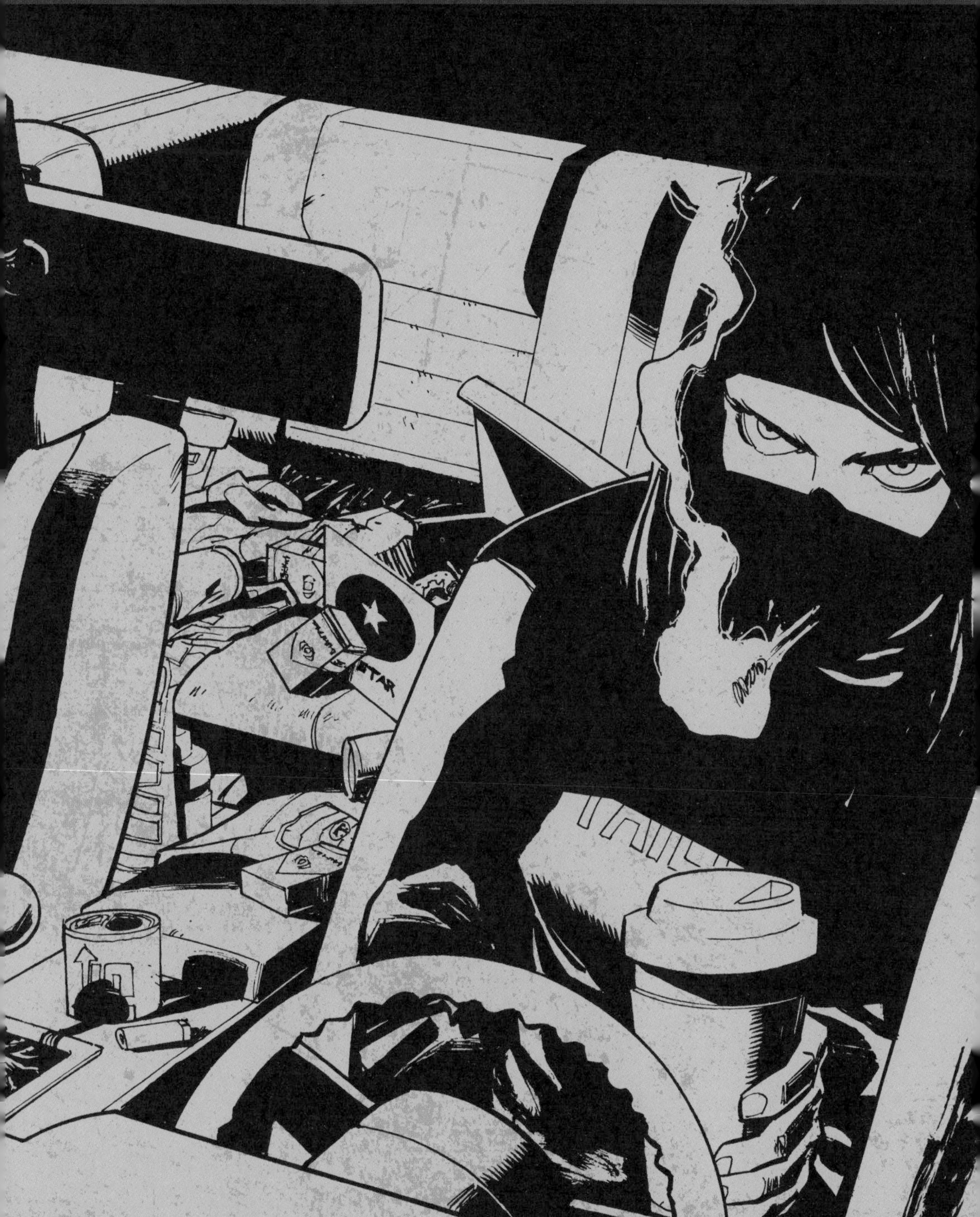

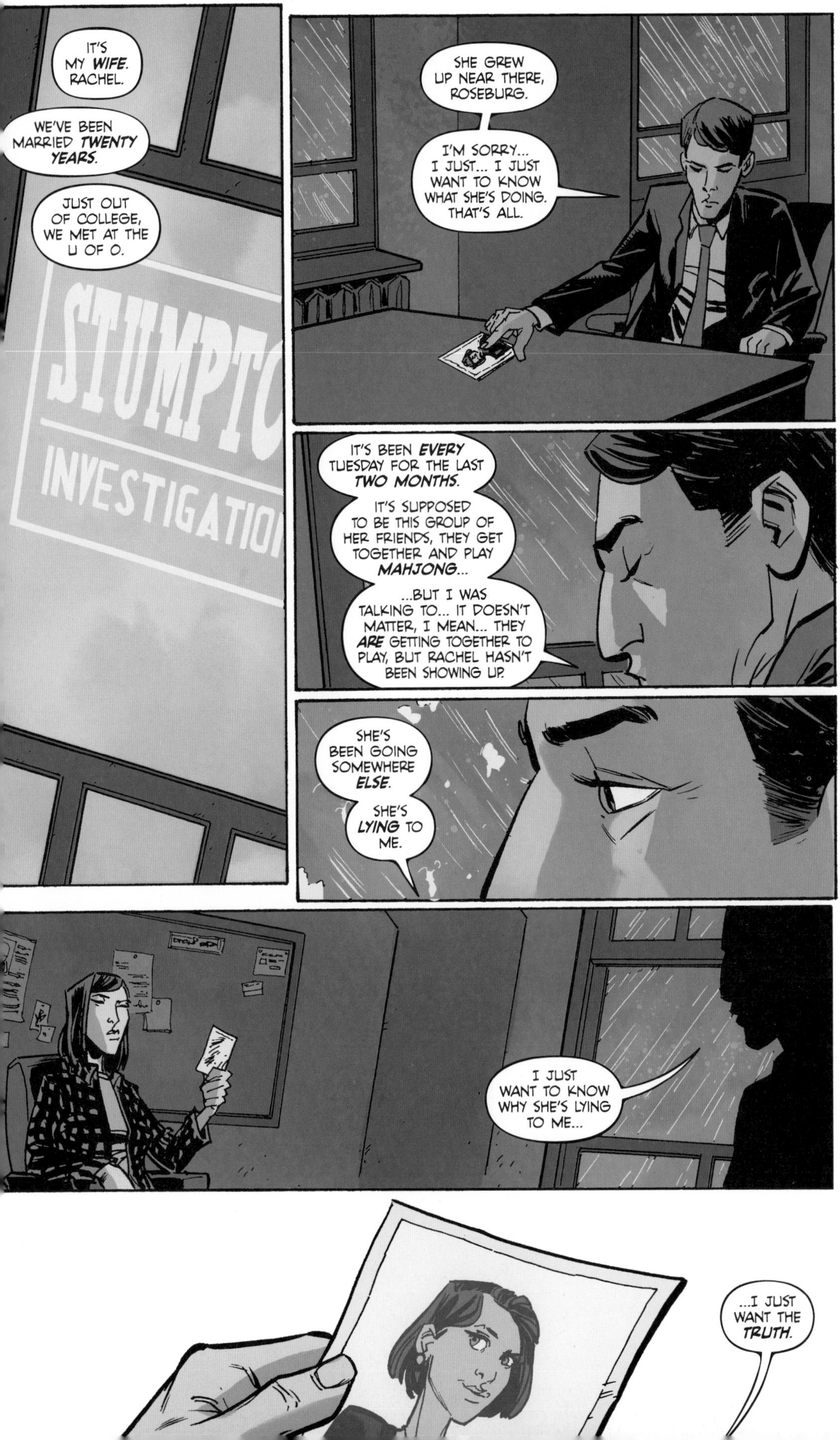
IT'S MY WIFE. RACHEL.
WE'VE BEEN MARRIED TWENTY YEARS.
JUST OUT OF COLLEGE, WE MET AT THE U OF O.
STUMPTO
INVESTIGATIO
SHE GREW UP NEAR THERE, ROSEBURG.
I'M SORRY... I JUST... I JUST WANT TO KNOW WHAT SHE'S DOING. THAT'S ALL.
IT'S BEEN EVERY TUESDAY FOR THE LAST TWO MONTHS.
IT'S SUPPOSED TO BE THIS GROUP OF HER FRIENDS, THEY GET TOGETHER AND PLAY MAHJONG...
...BUT I WAS TALKING TO... IT DOESN'T MATTER, I MEAN... THEY ARE GETTING TOGETHER TO PLAY, BUT RACHEL HASN'T BEEN SHOWING UP.
SHE'S BEEN GOING SOMEWHERE ELSE.
SHE'S LYING TO ME.
I JUST WANT TO KNOW WHY SHE'S LYING TO ME...
...I JUST WANT THE TRUTH.

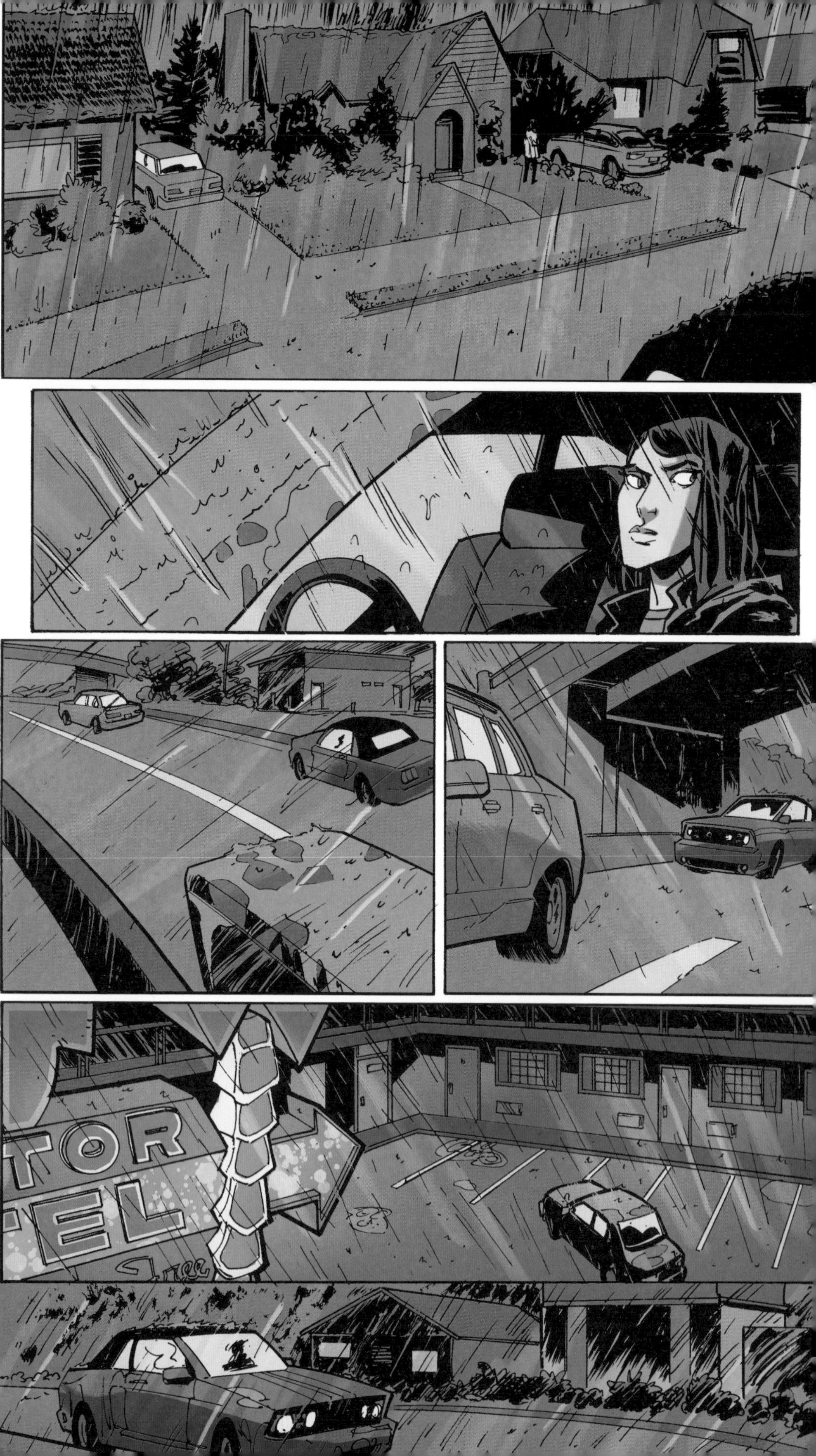

TOR
EL

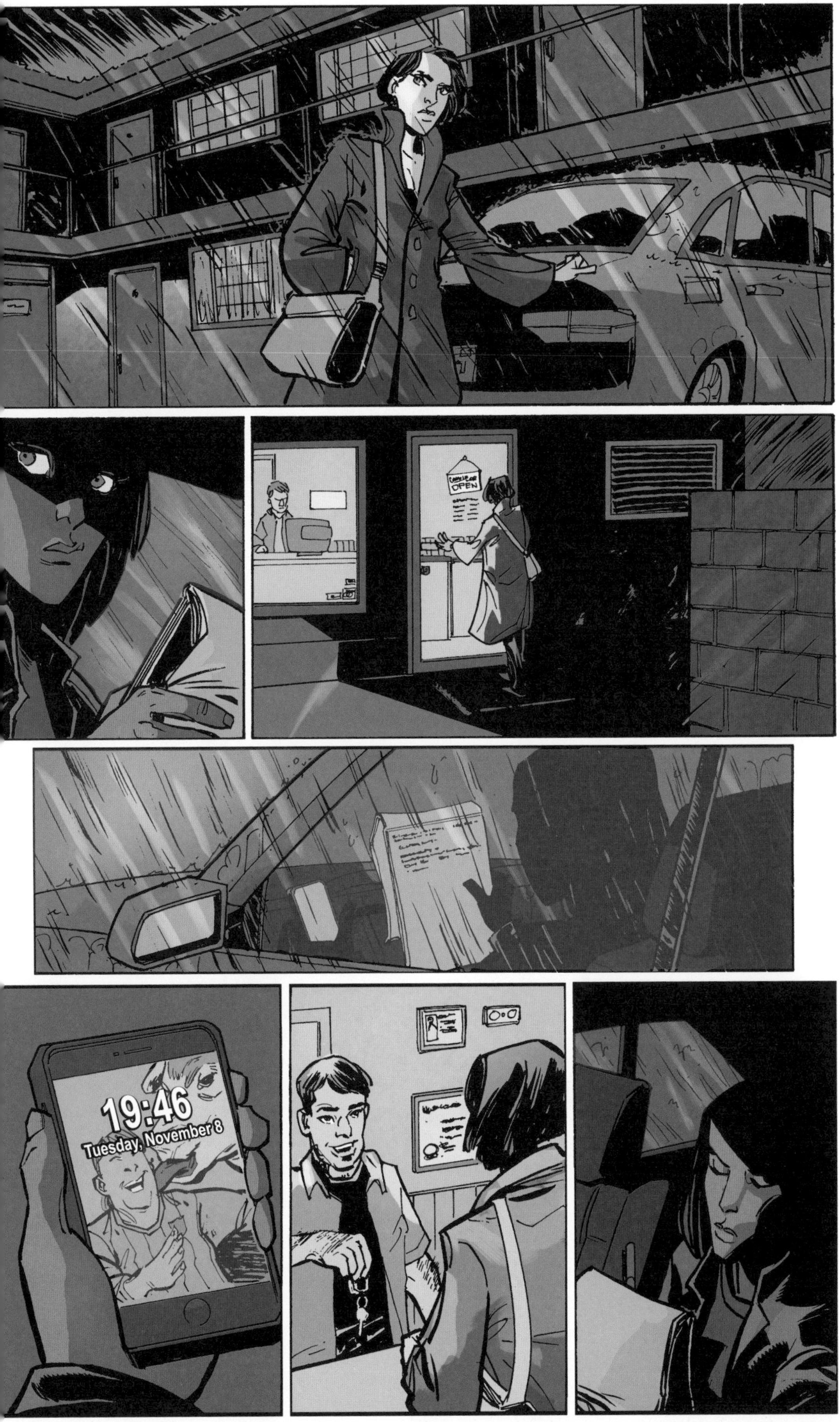
OPEN
19:46
Tuesday, November 8

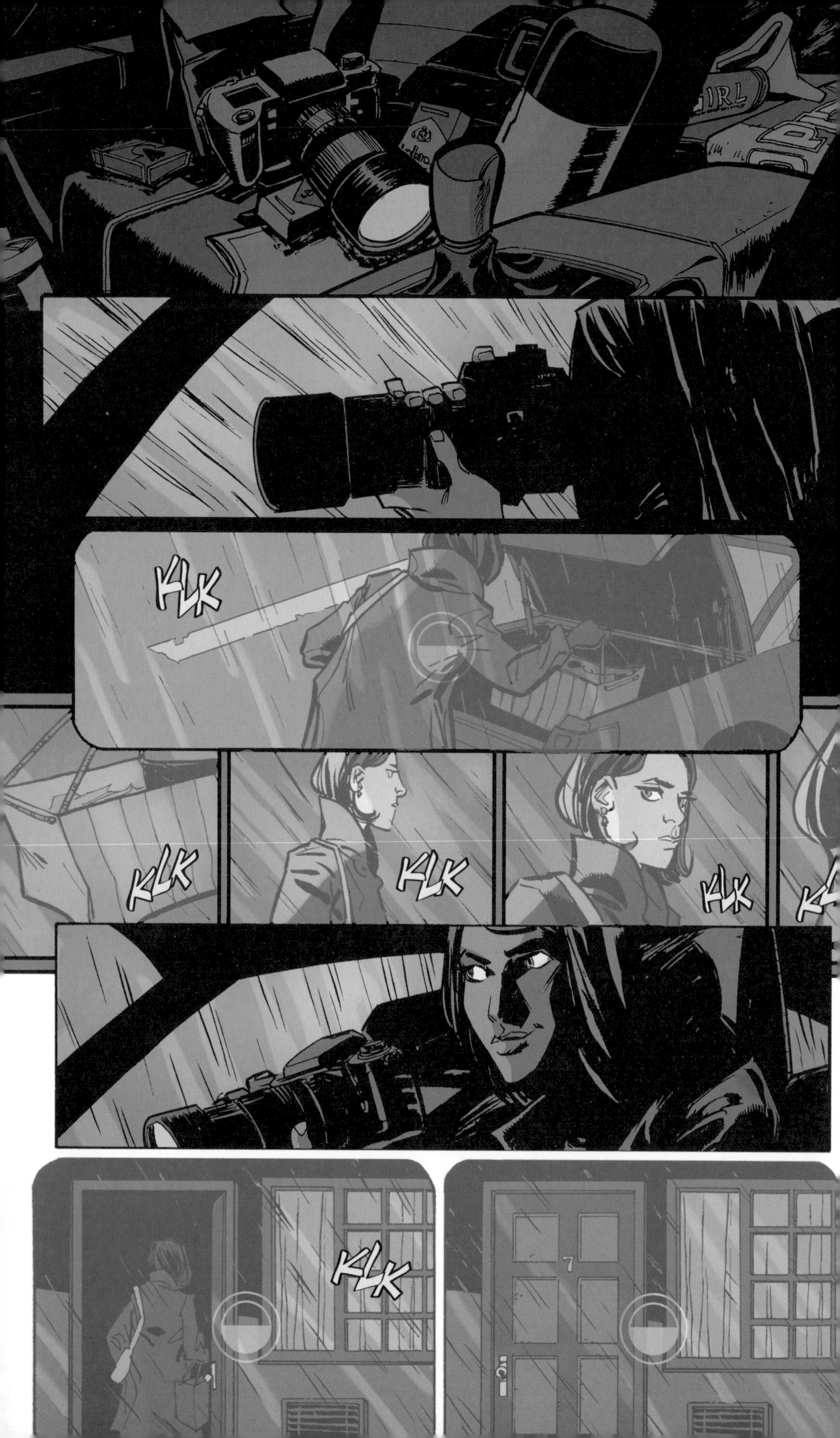
GIRL
KLK
KLK
KLK
KLK
KLK
7

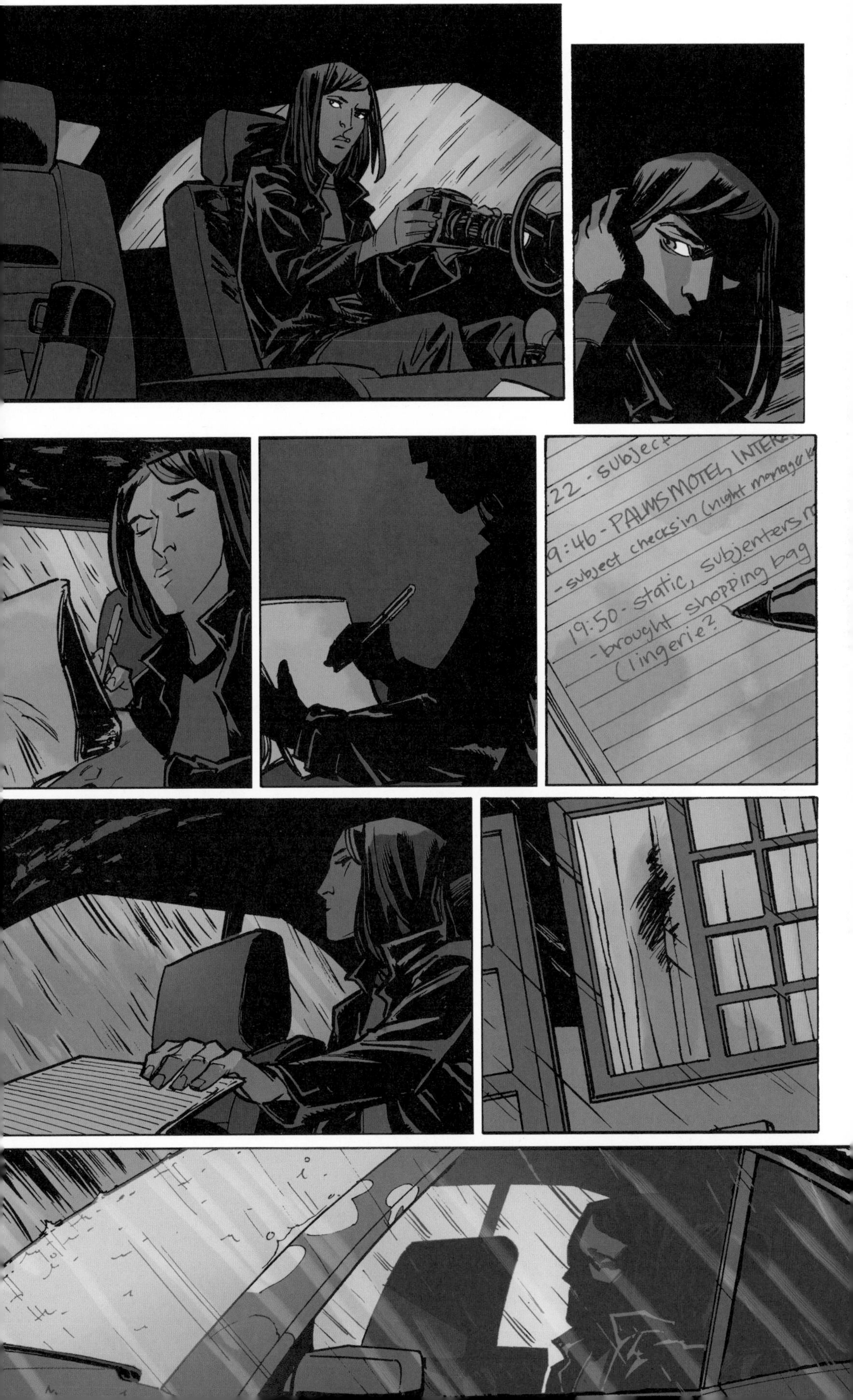
.22 - subject
9:46 - PALMS MOTEL, INTER
- subject checks in (night manager
19:50 - static, subj enters
- brought shopping bag
(lingerie?

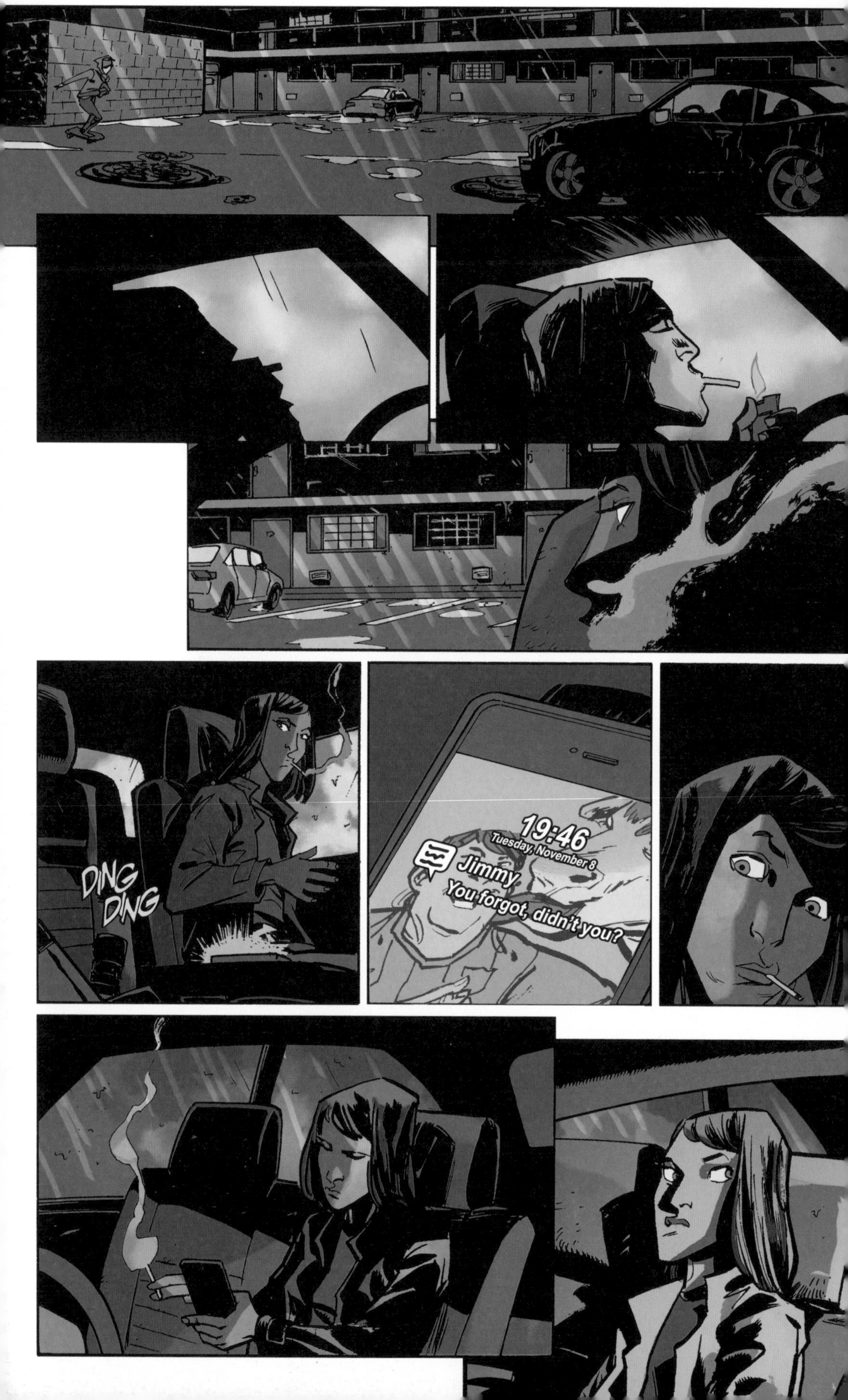
DING DING
19:46
Tuesday, November 8
Jimmy
You forgot, didn't you?

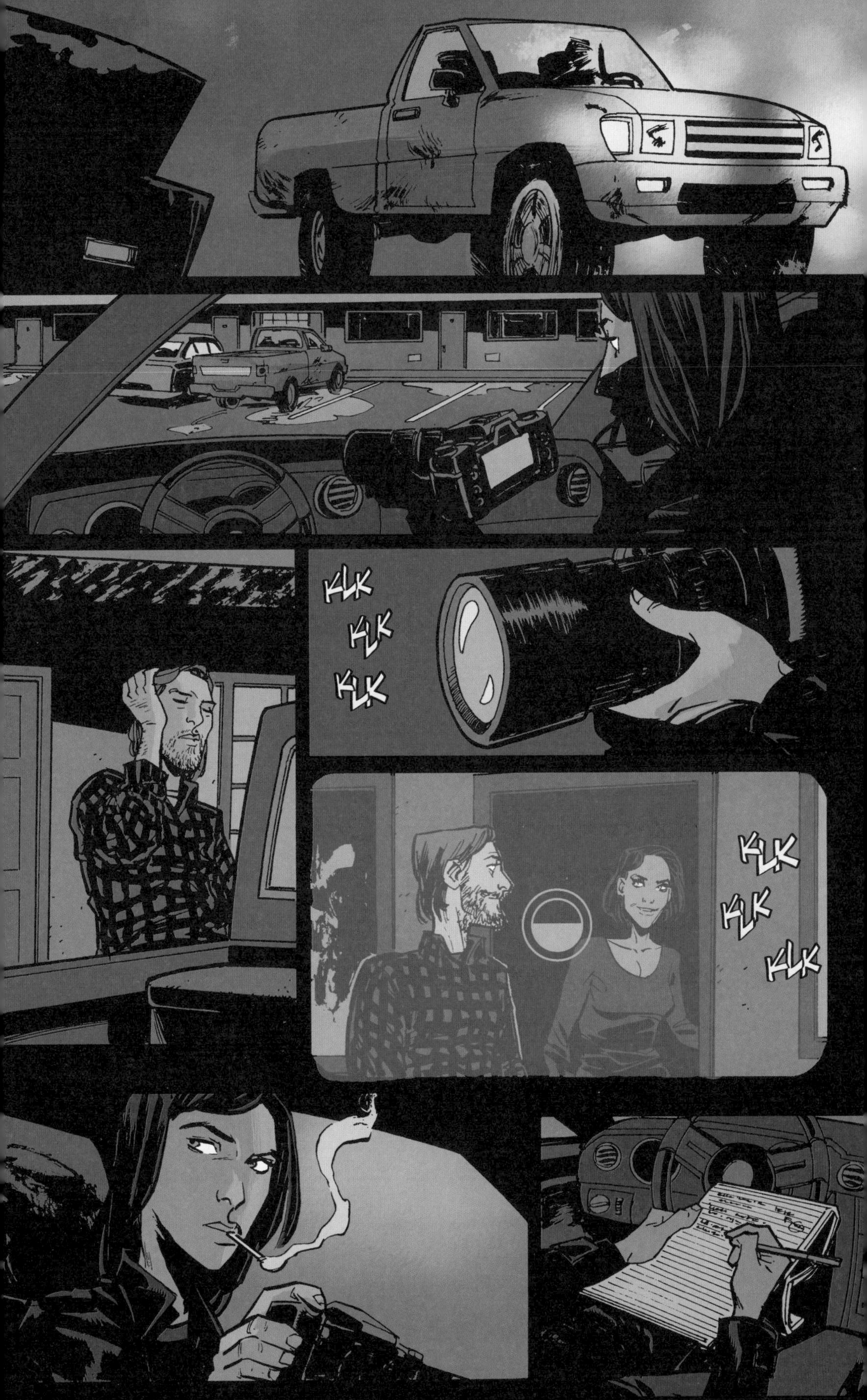
KLK
KLK
KLK
KLK
KLK
KLK

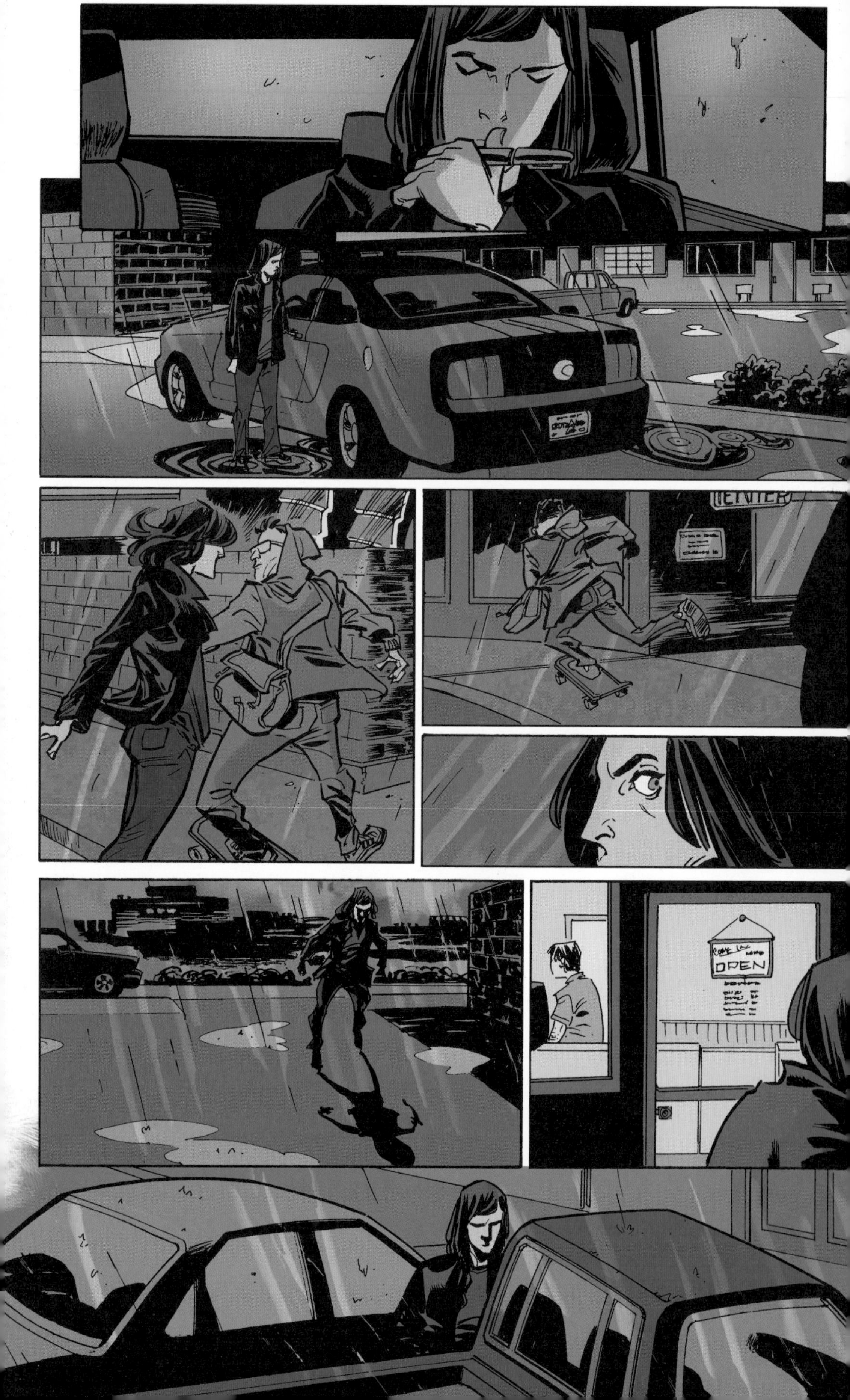

OPEN

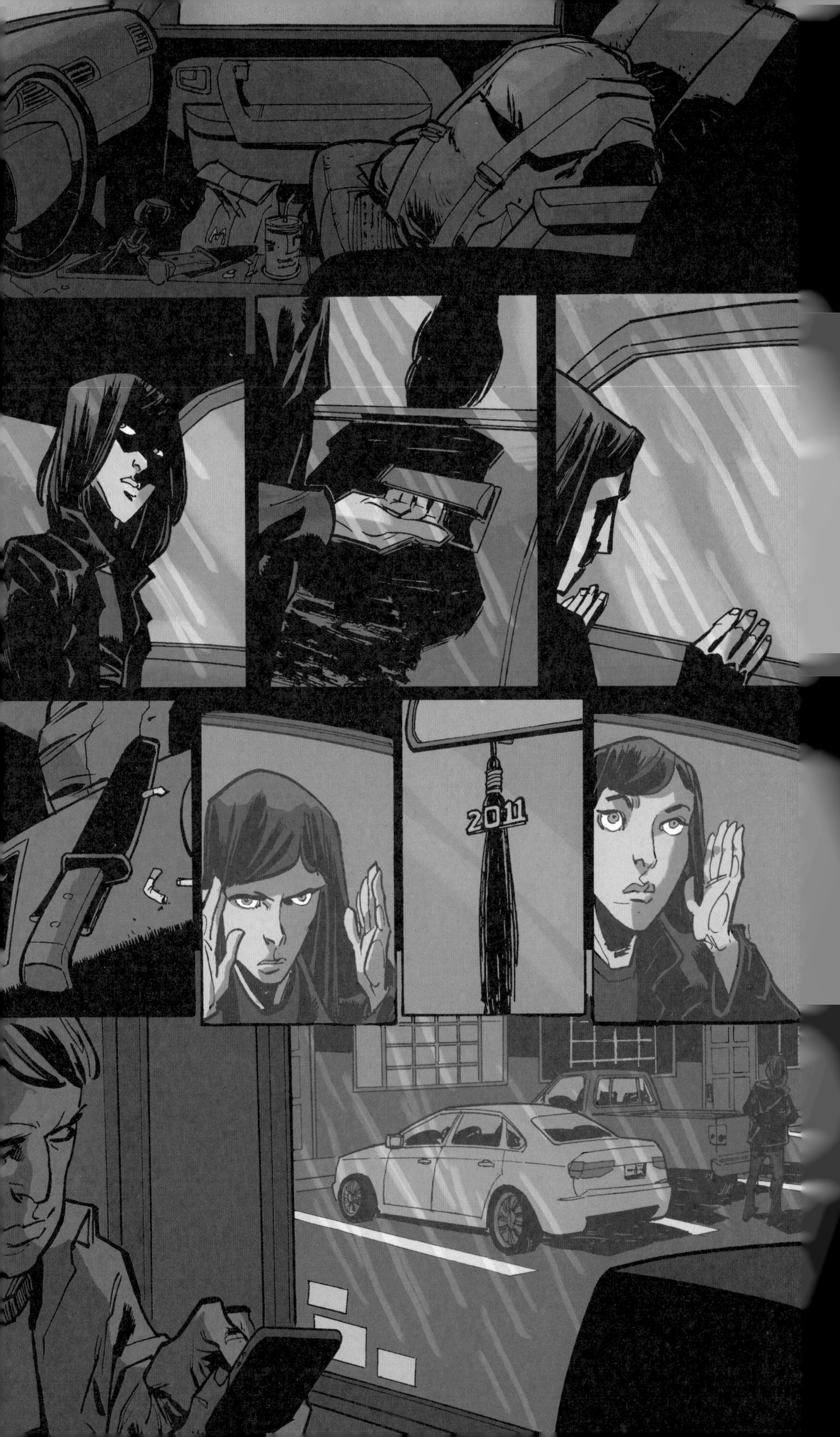
2011

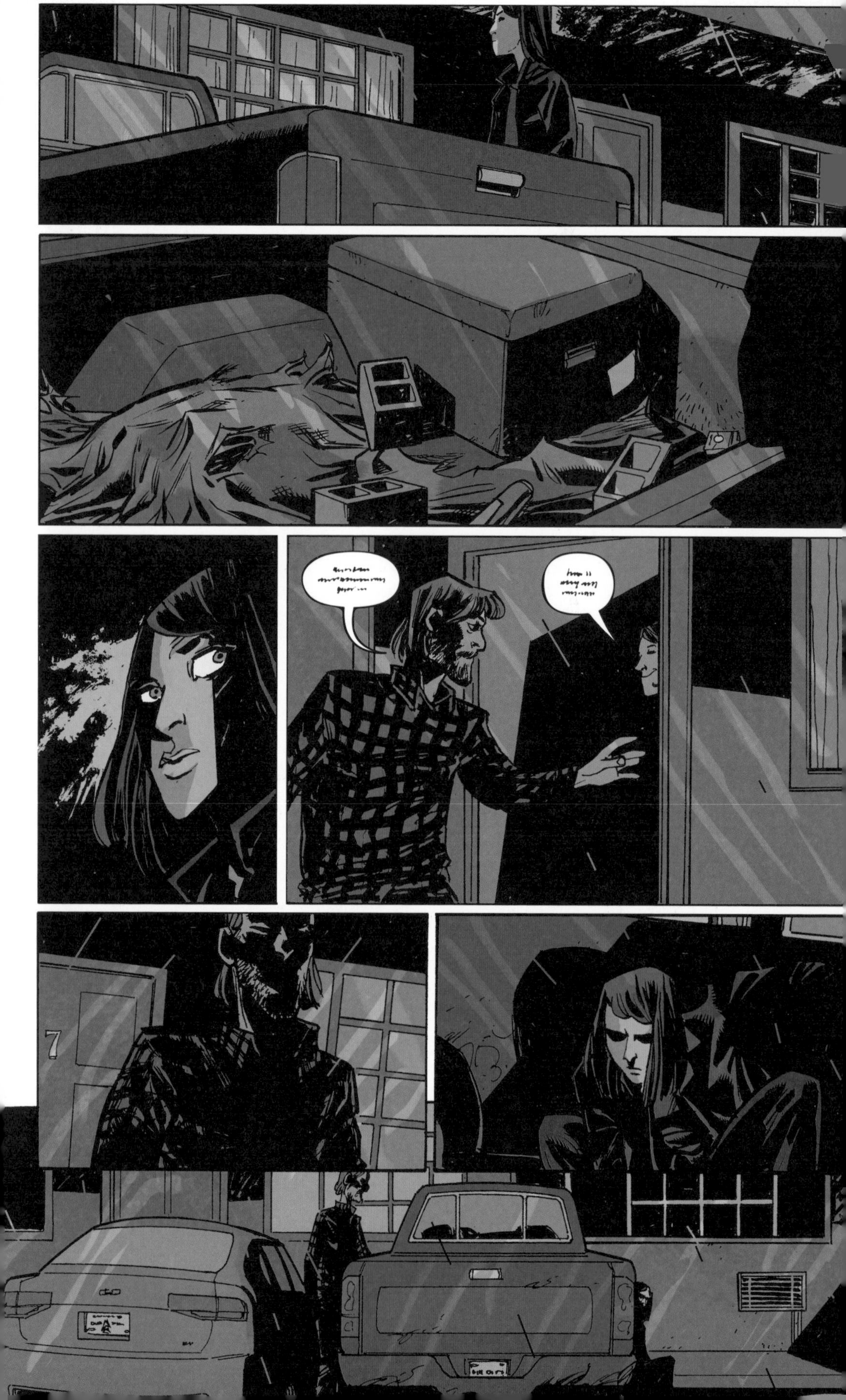
7

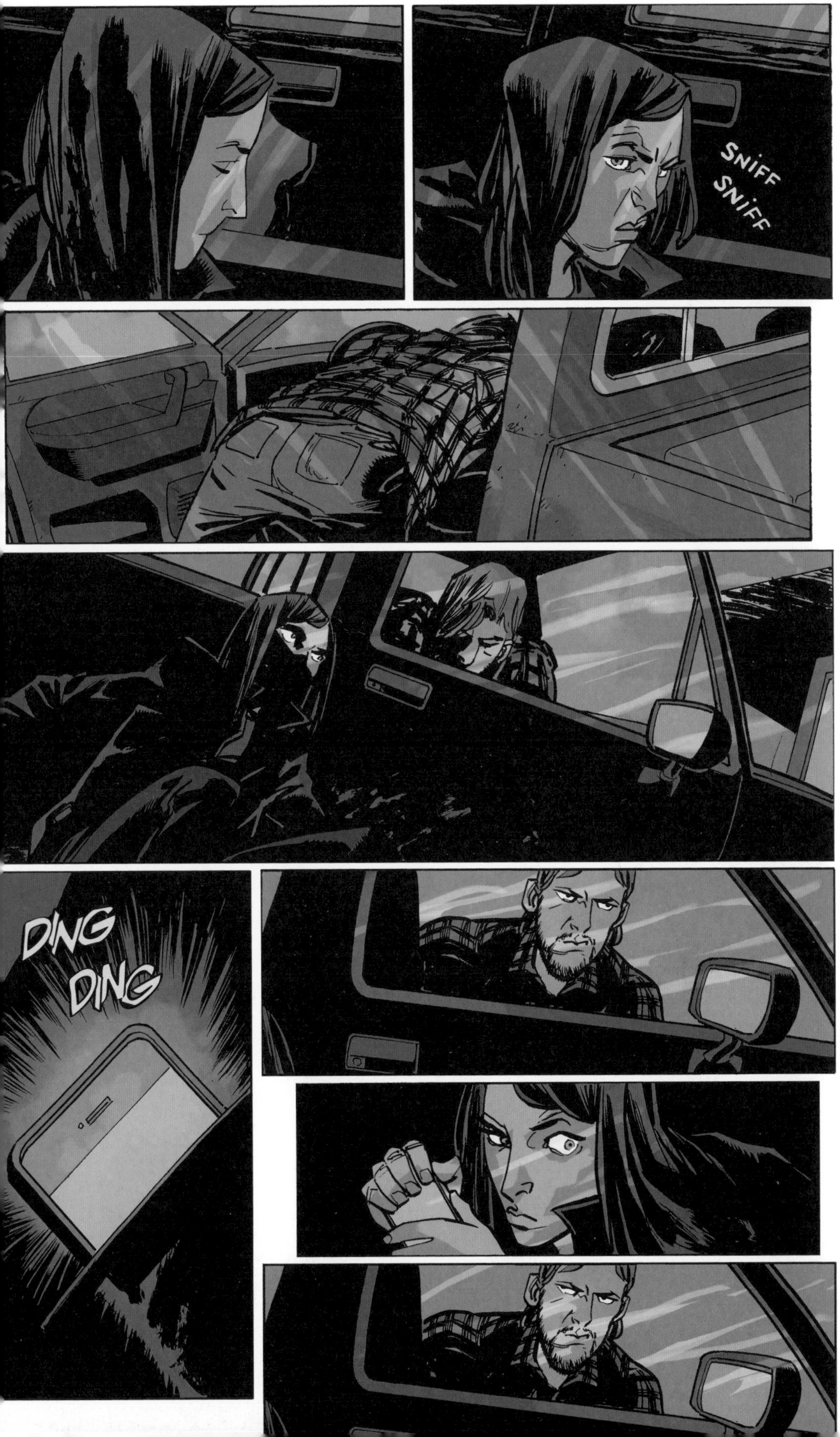
SNIFF
SNIFF
DING
DING

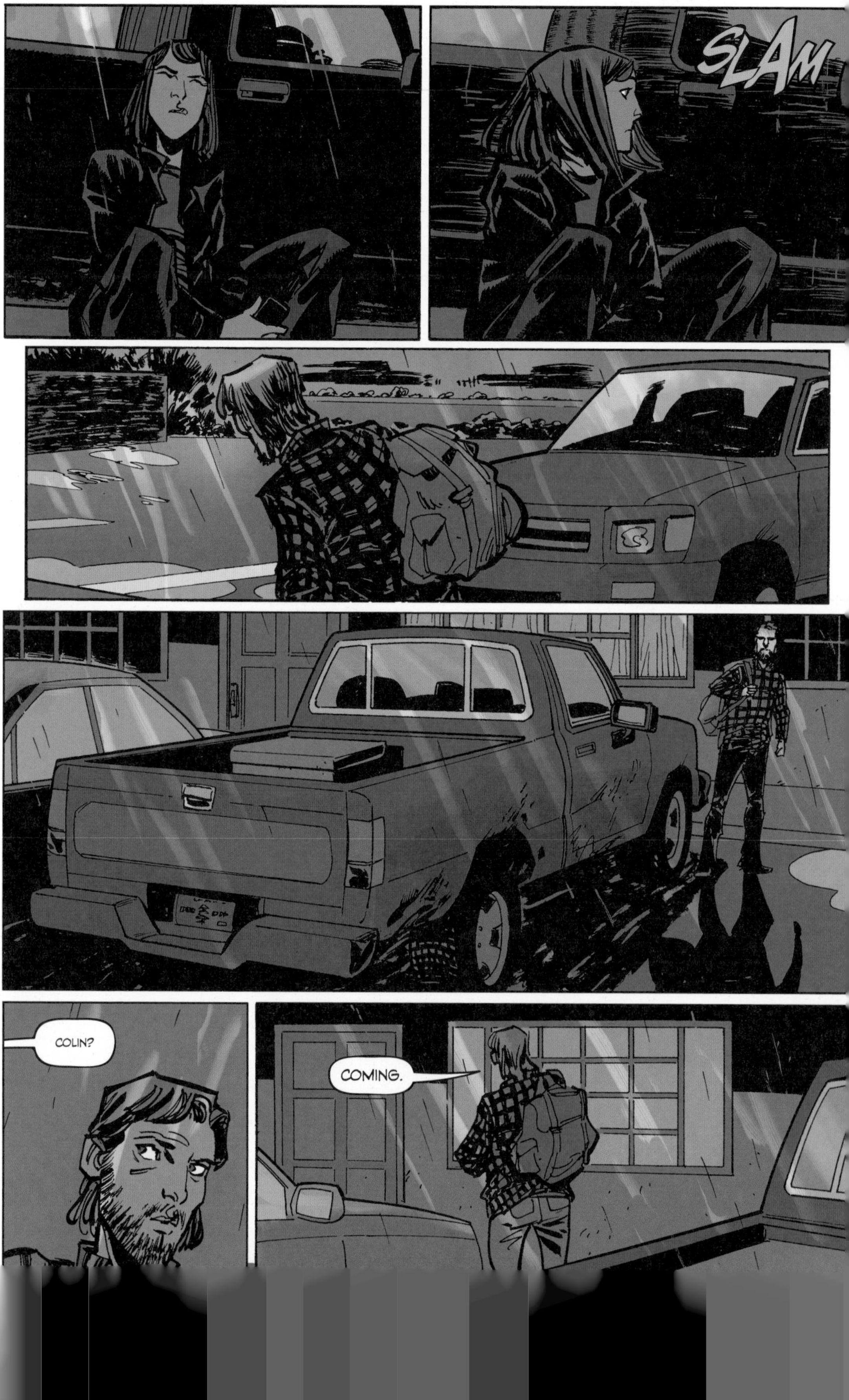
SLAM
COLIN?
COMING.

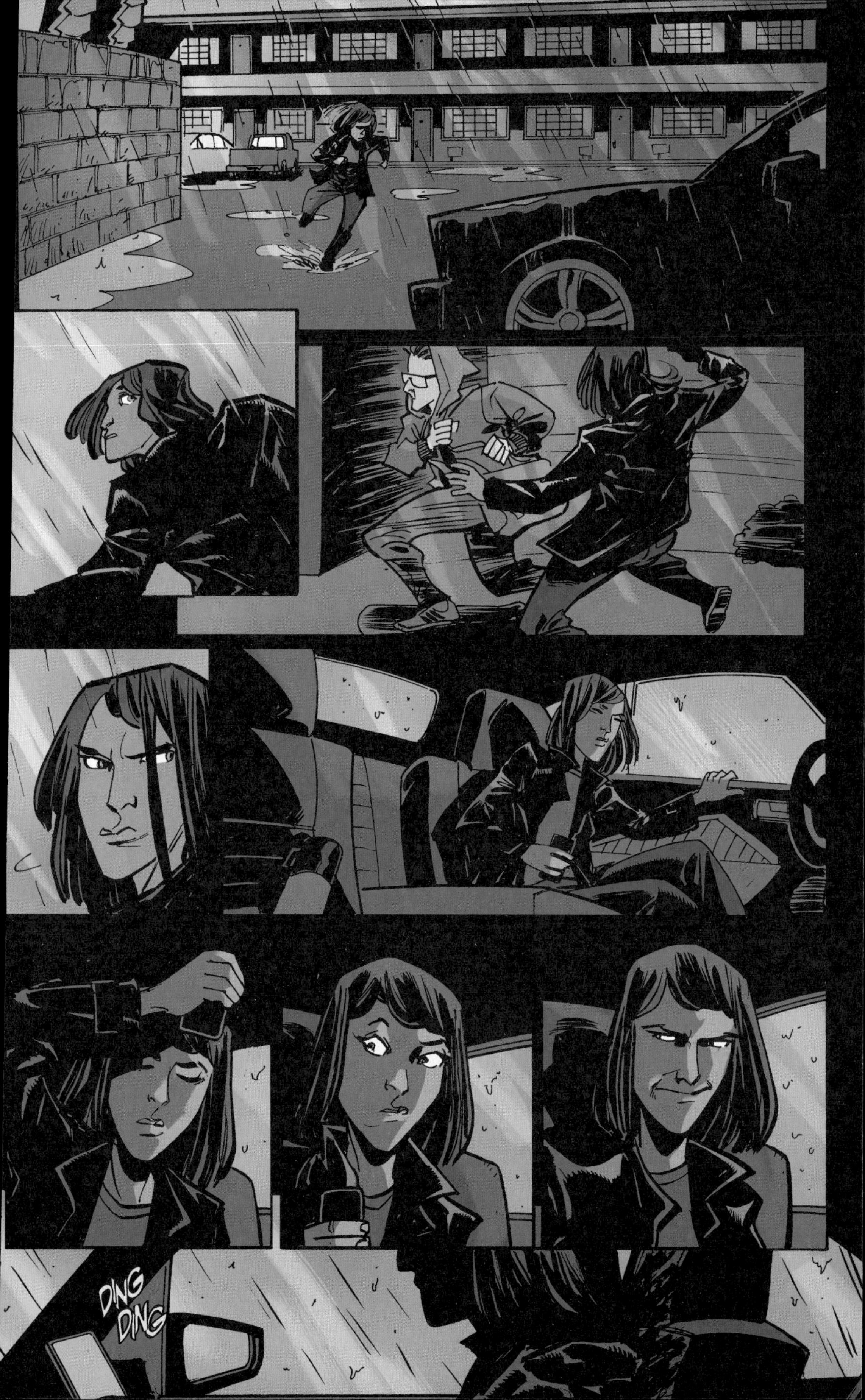
DING DING

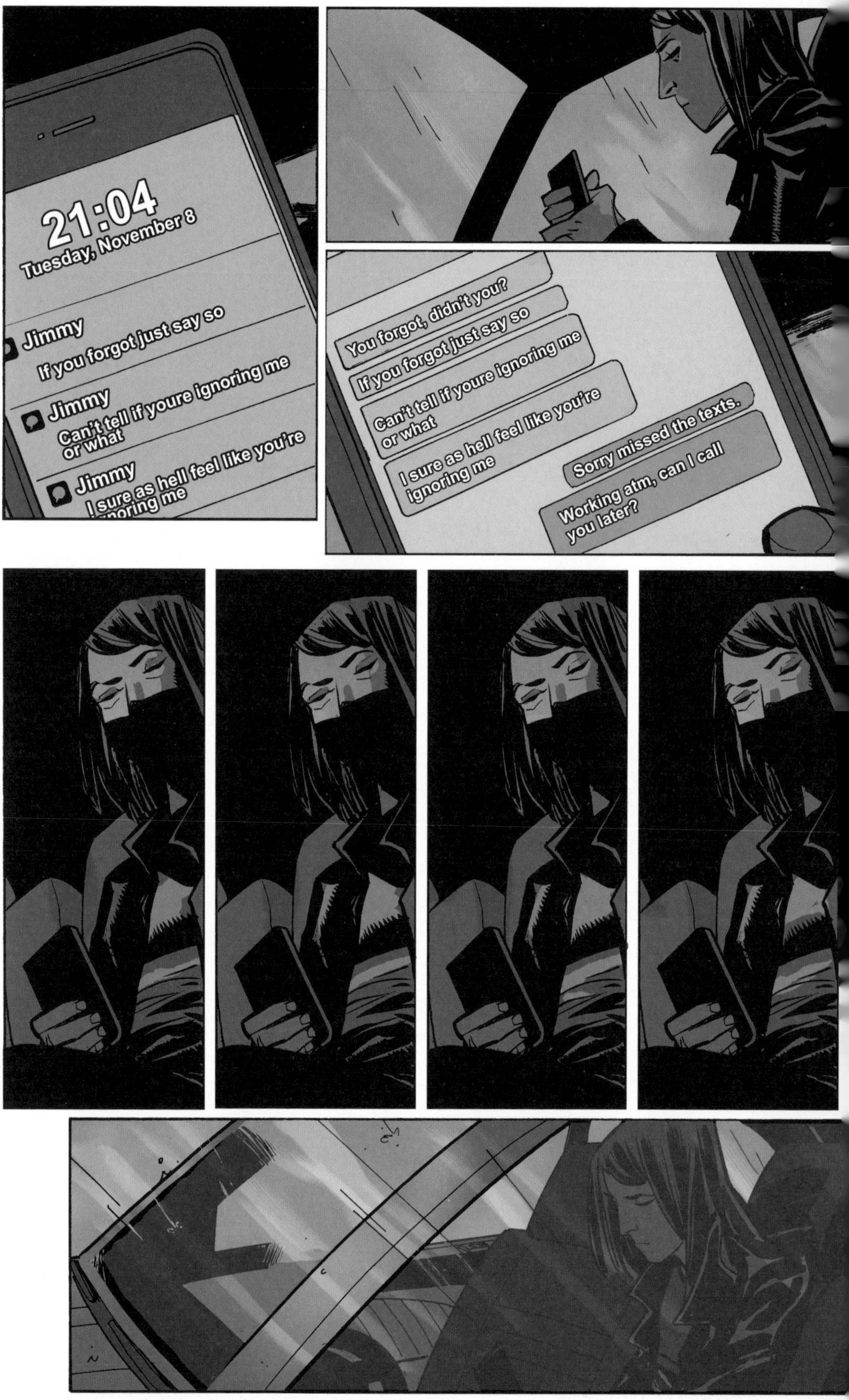
21:04
Tuesday, November 8
Jimmy
If you forgot just say so
Jimmy
Can't tell if youre ignoring me or what
Jimmy
I sure as hell feel like you're ignoring me
You forgot, didn't you?
If you forgot just say so
Can't tell if youre ignoring me or what
I sure as hell feel like you're ignoring me
Sorry missed the texts.
Working atm, can I call you later?

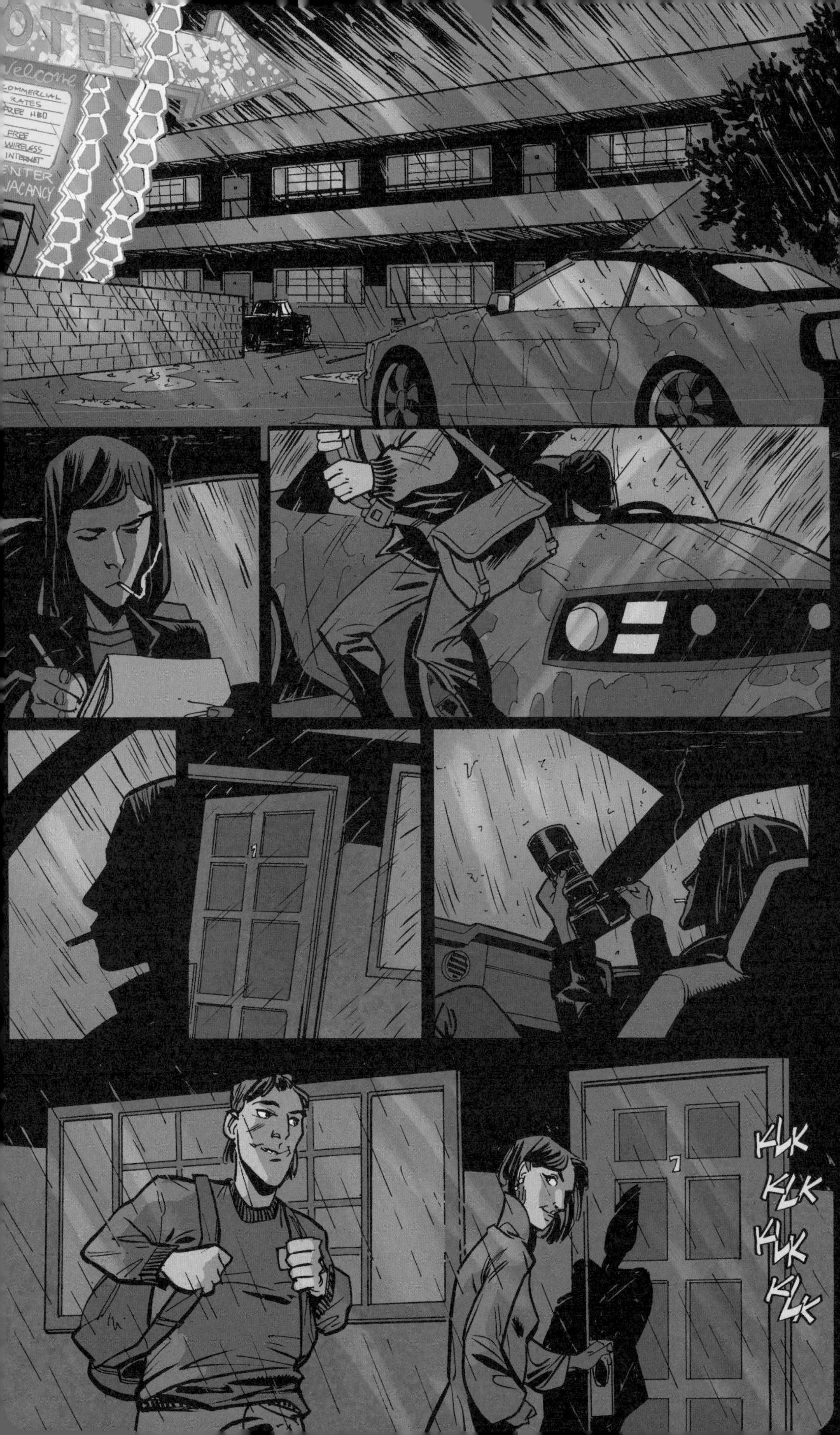
TEL
FREE HBO
FREE
WIRELESS
INTERNET
KLK
KLK
KLK
KLK

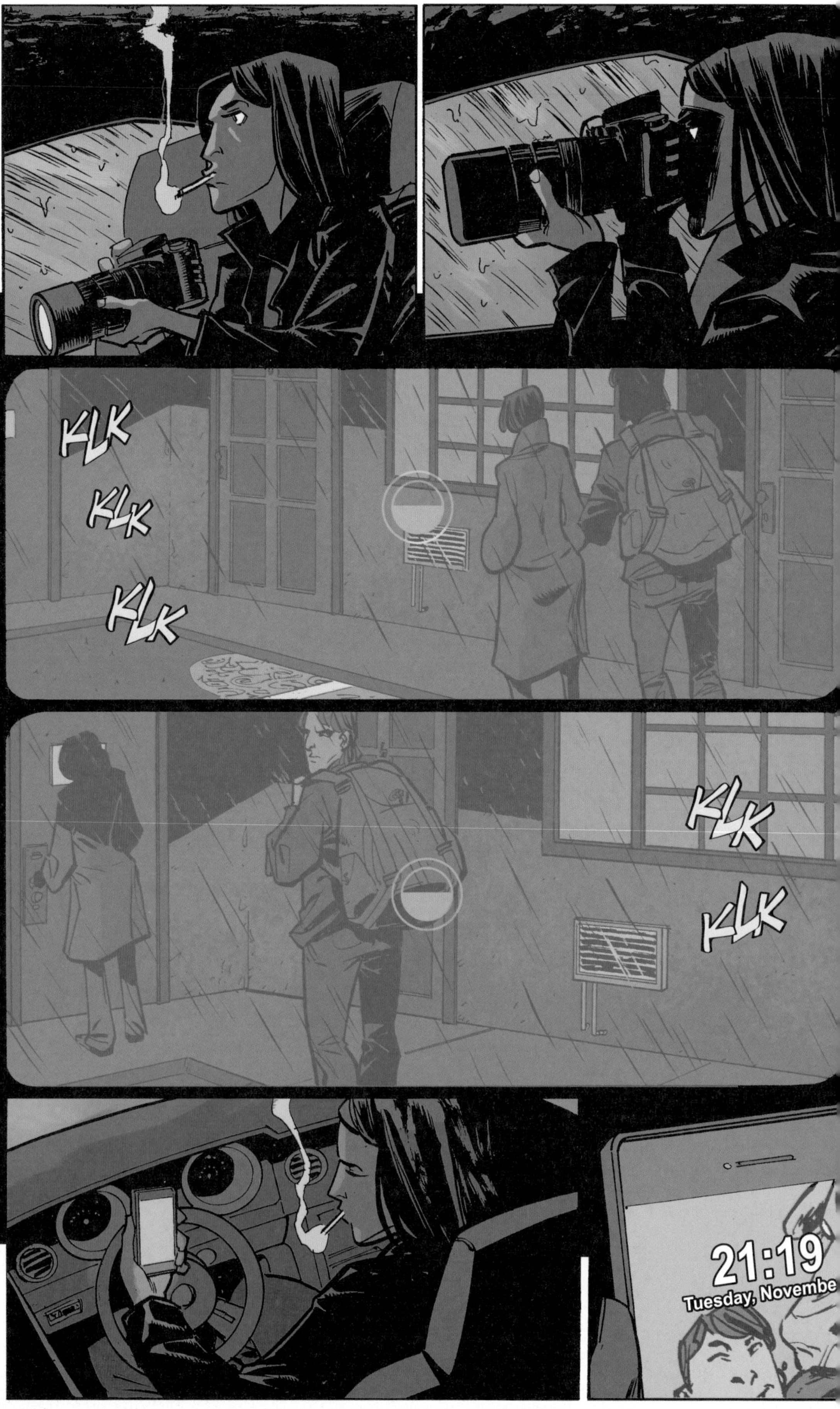
KLK
KLK
KLK
KLK
KLK
21:19
Tuesday, Novembe

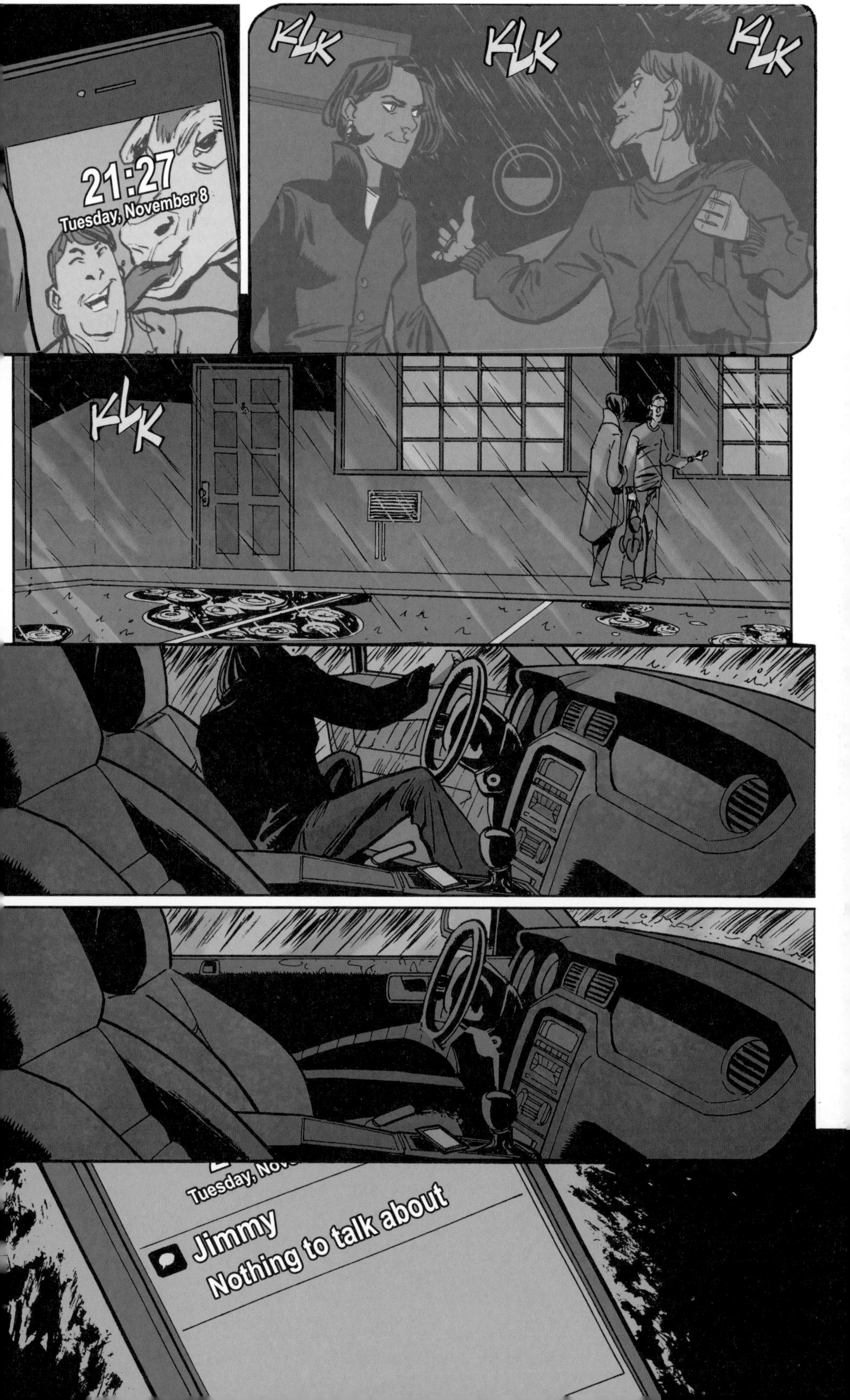

21:27
Tuesday, November 8
KLK
KLK
KLK
KLK
Tuesday, Nove
Jimmy
Nothing to talk about

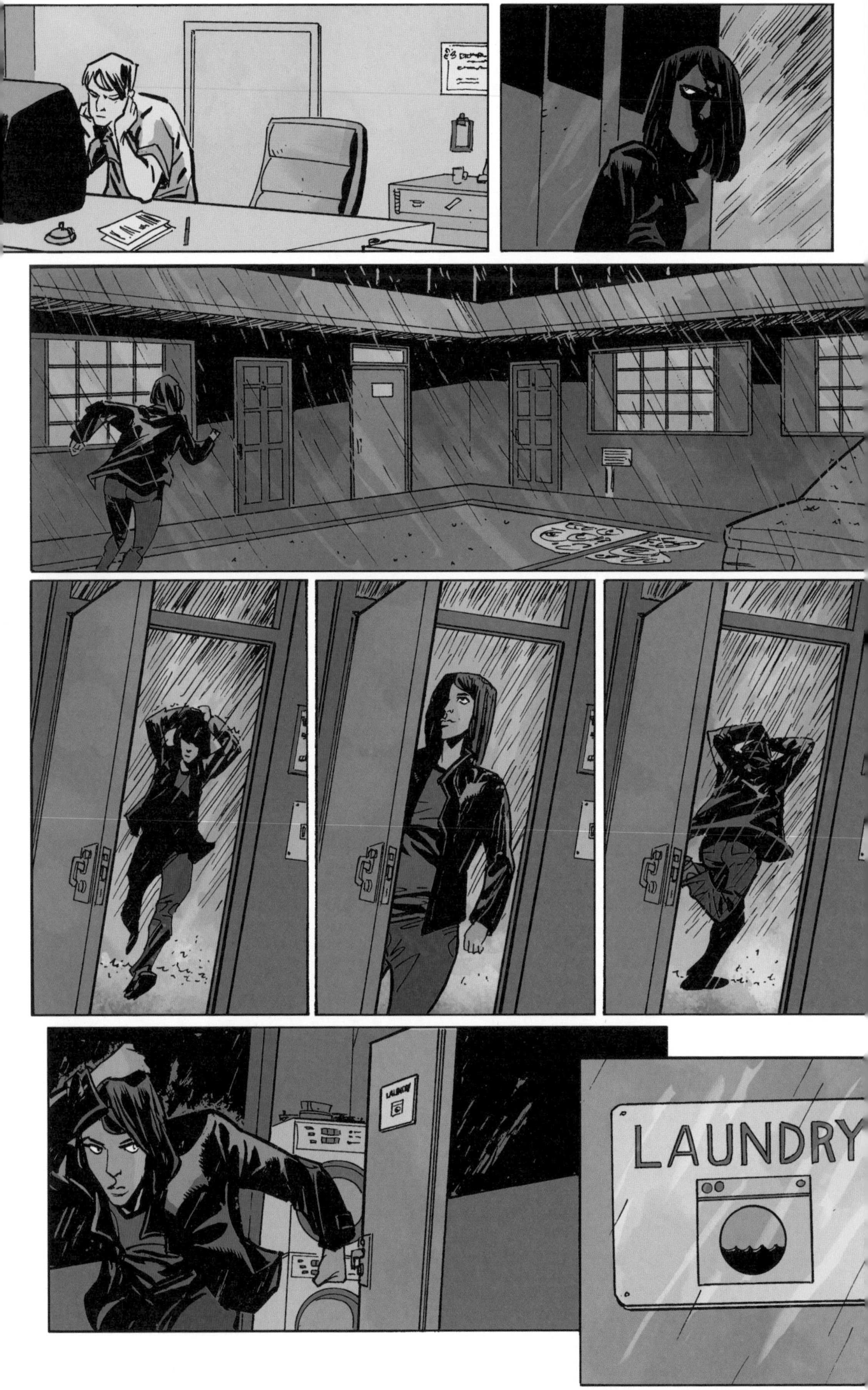
LAUNDRY

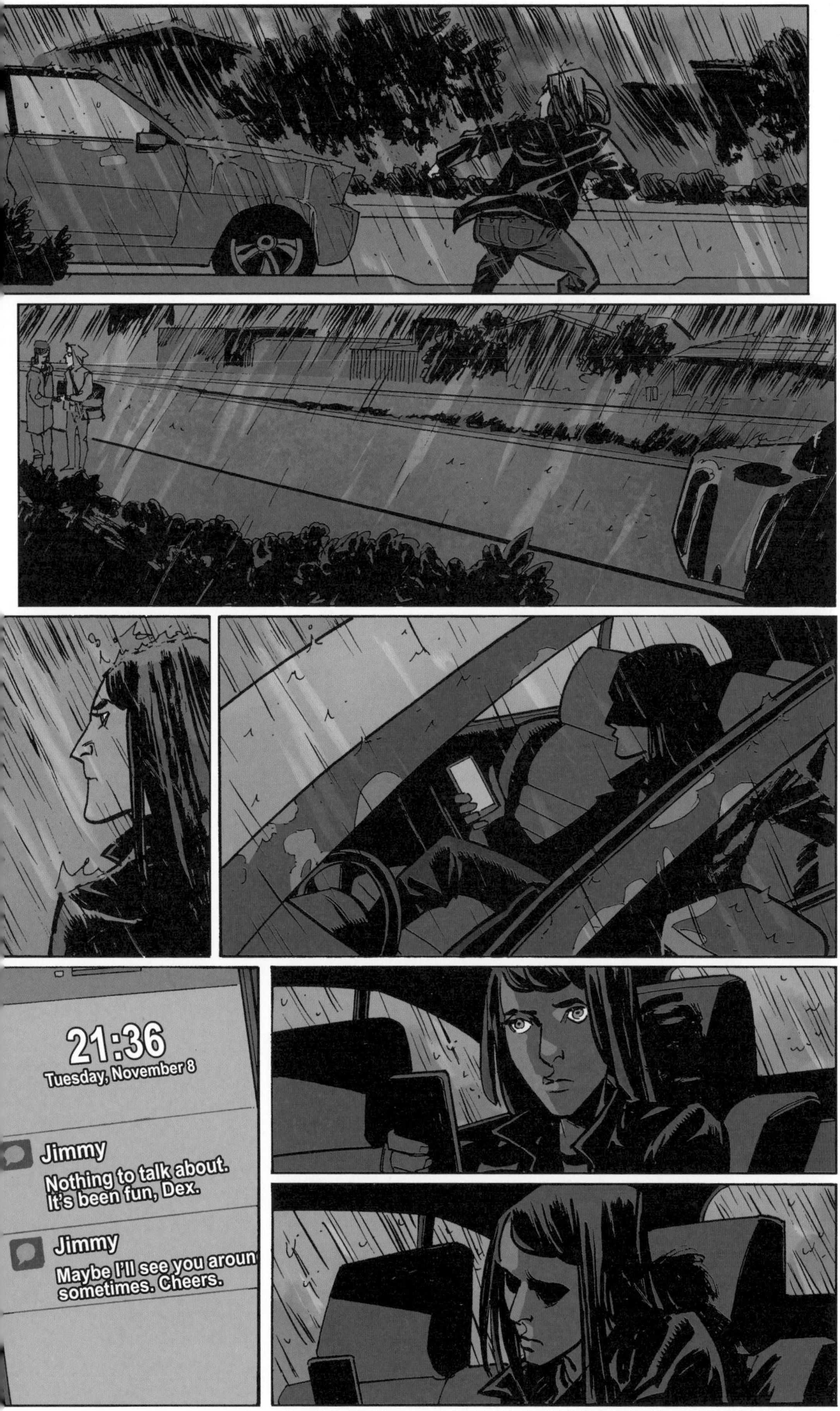
21:36
Tuesday, November 8
Jimmy
Nothing to talk about. It's been fun, Dex.
Jimmy
Maybe I'll see you aroun
sometimes. Cheers.

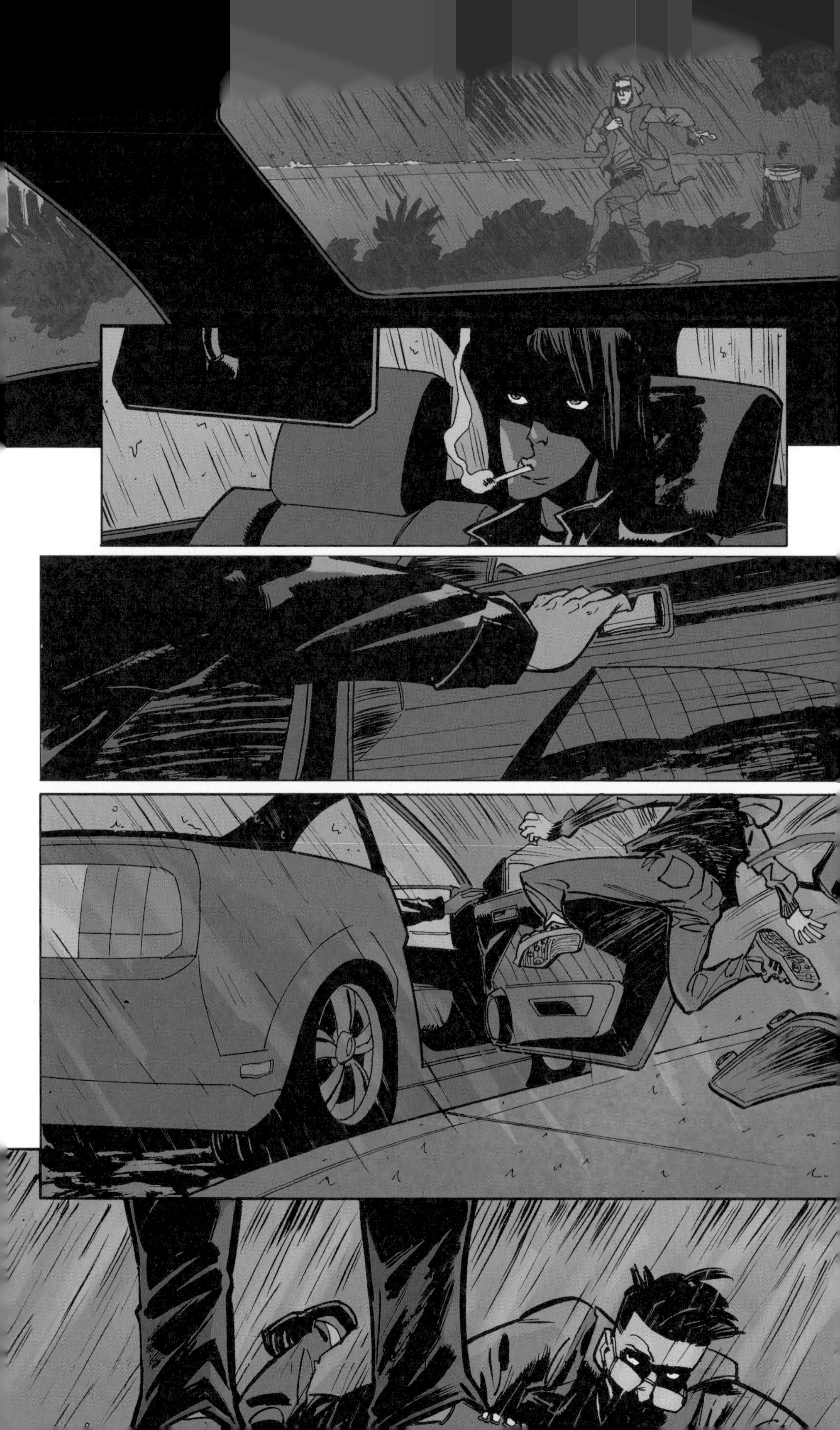

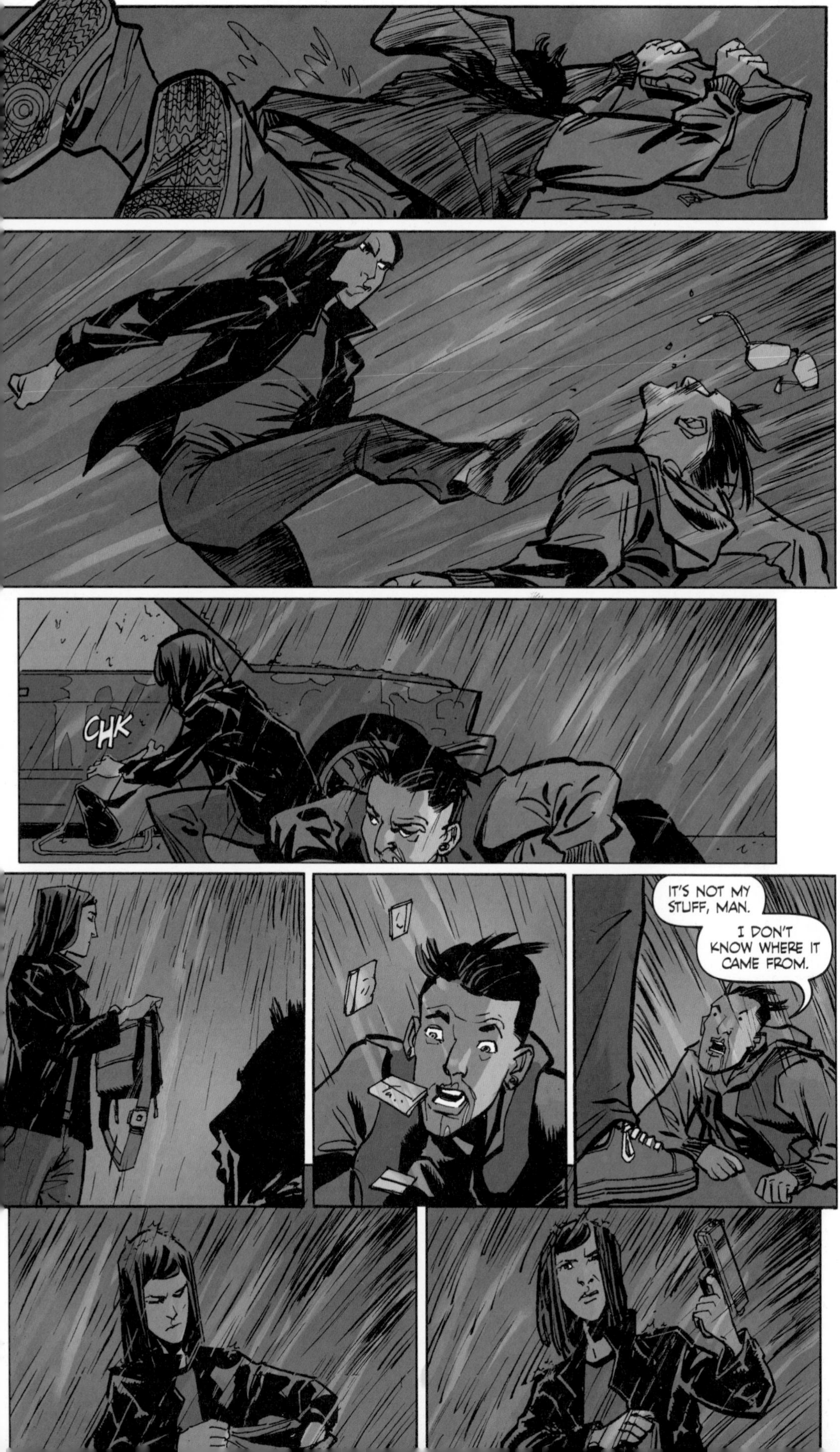
CHK
IT'S NOT MY STUFF, MAN.
I DON'T KNOW WHERE IT CAME FROM.

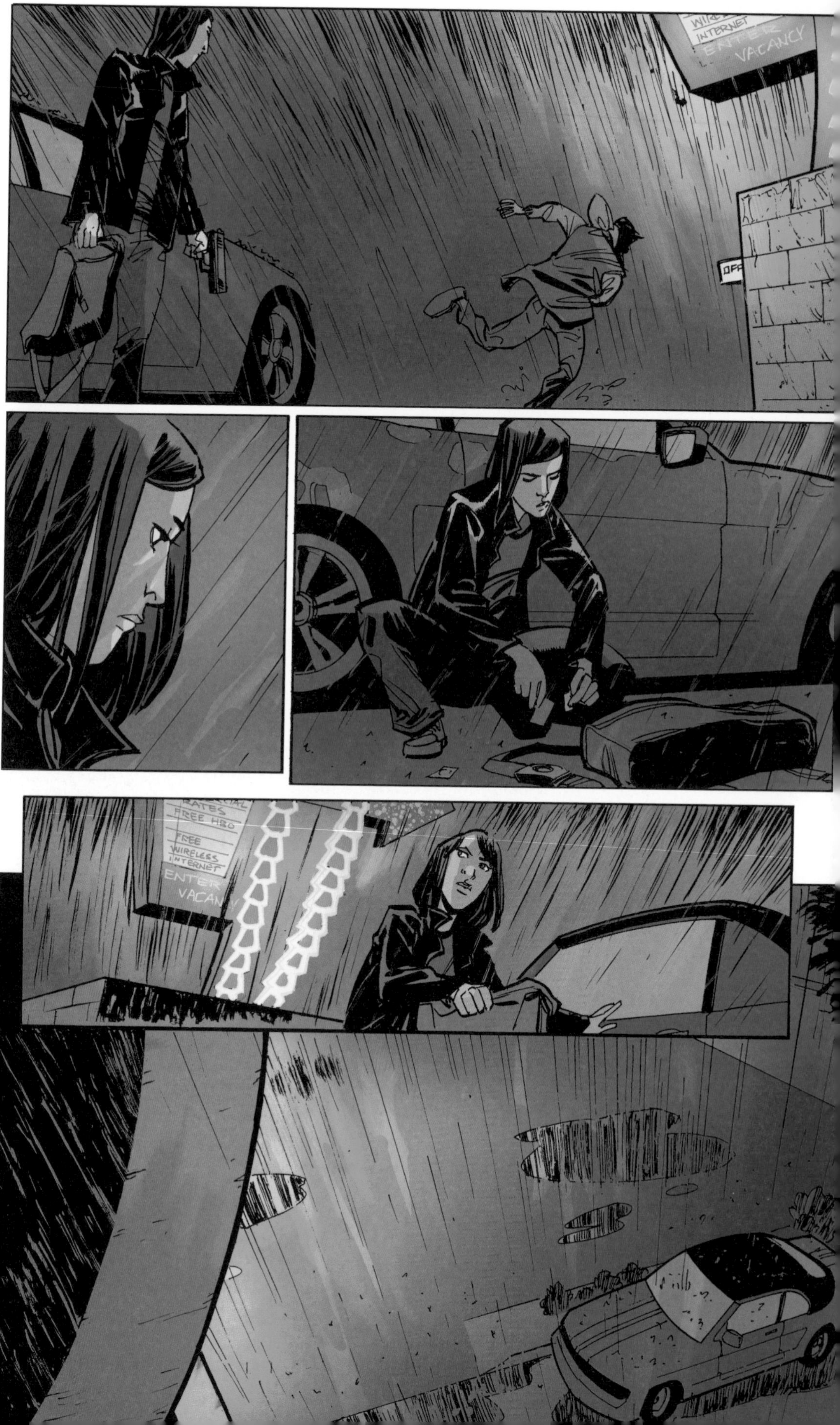
INTERNET
VACANCY
RATES
FREE HBO
FREE
WIRELESS
INTERNET
ENTER

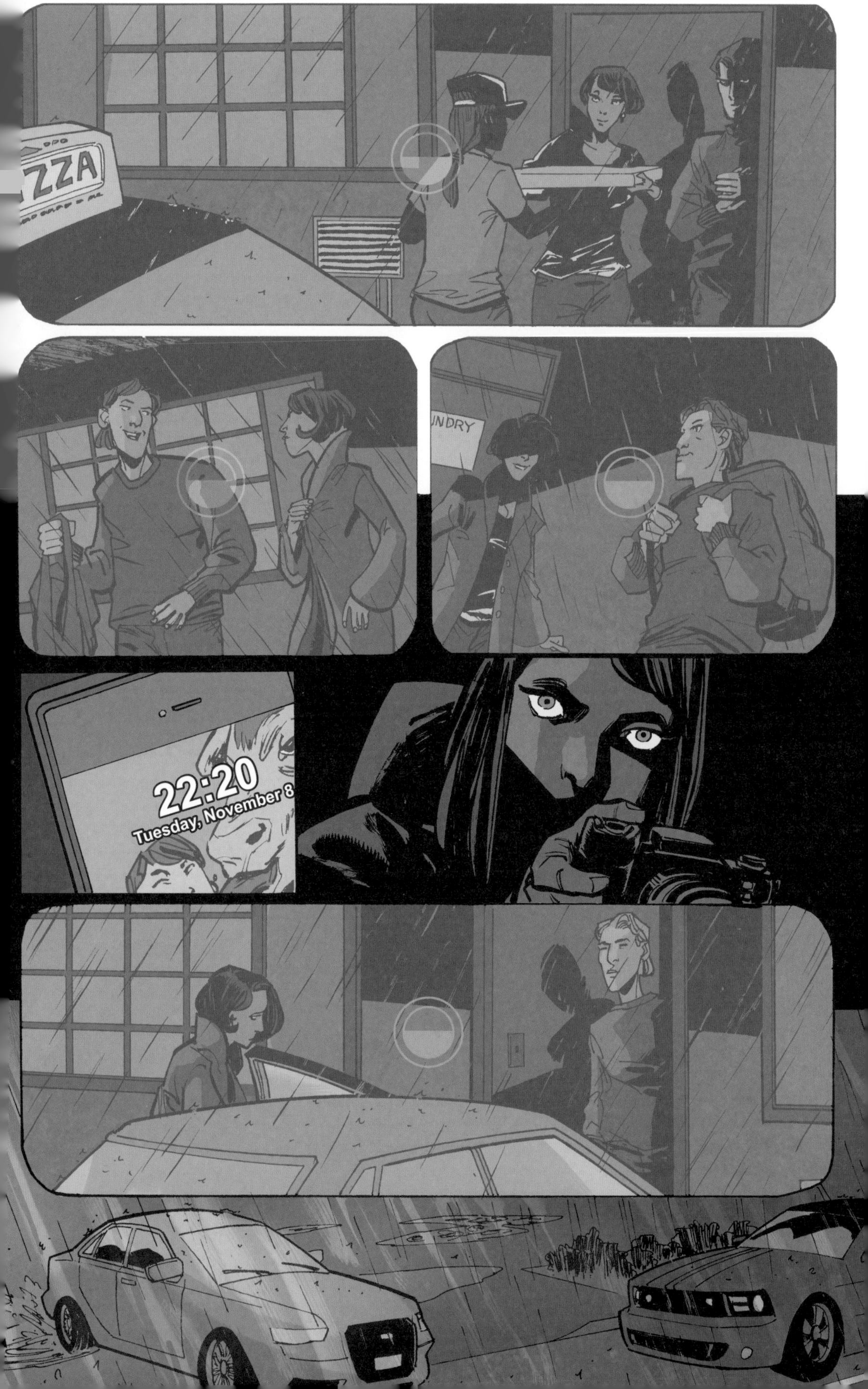

ZZA
UNDRY
22:20
Tuesday, November 8

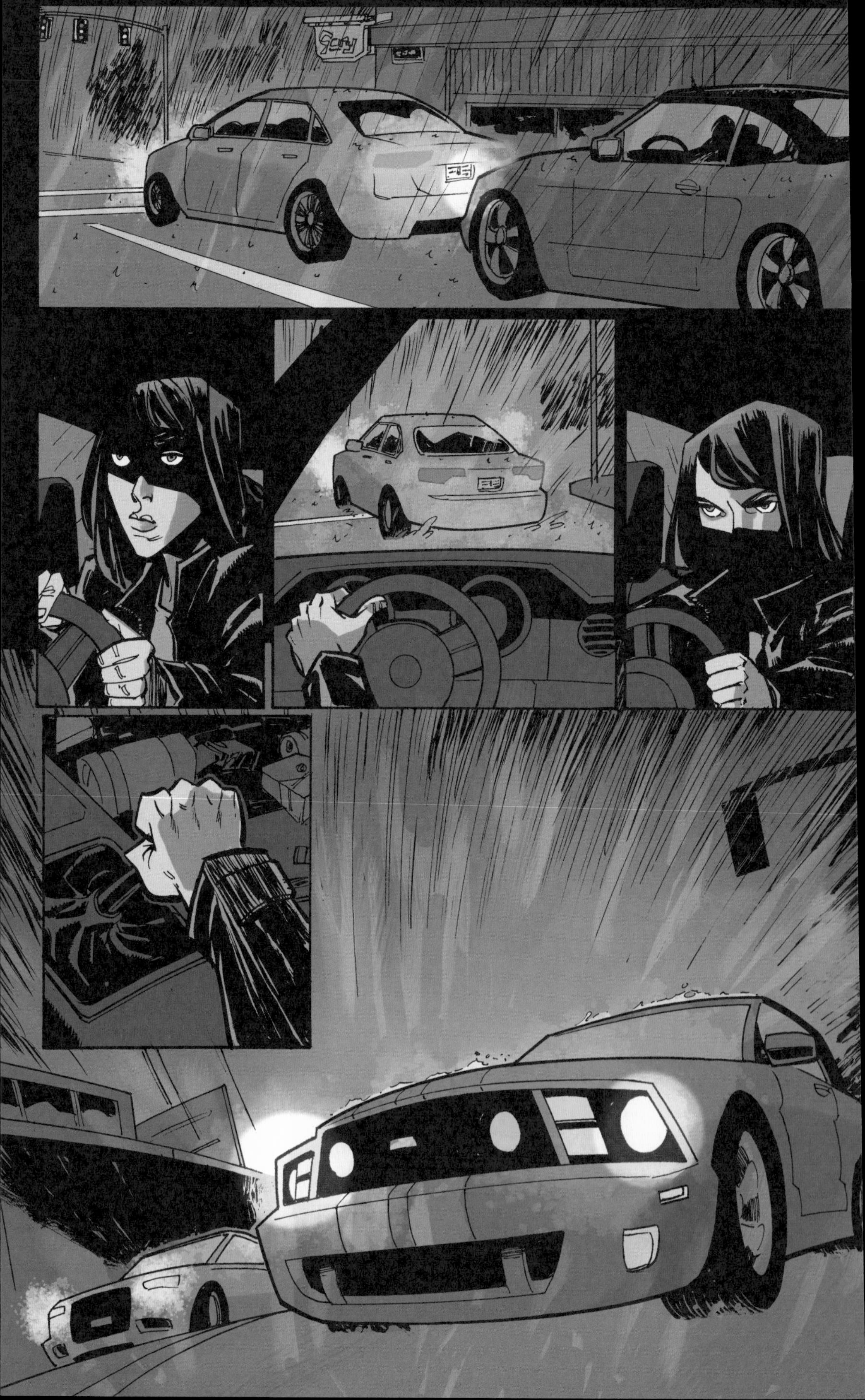

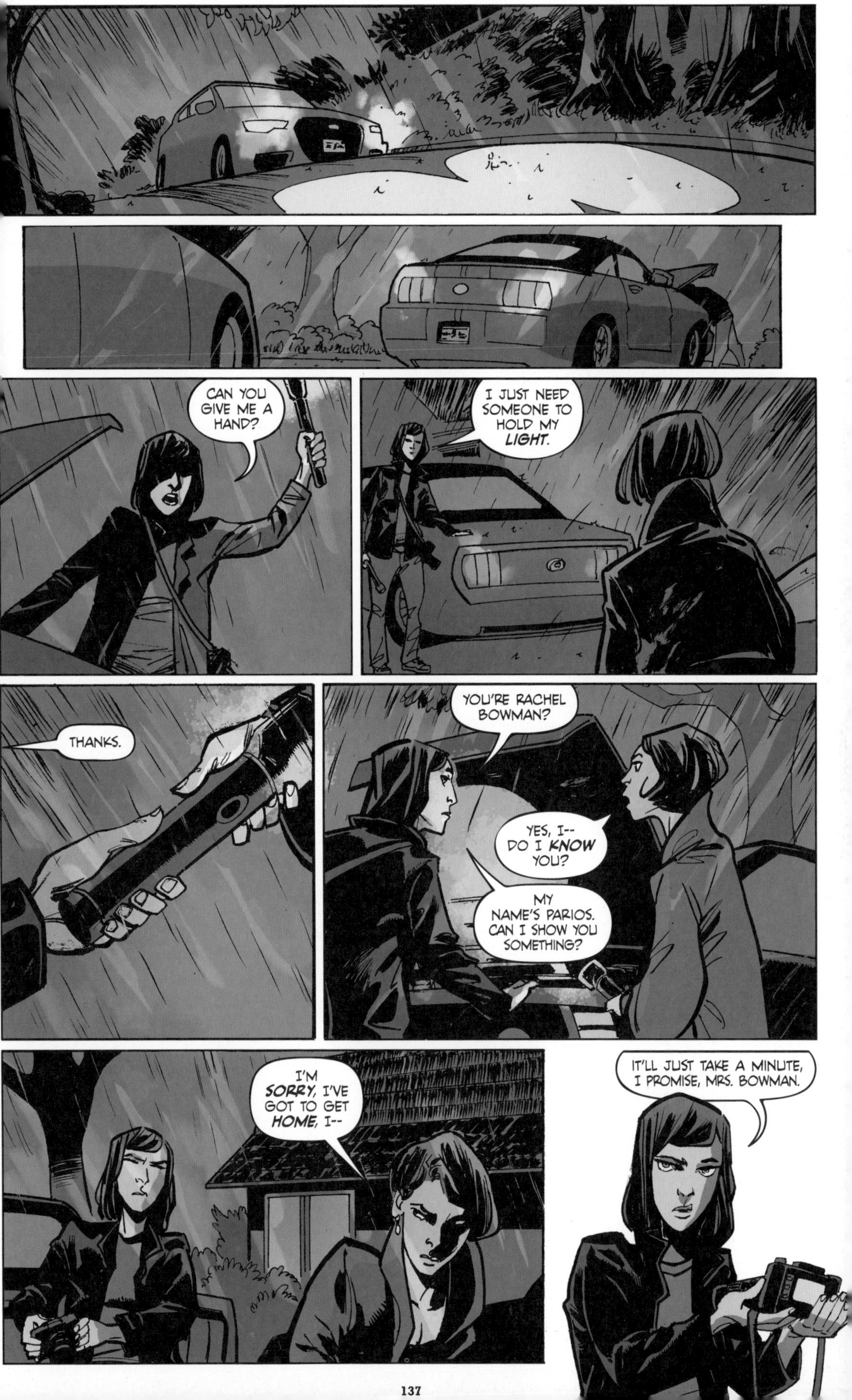
CAN YOU GIVE ME A HAND?
I JUST NEED SOMEONE TO HOLD MY LIGHT.
THANKS.
YOU'RE RACHEL BOWMAN?
YES, I-- DO I KNOW YOU?
MY NAME'S PARIOS. CAN I SHOW YOU SOMETHING?
I'M SORRY, I'VE GOT TO GET HOME, I--
IT'LL JUST TAKE A MINUTE, I PROMISE, MRS. BOWMAN.

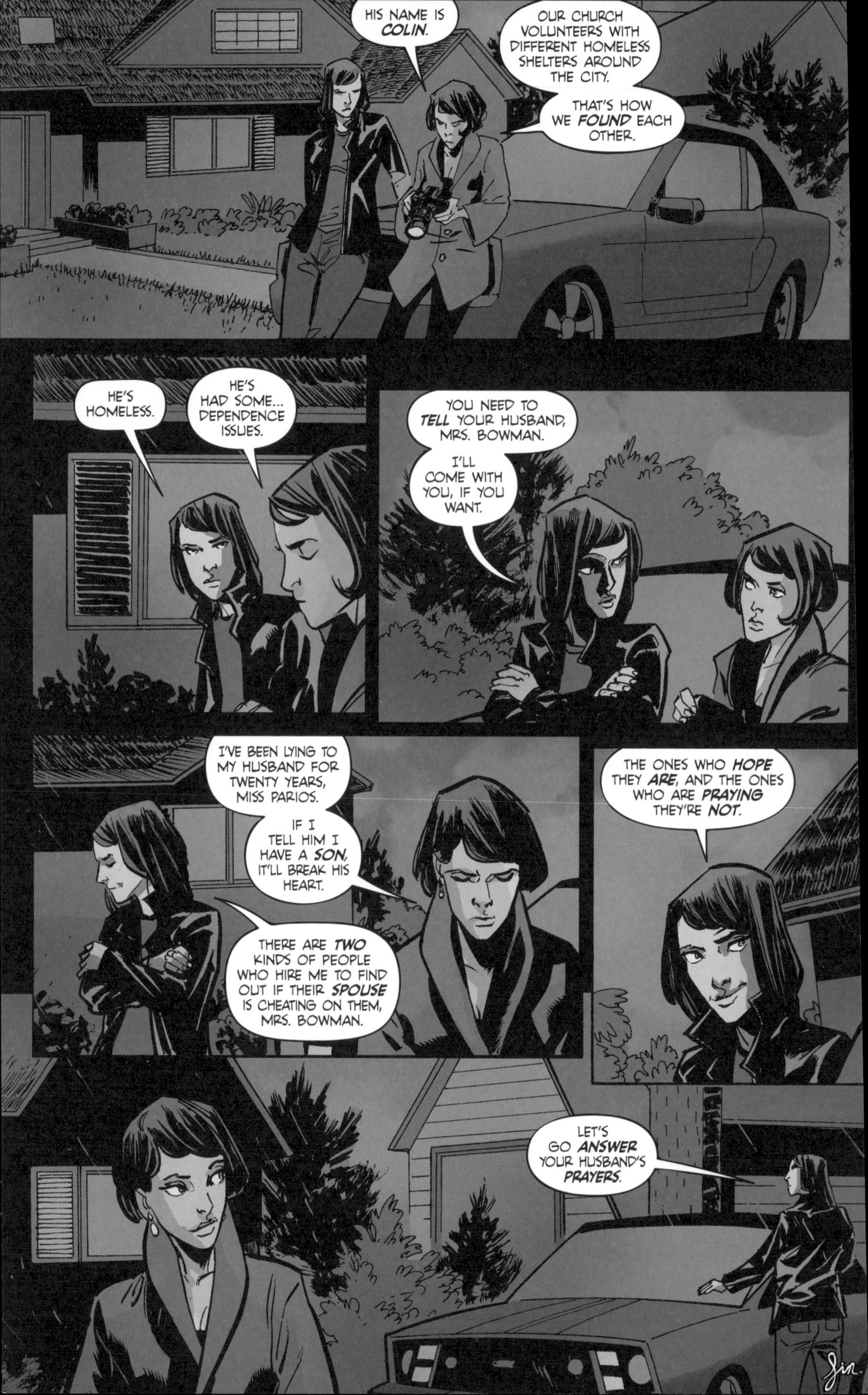
HIS NAME IS COLIN.
OUR CHURCH VOLUNTEERS WITH DIFFERENT HOMELESS SHELTERS AROUND THE CITY.
THAT'S HOW WE FOUND EACH OTHER.
HE'S HOMELESS.
HE'S HAD SOME... DEPENDENCE ISSUES.
YOU NEED TO TELL YOUR HUSBAND, MRS. BOWMAN.
I'LL COME WITH YOU, IF YOU WANT.
I'VE BEEN LYING TO MY HUSBAND FOR TWENTY YEARS, MISS PARIOS.
IF I TELL HIM I HAVE A SON, IT'LL BREAK HIS HEART.
THERE ARE TWO KINDS OF PEOPLE WHO HIRE ME TO FIND OUT IF THEIR SPOUSE IS CHEATING ON THEM, MRS. BOWMAN.
THE ONES WHO HOPE THEY ARE, AND THE ONES WHO ARE PRAYING THEY'RE NOT.
LET'S GO ANSWER YOUR HUSBAND'S PRAYERS.
Jin.

Artist Bios

GREG RUCKA was born in San Francisco and raised on the Central Coast of California, in what is commonly referred to as "Steinbeck Country." He began his writing career in earnest at the age of 10 by winning a county-wide short-story contest, and hasn't let up since. He graduated from Vassar College with an A.B. in English, and from the University of Southern California's Master of Professional Writing program with an M.F.A.

He is the author of nearly a dozen novels, six featuring bodyguard Atticus Kodiak, and three featuring Tara Chace, the protagonist of his *Queen & Country* series. Additionally, he has penned several short-stories, countless comics, and the occasional non-fiction essay. In comics, he has had the opportunity to write stories featuring some of the world's best-known characters—Superman, Batman, and Wonder Woman—as well as penning several creator-owned properties himself, such as *Whiteout* and *Queen & Country*, both published by Oni Press. His work has been optioned several times over, and his services are in high-demand in a variety of creative fields as a story-doctor and creative consultant.

Greg resides in Portland, Oregon, with his wife, author Jennifer Van Meter, and his two children. He thinks the biggest problem with the world is that people aren't paying enough attention.

JUSTIN GREENWOOD is knee-deep in a lifelong love affair with comic books. Born and raised in the Northern California Bay Area, he attended the Academy of Art University in San Francisco and graduated with a BFA in Illustration. His first professional work was with Oni Press, contributing to series like *Wasteland* and *Resurrection*, as well as projects like *Masks and Mobsters*, *Ghost Town*, and *Continuum: The War Files* for various other publishers. In those very rare occasions when he is not drawing, he can be found running around the East Bay with his wife Melissa and their dual wildlings, tracking down small produce markets and high intensity card games with equal vigor.

RYAN HILL lives in Portland, Oregon and has worked in comics in some form or another for over a decade. He's been coloring for the last few years and hopes he's good at it. He knows Dex tends to roam around Alberta a lot, but thinks at some point she should try drinking North around 50th and Division, 'cause that's his favorite bar.

MORE GRAPHIC NOVEL EXCELLENCE FROM GREG RUCKA, JUSTIN GREENWOOD & ONI PRESS...

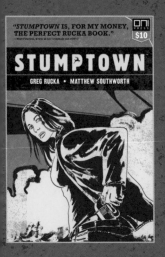

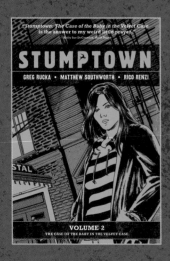

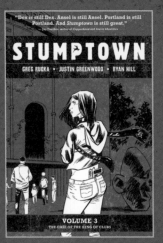

STUMPTOWN, VOLUME 1
By Greg Rucka and Matthew Southworth
160 pages, softcover, color interiors
ISBN 978-1-62010-599-3

STUMPTOWN, VOLUME 2
By Greg Rucka and Matthew Southworth
144 pages, softcover, color interiors
ISBN 978-1-62010-480-4

STUMPTOWN, VOLUME 3
By Greg Rucka, Justin Greenwood,
and Ryan Hill
144 pages, softcover, color interiors
ISBN 978-1-62010-539-9

STRINGERS
By Marc Guggenheim, Justin Greenwood,
and Ryan Hill
160 pages, softcover, color interiors
ISBN 978-1-62010-291-6

QUEEN & COUNTRY
DEFINITIVE EDITION, VOL. 1
By Greg Rucka, Steve Rolston,
Brian Hurtt, and Leandro Fernandez
376 pages, softcover, B&W interiors
ISBN 978-1-932664-87-4

WASTELAND COMPENDIUM
By Antony Johnston, Christopher Mitten,
and Justin Greenwood
744 pages, softcover, B&W interiors
ISBN 978-1-62010-412-5

For more information on these and other fine Oni Press comic books and graphic novels visit www.onipress.com.
To find a comic specialty store in your area visit www.comicshops.us.

MORE CRIME & MYSTERY FROM ONI PRESS!

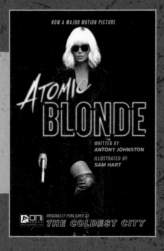

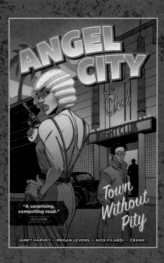